A HISTORY OF THE SOCIAL SCIENCES
IN 101 BOOKS

A HISTORY OF THE SOCIAL SCIENCES IN 101 BOOKS

EDITED BY CYRIL LEMIEUX,
LAURENT BERGER, MARIELLE MACÉ,
GILDAS SALMON, AND CÉCILE VIDAL

translated by Adrian Morfee

The MIT Press
Cambridge, Massachusetts
London, England

© 2023 EHESS

Originally published as *Pour les sciences sociales: 101 livres en temps & lieux* © Editions EHESS 2017

English translation © EHESS 2021

All rights reserved. No part of this book may be reproduced in any form by any electronic or mechanical means (including photocopying, recording, or information storage and retrieval) without permission in writing from the publisher.

This book was set in Adobe Garamond Pro by New Best-set Typesetters Ltd. Printed and bound in the United States of America.

Library of Congress Cataloging-in-Publication Data

Names: Lemieux, Cyril, 1967– editor. | Berger, Laurent, editor. | Macé, Marielle, editor.
Title: A history of the social sciences in 101 books / edited by Cyril Lemieux, Laurent Berger, Marielle Macé, Gildas Salmon, and Cécile Vidal.
Other titles: Pour les sciences sociales. English | A history of the social sciences in one hundred and one books
Description: Cambridge, Massachusetts : The MIT Press, [2023]
Identifiers: LCCN 2022030945 (print) | LCCN 2022030946 (ebook) | ISBN 9780262048088 (hardcover) | ISBN 9780262374392 (epub) | ISBN 9780262374408 (pdf)
Subjects: LCSH: Social sciences—Research—History. | Social sciences—History. | Social sciences—Bibliography.
Classification: LCC HM588 .P67813 2023 (print) | LCC HM588 (ebook) | DDC 301.072—dc23/20220822
LC record available at https://lccn.loc.gov/2022030945
LC ebook record available at https://lccn.loc.gov/2022030946

10   9   8   7   6   5   4   3   2   1

Contents

Introduction: Revisiting the Social Science Library   *xiii*

1947 *DIALECTIC OF ENLIGHTENMENT*: ADORNO AND HORKHEIMER DIAGNOSE THE SELF-DESTRUCTION OF THE ENLIGHTENMENT   *1*

1948 *SITUATIONS II*: SARTRE HOLDS LITERATURE TO ACCOUNT   *4*

1949 *THE MEDITERRANEAN AND THE MEDITERRANEAN WORLD IN THE AGE OF PHILIP II*: BRAUDEL'S INTERLOCKING DURATIONS   *7*

1949 *THE ELEMENTARY STRUCTURES OF KINSHIP*: LÉVI-STRAUSS FOUNDS KINSHIP ON MATRIMONIAL EXCHANGE   *10*

1949 *MALE AND FEMALE*: MEAD DENATURALIZES THE DIFFERENCE BETWEEN THE SEXES   *13*

1949 *SOCIAL THEORY AND SOCIAL STRUCTURE*: MERTON SUGGESTS A CODE OF CONDUCT FOR SOCIOLOGY   *16*

1950 *SOCIOLOGIE ET ANTHROPOLOGIE*: MAUSS AND THE CONSECRATION OF THE SOCIAL UNCONSCIOUS   *19*

1951 *THE ORIGINS OF TOTALITARIANISM*: ARENDT AND THE RADICAL NOVELTY OF TOTALITARIANISM   *23*

1952 *KNOWLEDGE OF LIFE*: CANGUILHEM REDEFINES THE PRINCIPLE OF LIFE   *26*

1953 *COMBATS POUR L'HISTOIRE*: FEBVRE ANNOUNCES HISTORY'S FUTURE   *29*

1954 *POLITICAL SYSTEMS OF HIGHLAND BURMA*: LEACH EXPLODES THE STABILITY OF SOCIAL STRUCTURE *32*

1955 *MEANING IN THE VISUAL ARTS*: PANOFSKY REPLACES BEAUTY WITH MEANING *35*

1955 *THE SOCIOLOGY OF BLACK AFRICA*: BALANDIER SOCIOLOGIZES AFRICA *38*

1956 *THE POWER ELITE*: MILLS AND THE CONFISCATION OF POWER *41*

1957 *THE USES OF LITERACY*: HOGGART FINALLY CASTS LIGHT ON WORKING-CLASS CULTURES *44*

1957 *MYTHOLOGIES*: BARTHES DEPLOYS SEMIOLOGY TO DEMYSTIFY MYTH *47*

1957 *THE KING'S TWO BODIES*: KANTOROWICZ AND THE MYSTIQUE OF POLITICS *50*

1958 *THE AFFLUENT SOCIETY*: GALBRAITH AND THE HERALDED END OF POVERTY *53*

1959 *THE PRESENTATION OF SELF IN EVERYDAY LIFE*: GOFFMAN TURNS DAILY LIFE INTO THEATER *56*

1960 *CENTURIES OF CHILDHOOD*: ARIÈS REDISCOVERS THE FEELING OF CHILDHOOD *59*

1961 *HISTORY OF MADNESS*: FOUCAULT REENDOWS MADNESS WITH ITS DESTABILIZING POWER *62*

1962 *HOW TO DO THINGS WITH WORDS*: AUSTIN AND LANGUAGE AS ACTION *65*

1962 *THE STRUCTURAL TRANSFORMATION OF THE PUBLIC SPHERE*: HABERMAS AND THE DECADENCE OF "PUBLICNESS" *68*

1962 *THE STRUCTURE OF SCIENTIFIC REVOLUTIONS*: KUHN CONCEIVES OF SCIENCE AS WORK COMMUNITIES *71*

1963 *THE MAKING OF THE ENGLISH WORKING CLASS*: THOMPSON RESTORES THE EXPERIENCE OF THE WORKING CLASS *74*

1964 *GESTURE AND SPEECH*: LEROI-GOURHAN LINKS UP GESTURE AND SPEECH *77*

1965 *MYTH AND THOUGHT AMONG THE GREEKS*: VERNANT AND THE EXPERIENCE OF THE GREEKS *80*

1965 *READING CAPITAL*: ALTHUSSER AND THE SILENCES OF CAPITAL *83*

1966 *PURITY AND DANGER*: DOUGLAS USHERS CONTEST INTO THE HEART OF THE SYMBOLIC ORDER *86*

1966 *PROBLEMS IN GENERAL LINGUISTICS*: BENVENISTE MOVES BEYOND STRUCTURALISM *89*

1966 *THE SOCIAL CONSTRUCTION OF REALITY*: BERGER AND LUCKMANN LAY THE BASES OF CONSTRUCTIVISM *92*

1967 *OF GRAMMATOLOGY*: DERRIDA INVENTS A WRITING PRECEDING SIGNS *95*

1967 *STUDIES IN ETHNOMETHODOLOGY*: GARFINKEL AND THE PHENOMENOLOGY OF THE SOCIAL *98*

1968 *MYTHE ET ÉPOPÉE*: DUMÉZIL VIEWS MYTH AS EXPRESSING SOCIAL ORGANIZATION *101*

1969 *THE POST-INDUSTRIAL SOCIETY*: TOURAINE AND THE ONSET OF A NEW TYPE OF SOCIETY *104*

1969 *THE COURT SOCIETY*: ELIAS DEFINES COURT SOCIETY AS THE CRUCIBLE FOR THE CIVILIZING PROCESS *107*

1969 *ETHNIC GROUPS AND BOUNDARIES*: BARTH DESUBSTANTIALIZES THE IDEA OF ETHNIC GROUPS *110*

1970 *EXIT, VOICE, AND LOYALTY*: HIRSCHMAN THEORIZES THE EXPRESSION OF DISCONTENT *113*

1971 *THE VISION OF THE VANQUISHED*: WACHTEL SWITCHES PERSPECTIVE ON THE SPANISH CONQUEST *116*

1972 *LANGUAGE IN THE INNER CITY*: LABOV DEFENDS A UNIFIED THEORY OF LANGUAGE AND ITS SOCIAL USES *119*

1972 *STONE AGE ECONOMICS*: SAHLINS OVERTHROWS THE PRODUCTIVIST HYPOTHESIS *122*

1973 *THE LEGEND OF BOUVINES*: DUBY DOES BATTLE WITH EVENTS-BASED HISTORY *125*

1973 *THE INTERPRETATION OF CULTURES*: GEERTZ TURNS CULTURES INTO TEXTS TO BE INTERPRETED *128*

1974 *THE MODERN WORLD-SYSTEM*: WALLERSTEIN AND THE PLANETARY EXPANSION OF MODERN CAPITALISM *131*

1975 *MAIDENS, MEALS, AND MONEY*: MEILLASSOUX AND THE ALIMENTARY STRUCTURES OF KINSHIP *134*

1976 *THE CHEESE AND THE WORMS*: GINZBURG LAUNCHES MICROHISTORY *137*

1976 *BREAD AND CIRCUSES*: VEYNE AND THE LOGIC OF GOOD DEEDS *140*

1977 *DEADLY WORDS*: FAVRET-SAADA CASTS A SPELL ON POSITIVISM *143*

1977 *THE DOMESTICATION OF THE SAVAGE MIND*: GOODY EXPLORES THE INTELLECTUAL TECHNOLOGIES CONNECTED TO WRITING *146*

1978 *INTERPRETING THE FRENCH REVOLUTION*: FURET CONSIGNS THE REVOLUTION TO THE PAST *149*

1978 *ORIENTALISM*: SAID VIEWS THE ORIENT IN THE MIRROR OF THE WEST *152*

1979 *FUTURES PAST*: KOSELLECK SETS OUT HIS THEORY OF HISTORICAL TIME *155*

1979 *DISTINCTION*: BOURDIEU AND THE SOCIAL PRODUCTION OF TASTE *158*

1980 *THE PRACTICE OF EVERYDAY LIFE*: DE CERTEAU AND THE CREATIVITY OF ORDINARY PRACTICE *161*

1981 *PORTRAIT OF THE KING*: MARIN AND THE POWER OF REPRESENTATION *164*

1981 *L'EXERCICE DE LA PARENTÉ*: HÉRITIER UNIFIES THE FIELD OF KINSHIP *167*

1982 *SLAVERY AND SOCIAL DEATH*: PATTERSON DEFINES SLAVERY AS SOCIAL DEATH *170*

1982 *ART WORLDS*: BECKER TURNS ART INTO A JOB LIKE ANY OTHER *173*

1982 *THE FOUL AND THE FRAGRANT*: CORBIN ENDOWS OUR SENSES WITH A HISTORY *176*

1982 *THE MAKING OF GREAT MEN*: GODELIER AND THE MULTIPLE FORMS OF DOMINATION *179*

1983 *ELEMENTARY ASPECTS OF PEASANT INSURGENCY IN COLONIAL INDIA*: GUHA REHABILITATES THE POLITICAL CONSCIOUSNESS OF SUBALTERNS *182*

1983 *ESSAYS ON INDIVIDUALISM*: DUMONT PLACES WESTERN EXCEPTION IN PERSPECTIVE *185*

1983 *IMAGINED COMMUNITIES*: ANDERSON UNVEILS NATIONS' FICTIONAL UNDERPINNINGS *188*

1984 *THE PASTEURIZATION OF FRANCE*: LATOUR MAKES ROOM FOR THE NONHUMAN *191*

1985 *TIME AND NARRATIVE*: RICŒUR REFIGURES TIME *194*

1986 *RISK SOCIETY*: BECK ANNOUNCES SCIENCE'S SELF-DISENCHANTMENT *197*

1987 *THE CULTURAL USES OF PRINT IN EARLY MODERN FRANCE*: CHARTIER AND THE CULTURAL HISTORY OF THE SOCIAL REALM *200*

1987 *FAMILY FORTUNES*: DAVIDOFF AND HALL ANALYZE THE CO-CONSTRUCTION OF GENDER AND CLASS *203*

1988 *THE GENDER OF THE GIFT*: STRATHERN TURNS GENDER INTO A CAPACITY FOR ACTION *207*

1989 *PRIMATE VISIONS*: HARAWAY FINDS IN PRIMATOLOGY TOOLS FOR RADICAL PROTEST *210*

1990 *GENDER TROUBLE*: BUTLER SOWS TROUBLE IN GENDER *213*

1990 *LE CARREFOUR JAVANAIS*: LOMBARD RESHUFFLES THE CARDS OF GLOBAL HISTORY *216*

1991 *THE MIDDLE GROUND*: RICHARD WHITE AND INTERCULTURAL ACCOMMODATIONS *219*

1992 *IDENTITY AND CONTROL*: HARRISON WHITE AND EMERGING SOCIAL FORMATIONS *222*

1993 *THE POLITICS OF LARGE NUMBERS*: DESROSIÈRES INVESTIGATES THE ONTOLOGY OF STATISTICAL KNOWLEDGE *225*

1994 *THE AGE OF EXTREMES*: HOBSBAWM RECOUNTS THE END OF NINETEENTH-CENTURY BOURGEOIS SOCIETY *228*

1995 *FROM MANUAL WORKERS TO WAGE LABORERS*: CASTEL AND THE EROSION OF THE WAGE SYSTEM *231*

1996 *SAINT LOUIS*: LE GOFF MEETS SAINT LOUIS *234*

1997 *THE DIVIDED CITY*: LORAUX SHOWS FORGETTING IS CENTRAL TO POLITICS *237*

1998 *ART AND AGENCY*: GELL REDEFINES ART INDEPENDENTLY OF AESTHETICS *240*

1999 *THE NEW SPIRIT OF CAPITALISM*: BOLTANSKI AND CHIAPELLO READDRESS THE ENIGMA OF CAPITALISM *243*

2000 *THE GREAT DIVERGENCE*: POMERANZ EXPLAINS WHY CHINA "LAGGED" BEHIND THE WEST *246*

2001 *ACTING IN AN UNCERTAIN WORLD*: CALLON, LASCOUMES, AND BARTHE RETHINK DEMOCRACY *249*

2002 *THE SURVIVING IMAGE*: DIDI-HUBERMAN MAKES TIME THE FUNDAMENTAL DIMENSION OF IMAGES *252*

2003 *THE PRICE OF MONOTHEISM*: ASSMANN AND THE VIOLENCE OF MONOTHEISM *255*

2003 *LAW AND REVOLUTION*: BERMAN AND THE REVOLUTIONS OF WESTERN LAW *258*

2003 *REGIMES OF HISTORICITY*: HARTOG AND EXPERIENCE OF THE PRESENT   *261*

2004 *LA SERVITUDE VOLONTAIRE*: TESTART, THE GENESIS OF INEQUALITIES AND THE EMERGENCE OF THE STATE   *264*

2005 *EXPLORATIONS IN CONNECTED HISTORY*: SUBRAHMANYAM CONNECTS THE EURO-ASIAN WORLDS   *267*

2005 *BEYOND NATURE AND CULTURE*: DESCOLA STEERS NATURE INTO THE SOCIAL SCIENCES   *270*

2006 *CHARONNE, 8 FÉVRIER 1962*: DEWERPE AUTOPSIES STATE VIOLENCE   *273*

2007 *THE YEARS OF EXTERMINATION*: FRIEDLÄNDER PUTS THE HOLOCAUST AT THE HEART OF SCHOLARSHIP ON NAZISM   *276*

2008 *VIOLENCE*: COLLINS MAKES VIOLENCE AN EFFECT OF SITUATION   *279*

2009 *THE ART OF NOT BEING GOVERNED*: SCOTT AND THE ANTHROPOLOGICAL OUTCOME OF AN ANARCHIST HISTORY   *282*

2010 *HOW CHIEFS BECAME KINGS*: KIRCH ENDOWS POLYNESIA WITH ITS OWN ARCHAIC STATE   *285*

2011 *DEBT*: GRAEBER WISHES TO END THE VIOLENCE OF DEBT   *288*

2012 *THROUGH THE EYE OF A NEEDLE*: BROWN RETURNS TO THE ROOTS OF THE CHRISTIAN PROBLEM OF WEALTH   *291*

2013 *CAPITAL IN THE TWENTY-FIRST CENTURY*: PIKETTY DECRYPTS SHIFTS IN ECONOMIC INEQUALITIES OVER THE CENTURIES   *294*

2014 *THE USE OF BODIES*: AGAMBEN AND LIFE AS USE   *297*

2015 *THE MUSHROOM AT THE END OF THE WORLD*: TSING TRACKS LIFE IN THE RUINS OF CAPITALISM   *300*

2016 *MONEY*: AGLIETTA UNVEILS THE CONTRADICTORY NATURE OF MONEY   *303*

List of Books Covered   *307*
List of Contributors   *311*

xi   *Contents*

Introduction: Revisiting the Social Science Library

The purpose driving this work is to reread 101 books, published since the Second World War, that have left their mark on how the social sciences have been built, year after year, in France and around the world. In so doing, we shall encounter countless objects of study, names, tenets, and debates. We shall witness the birth of concepts now central to how we apprehend and intervene in the social world. We shall follow solidly woven lines of thought and look on as others fray and fall apart. From the cultural diagnosis of Theodor W. Adorno to the gender trouble introduced by Judith Butler, from the long time frame of Fernand Braudel's "Mediterranean" to Randall Collins's analysis of micro-situations of violence, from Claude Lévi-Strauss's kinship systems to Anna Tsing's mushroom growing amid the ruins of capitalism—this book portrays the discontinuous, multifaceted endeavor of the social sciences while showing it to be a pursuit sustained by a common effort and project.

Strikingly, no one has addressed this challenge before. It is as though the social sciences, despite being constituted as such for nearly a century and a half, still struggle to grasp what confers their unity. To portray their development, they have relied on discipline-specific retrospectives and anthologies rather than focusing on how they conjointly drive a movement that is central to contemporary thought. And it is precisely this whole, composed of many different fields, that we seek to capture. For, in addition to being connected by intellectual dynamics, transfers, and debates, these disciplines share a common position vis-à-vis the life sciences and, above all, partake in a common project—adding to the collective reflexivity of contemporary societies and furthering our critiques of ethnocentric bias.

This emancipating project is, to our minds, the crucial element. If the social sciences merit the energies expended on them, it is because they increase our collective capacity to view our societies and their institutions in a denaturalizing light. The movement by which they tirelessly explore the infinite variety of human practices, via the methods and techniques they have devised, is in fact related to their capacity to peel away the veneer of obviousness overlaying our behavior and reveal that a form of necessity, yet equally of arbitrariness, influences our collective organization. This is the emancipating effect of the social sciences—an effect they could not relinquish if they wished to. In studying human life in all its diverse manifestations, the social sciences bring to light its foundations, which, though biologically determined, are fashioned perhaps primarily by sociohistorical forces.

DOING SOCIAL SCIENCE

Paying tribute to this emancipating effect entails exhibiting the shape it takes in each book presented. It also demands that we address not just a specialist readership but all those who appreciate the social sciences for the knowledge and freedom they bring. But making these books simpler and more accessible does not imply forgoing discussion of their technical dimensions, particularly the place held by the (at times difficult) problems of method in the debates driving the social sciences. Any attempt to erase what makes them more than simple statements about the social world would belie them. Our discussion thus necessarily covers investigation protocols, data-gathering techniques, critical analysis of sources, and tools for comparison and analysis, taking in, as a corollary, the production of concepts and theoretical frameworks. This technical aspect is what "disciplines" each social science, based on established procedures for investigation and reflexivity. These dimensions also relate to the fundamentally collective nature of working in the social sciences (even when the undertaking crystallizes around a name) and to the existence of research communities, whose development and autonomy of judgment undergird advances in knowledge.

xiv   *Introduction*

In addition to focusing on what these books state, it is thus important to further examine how they ground what they say. It is likewise important to pay attention to how each partakes in a series of research debates preceding it, often modifying the parameters and subsequent course of these debates, which amounts to raising the issue of the cumulative nature of knowledge in the social sciences.

We have called on some of the leading specialists currently working in France and elsewhere in the various disciplinary fields and objects of study. They go over how the publication of each book represented an event in its field, explain the effects the book produced on scientific debate, and specify where the interest lies today, without immuring each book from the living context of research or enshrining it as a museum piece cut off from any scientific tradition or collective undertaking.

This approach is intended as a dual tribute to the social sciences community. First, in bringing these books and researchers together, we wished to emphasize intergenerational solidarity. From the Second World War through to the present day, each new generation of researchers has received from the preceding one the technical and intellectual training without which they would have been incapable of producing their own works. This solidarity, however, is not merely a matter of acknowledging this legacy: rather, it entails appropriation through critique, carrying the legacy forward by building up a distance from predecessors' thought and approach, thereby opening up new vistas. Second, by calling on so many authors, we also wished to profess our vision of the social sciences as a unified whole. Such a vision is currently imperiled by the ongoing trend toward specialization, in which researchers in the social sciences are increasingly viewed as mere "experts" on a given question or domain. This reveals the full extent of the changes to research practices over the past seventy years, illustrating how the advent of mass higher education and, more recently, the managerialization of research output have radically altered what it means to be a researcher in the social sciences, affecting career training, the processes of intellectual consecration, investigation practices, the transmission of research techniques, publication modes, and even the very ethos of the researcher and associated professional ideal. But the interdisciplinary solidarity that we hold dear has not disappeared. A hundred or so researchers have recognized our approach as their own, and the existence of this book may be viewed as an act of resistance, an assertive reminder that the social sciences form a unitary endeavor. Further, this book can be seen as proof that such a project still makes sense to many of us, at a time when other approaches to scientific work—promoting the fragmentation of research fields, emphasizing individual strategies and expertise—are being paraded as a universal model. No doubt projects such as ours will garner ever more support in the future, as the need is felt to move beyond the dynamic of hyper-specialization that bleeds all reflexivity dry and turns the social sciences away from their emancipatory project.

BETTER THAN A PANTHEON

It took an institutional event to trigger the opportunity to profess this unitary and emancipatory vision and to tackle this challenge—namely, the seventieth anniversary in 2017 of the creation of a new department devoted to "economic and social sciences" at the École pratique des hautes études (EPHE). As is widely recognized, the department's creation in 1947 was of major scientific importance in France at that time. It is equally acknowledged that this was the kernel of the institution that developed and then acquired autonomy in 1975 as the École des hautes études en sciences sociales (EHESS), where the editors of this book work. This fortuitous occasion to go back over the previous seventy years of the social sciences was the germ whence this book grew.

Our readers will thus better understand why we settled on the period 1947–2017. But we still need to explain how we went about our undertaking—that is, how we selected, chose, and prioritized such and such a book. To tackle this obviously irresoluble problem, the five editors met on numerous occasions in 2016. During these meetings, our group engaged in fierce discussions. Although we had fixed the objective of drawing up a list of 100 or so books published since 1947, new and "indispensable" books kept on coming and asserting their right to be included. It was only very gradually, painfully, that we whittled down our list to 101 titles, rather than 100, which is too neat, too tidy a number. The figure also invites others to continually reopen and enrich this selection and, as far as possible, lessens the impression inherent to this type of project that the works listed are somehow the "best."

There was never any question in our minds of restricting our selection to an abridged series of canonized authors, supposedly equating to some golden age of the social sciences around the 1960s and 1970s. Rather, it was a matter of following the social sciences as an ongoing endeavor, characterized by its ups and downs, surprises, and fluctuations in intensity. We decided that each year was to be represented, and no author, however influential, was to appear more than once. We also opted to follow these disciplines through to the present day while remaining alert to the difficulties occasioned by lacking the requisite distance to pick our way surely through the most recent output. Lastly, we wished to limit imbalances between disciplines, between French and non-French authors, between men and women, and between histor-ical periods and cultural areas, though our selection is obviously marked by the social conditions of research—mostly male, mostly European and American—during the period under consideration and by our project hav-ing been carried out at the heart of a French institution.

So, this work is not a little pantheon. It is less monumental and less fettered. Our readers are invited to circulate freely among the books, not to admire them. Nor is it the result of a selection that could be described as objective, as if criteria could exist wholly detached from the sociohis-torical situation of those choosing. We have no such radical conception of objectivity. It is clear to our minds that our choices are necessarily situated. First, our choices are situated in time, for it is necessarily from where our disciplines now stand that we have scrutinized their pasts, looking for works that have come down through the years, standing out as "noteworthy" or "remarkable," even as "foundational" or "representative" of a current they themselves did not envisage. But rather than engaging with the works of the past from the standpoint of our expectations, we have reconsidered them from theirs—thus arguments that have become self-evident are rehearsed afresh with the novelty they had when formulated. Second, our selections are situated in space, for our enterprise, conducted in a French research establishment, which assumes a standpoint toward the global history of the social sciences (no doubt a very different one from that our American colleagues would have assumed if asked to draw up such a list). However, we considered the importance attached to the selected titles in places outside France and Europe. Thus, though clearly "situated," our approach is driven by a constant effort to decenter it in both time and space.

CLASHES AND CHOICES

Our overall line led us to embrace a certain number of deliberate choices. The first and main such choice is to adopt the standpoint of the social sciences rather than of a particular discipline. That does not mean championing some flat, bland vision of the social sciences. Rather, we profess a more structured vision, drawing notably on the history of the EPHE economics and social science department and what it owed to the Annales school.[1] We are mindful of what Jean-Claude Passeron has called the "epistemological indiscernibility"[2] of the three disciplines underpinning the social sciences—history, anthropology, and sociology. Around this base is a constellation of other disciplines with fundamentally different epistemologies—law, linguistics, philosophy, the history of art, literary studies, economics, the cognitive sciences, and so on. The whole interest of their interaction with the three underpinning disciplines springs, of course, from this difference. Admittedly, placing certain disciplines at the center and others on the periphery is in itself controversial. Clearly, the way in which the social sciences figure the relationships between their constitutive fields sparks clashes. Additionally, while these three disciplines are the main force behind the social sciences, it is only conjointly, not singly, that they impart this drive, drawing on the exchanges, theoretical debates, and questionings issuing from the surrounding disciplines grounded in another epistemology and affecting them. One has only to think, for example, of the emblematic role played by linguistics in the 1960s.

A second deliberate choice, which is important to us, is to honor a particular form of scholarship—namely, books published under the author's (or authors') name. Changes currently favor the article and, to a lesser extent, chapter in a joint volume from a conference or colloquium. For its part, the world of publishing encourages social science researchers to produce brief essays, textbooks, and other "contributions." All these formats have their merits, meeting the requirements of different publics while adding to the production and raising the profile of the social sciences. But historically, the publication of books has assuredly been central to building the social sciences, and it is the main means by which they have forged their reputation with the general public. Our choice to privilege books as the preeminent form of scholarly output explains why a certain number of important works—particularly articles—do not figure on our list, and nor do specific journal issues, dictionaries, or encyclopedias. This place granted to books does not issue solely from one of the essential differences between the social sciences and the natural sciences (in which the seminal format is the article). It also expresses the tie linking them—from the outset—to the world of the literature.[3] The social sciences have an irreducibly hermeneutic and narrative dimension that stems not solely from their object of study (human activities and their historical transformations) but also from the type of labor they require, which entails framing reality as an enigma, seeking to "speak true." This demands, or should demand, that none shirk the task of voicing and being mindful of the issues involved in describing and categorizing reality. Here once again, not everyone will agree. Within our little editorial group, for that matter, the literary question gave rise to lively debates—and the place accorded to matters of form, the feeling that the "essay" is an inherently dignified genre, or the belief that the effort involved in writing is central to all thinking, did not always emerge victorious. Claiming that one format of scholarly output has primacy, or denouncing how it is treated by our epoch, necessarily figures among the issues at stake in clashes within the highly diverse world of research and could not transpire in a different light.

WHICH HISTORY OF THE SOCIAL SCIENCES?

In offering a renewed, updated, and internationalized perspective on the major (together with some lesser known) works in the repository of knowledge built up by the social sciences, the panorama we sketch allows us to gauge changes in these sciences, together with the directions in which they have evolved. This book assumes these constraints and, thanks to its collaborative nature, is strongly placed to set out these discontinuities and attendant effects of convergence and densification, thus highlighting the major lines of change.

One of the lines of change—perhaps the most flagrant, and in no way a discovery, but with a notable inflection over the decades studied here—is the curve traced by structuralist thought, from its emergence just after the Second World War through its domination in the 1960s, followed by its supposed decline. Did the social sciences, under the aegis of the idea of structure, manage to demonstrate their unity to themselves and triumph awhile, before researchers, naturally given to critique, set about dismantling this unifying belief? Some such nostalgic and disillusioned vision is hawked in accounts that abridge the social sciences to what they are held to have been in the 1960s—some "golden age" corresponding to that of their "great names." But the path we follow allows us to see things differently and to recognize in the very critique of structuralism (commencing in the 1970s and flourishing as of the 1980s), in its reappraisals and rereadings, a renewed expression of the unity of the social sciences. This critical movement borrows from one discipline to the next such similar schema (emphasizing agency, refusing totalizations, paying attention to situational constraints, etc.), makes methodological recommendations that so frequently converge, and operates on such a scale that we are fully entitled to view the phase on which the social sciences embarked thirty or so years ago in a different light. This view is no longer based on the idea of decline or crisis—characterized by dispersal, fragmentation, and powerlessness even—but on the conviction that this phase exhibits a multiform yet common effort to move beyond the limits of the structuralist enterprise and to take further the goal of denaturing the social world. Starting in the 1990s, on most university campuses around the world involved in teaching and practicing the social sciences, the common language across disciplines tended to center on the idea of "social constructs," which emerged as the most significant marker of these sciences' contribution to public debate.

From there, we may trace a second evolution, relating to the importance acquired by feminist studies, together with colonial, subaltern, and postcolonial studies. Feminist studies appeared in the late 1940s, and the others surfaced during the 1950s. It was only during the 1970s and the 1980s, however, that they genuinely took off in English-speaking academia. It took a while for them to reach France, where they were received critically. Yet here, too—though admittedly in the central disciplines of the social sciences rather than in the fields organized into "studies"—they sparked renewed interest in matters of sex, gender, colonization, empire, and domination, steering research in the social sciences toward rehabilitating the "agency" of the dominated. In this case, no doubt more than others, the social sciences show how they are united around a common project to increase reflexivity within societies: In enabling subjects to denaturalize traditional relations of domination, the transformations to these societies gave feminist, subaltern, and postcolonial arguments an ever-expanding audience and reach. In return, social science methods have been profoundly modified: confronting hitherto unsuspected practical difficulties, they now seek to better "symmetrize" the point of view of the dominant and the dominated and to avoid importing the prejudices of the dominant enswathed within their conceptualizations and research procedures.

Let us mention one final evolution, which arguably lies at the heart of how we experience the contemporary world: the change in how the social sciences apprehend humanity as a whole and the limits of our planet. Here, it is the questioning of the nation-state that is the crucial element. Constructivist thought once again played a prime role here, making it possible to flush out the overly naturalizing aspects in the conceptions that the social sciences (often unconsciously) favor for apprehending such entities as "nations," "societies," and "ethnic groups." Hence the effort to "deconstruct" these notions and conceive of the realities they overlay as performances rather than as givens. Hence, too, the devising of innovative instruments, primarily methodological, to successfully vary the scales of analysis for apprehending phenomena and for thinking of social activities in terms of "networks," without being hidebound by the preexisting blueprint afforded by social groups and borders. This is the viewpoint from which to understand the singular importance that, since the 2000s, the social sciences have attached to the dynamics of capitalism, the loss of state sovereignty, the failures in regulating (and thinking about) the ecological crisis, and the depletion of natural resources—all of which require us to extricate our analysis from a viewpoint centered on nation-states.

Here, once again, the social sciences show how they are connected to evolutions in the societies within which they develop. By taking globalization as their object and conceiving of their task within this movement, they summon us to be mindful of the sociohistorical conditions engendering them and assert their genuinely political role.

Cyril Lemieux, Laurent Berger, Marielle Macé, Gildas Salmon, and Cécile Vidal

NOTES

1. André Burguière, *L'école des Annales: Une histoire intellectuelle* (Paris: Odile Jacob, 2006). Translated into English by Jane Marie Todd as *The Annales School: An Intellectual History* (Ithaca, NY: Cornell University Press, 2009).

2. Jean-Claude Passeron, *Le raisonnement sociologique: Un espace non poppérien de l'argumentation* (Paris: Albin Michel ["Bibliothèque de 'L'évolution de l'humanité'"], [1991] 2006). Translated into English by Rachel Gomme as *Sociological Reasoning: A Non-Popperian Space of Argumentation* (Oxford: Bardwell Press, 2013).

3. See, for example, Wolf Lepenies, *Die Drei Kulturen* (Munich: Carl Hanser Verlag, 1985). Translated into English by R. J. Hollingdale as *Between Literature and Science: The Rise of Sociology* (Cambridge: Cambridge University Press, 1988).

1947

DIALECTIC OF ENLIGHTENMENT: ADORNO AND HORKHEIMER DIAGNOSE THE SELF-DESTRUCTION OF THE ENLIGHTENMENT

Dialektik der Aufklärung (*Dialectic of Enlightenment*), published in Amsterdam shortly after the Second World War, is the result of work jointly conducted by Theodor W. Adorno (1903–1969) and Max Horkheimer (1895–1973) when in exile in the United States. It sets out to understand "why humanity, instead of entering a truly human state, is sinking into a new kind of barbarism." Far from interpreting this as a return to some state of original savagery, they interpret it as expressing a contradiction at the heart of Enlightenment rationality. Though the Enlightenment (taken in the broad meaning of "thought in progress," above and beyond any chronological demarcation) had promised to free men of fear, it only progressed along this path by repressing this affective substratum and by reducing rationality to its instrumental component, obsessed with calculating means and pressed into the sole service of self-preservation. Reason, which was meant to work for humankind's emancipation, necessarily became the instrument of domination, divided by Adorno and Horkheimer into three registers: exercising reason has the prime aim of endowing humans, through work, with power over nature, which is perceived as a threat; the success of this program then implies that each individual interiorizes this domination, thereby mutilating everything internal, which nevertheless partakes in this very nature (a way, for the authors, to mark the decisive critical contribution of psychoanalysis); this structure of domination is then repeated within society, in the conflict inevitably thenceforth opposing dominant and dominated.

The authors set out a series of ways in which this "aporia" constituting "the self-destruction of reason" transpires. The ideals of the Enlightenment are denied in the standardized and stereotypical products of the "cultural industry," and "cultural goods," far from working to form autonomous individuals, promote the order of the market and reinforce the submission of the masses. As for anti-Semitism, its apparent irrationality is only the other side of the "limits" of Enlightenment rationality succumbing to paranoia: "the will to destroy spontaneously born of a false social order" is projected onto the Jews.

Over the course of these "philosophical fragments" (the title of the first non-trade version that Adorno and Horkheimer distributed to a few close associates in 1944), while building on and paving the way for more empirical research into authority and prejudice, three provocative ideas come into focus: Fascism, far from being a move backward or some aberrant deviation in the history of modernity, was in fact deeply rooted in the very dynamic of Western rationality. The progress of scientific rationality was not so much a means of resisting all forms of moral and political regression as it was a symptom, a lever even in this monstrous reversal of culture into barbarism. As for liberal democracies, they were too profoundly subject to the law of capitalism to constitute a rampart and thus just as adept as authoritarian regimes in "manipulating the masses."

It would, however, be mistaken to classify Adorno and Horkheimer as "anti-Enlightenment" thinkers, as their concern was to conduct an immanent critique of the *Aufklärung* by confronting it with its own concept, the better to denounce, in the name of reason, the blatant scandal of its unfulfilled promise. Is not the critical work conducted in this book sufficient proof of the positive function of reason once it manages to exert its capacity for self-reflection?

Like a "bottle thrown into the sea," *Dialectic of Enlightenment* was doubtless not intended to produce immediate effects but rather to safeguard the prospects for future critical thought. When it surfaced in the mid-1960s, the book resonated with critiques of consumer society, reinforcing many protests against colonial imperialism and strengthening nascent feminist demands. By placing the issue of domination at the heart of their analyses, Adorno and Horkheimer also expanded on traditional criticisms of economic exploitation through their reference to nature, feeding into criticism of a certain "productivism" from which Marxism had not necessarily managed to distance itself. Before Foucault (and, if we believe his subsequent avowals, without his knowledge), Adorno and Horkheimer brought to light how knowledge is inextricably bound up with power. They sketched the outlines of a sociology of domination, which, in the hands of Bourdieu—and irrespective of the methodological differences between his approach and their foundational work—went on to prove just how fertile it could be. As for the "notes and sketches" that form the final chapter (and which, in their deliberate dispersal, reinforce the fragmentary tenor of the whole), they are presented as a "dialectical anthropology" that, unlike psychology, examines not the individual but the new type of impersonal human being emerging at this stage in the history of capitalism.

Resolutely transgressing disciplinary divides, the better to make intelligible a reality whose irrationality seems to defy all attempts at elucidation, *Dialectic of Enlightenment* did not fail to spark controversy and polemical debate, including among those, such as Jürgen Habermas and Axel Honneth, who set about claiming the legacy of the "Frankfurt school," even though the work, in their eyes, embodied all the shortcomings of initial "critical theory," particularly because it promoted a pessimistic and apocalyptic "philosophy of history." No doubt the book deserves better than this status as a foil. By choosing to write this book together, and by opting for the form of a fragment, Adorno and Horkheimer resolutely distanced themselves from all systematic totalization and, through their micrological analyses punctuated with hyperbolic exaggerations, invented a theoretical style that remains as untimely as ever.

Jacques-Olivier Bégot

Theodor W. Adorno and Max Horkheimer, *Dialektik der Aufklärung* (Amsterdam: Querido, 1947). Translated into English as *Dialectic of Enlightenment*, trans. John Cumming (New York: Seabury Press, 1969) and trans. Edmund Jephcott (Stanford, CA: Stanford University Press, 2002).

1948

SITUATIONS II: SARTRE HOLDS LITERATURE TO ACCOUNT

Situations II contains—or used to contain (a new edition in 2010 divided up the *Situations* series differently)—a set of essays about the position of literature in the aftermath of the Second World War, originally published in the journal *Les Temps modernes* in 1947.

Under the pen of Walter Benjamin or Charles Péguy, the word "situation" had signaled that they placed literature within history, thereby politicizing writing. With Jean-Paul Sartre (1905–1980), the word became the most effective instrument for literature to confront the requisitions of the war. The collection opens with the very famous *Qu'est-ce que la littérature?* (What is literature?). This manifesto for freedom is where Sartre first theorized the notion of "*engagement*" (commitment). Though these pages are well known, we need to read them with a fresh sense of surprise, marveling particularly at how Sartre addresses the issue, taking writing not as a value but as an anonymous practice, inquiring into its semiotic nature, fundamental purpose, and social usage and intent: What does it mean to write; why write; for whom does one write?

How does Sartre treat these radically new questions? He repudiates the classics and, as Philippe Roussin observes, "puts an end to French literature's perceiving itself solely through its tradition." First, by relating literature to history and holding it to account—from the war and from the lessons of the Occupation and torture—he deduces the meaning of all prior literature. In the name of the war, he takes issue with the supposed gratuity of literary works, the separation of their language, the exceptionality of their authors. Combating literary "aristocracism," he argues that literature and the democratic form of life are mutually supporting, bound in a state of equal vulnerability: "The art of prose is bound up with the only regime in which prose has meaning: democracy. When one is threatened, the other is too." In judging literature in the light of its capacity to replicate reality, in sociologizing it, Sartre tears down its chimeras, probes its legitimacy, awakens feelings of its impropriety (1945 thus compounded the diagnosis of 1916, when, faced with "the silence of those on leave," language, and thereby literature, had been decreed powerless, seemingly incapable of rising to the collective experience).

But it was also by breaking with French national history that Sartre put an end to French literature's self-focusing bent. He took the American novel and played it off against French prose (American authors offered a different model, that of improper singularity, tussling with the common language), drew on international references, and paved the way for the awareness, formulated by Erich Auerbach, that "our philological home can no longer be the nation: it is the earth."

Yet, despite the subsequent fortune of some of its analyses—the distinction between prose and poetry, said to be *inengageable* (provocatively, if we remember Sartre's love of poems); the theorization of reading as something driven by freedom; the history of the relationship between a writer and his or her public—and despite the importance of a work that formed the baseline for all subsequent positions, including Maurice Blanchot's *La part du feu* (*The Work of Fire*), Roland Barthes's *Le degré zéro de l'écriture* (*Writing Degree Zero*), and third-worldist writings, what is a *literary essay* doing here among all these books forming the edifice of the social sciences?

In his essay, Sartre invents a critical practice that sets literature along the path *toward* the social world and *for* subjective freedom—from which literature emerged changed for good. His hatred of the classics, the charges he brings against the "autarky" of past literature (identified with prestige) and bourgeois writers (running after this prestige) established the line on which Bourdieu, in a scarcely submerged dialogue with the author of *L'idiot de la famille*, later built his *Les règles de l'art* [The Rules of Art] that likewise depicted "his Flaubert." Sartre established the literature to come—the literature he hoped for and that he wished his contemporaries capable of—as the spur to a critique of moral and cultural experience, summoning it as an ally against enslavement, working on a poetics of emancipation later taken up by Frantz Fanon, Edward Said, and Judith Butler, among others.

But perhaps this book also marks the end of a period when literature was a given. For, in asking what literature is, it holds the answer to be not self-evident, thus consigning literature to contingency. It also marks the end of the time when it was obvious that literary thought and literary practice partook in the manufacture of knowledge. This involvement had a name: the essay. Yet within the social sciences, nothing would subsequently be more suspect than "essayism." It is this essayism—connecting the *engagement* of writing, the critique of the present, and self-mobilization (in a landscape in which *Les Temps modernes* and *Critique*, generalist journals, albeit founded by writers, had assumed the mantle of the *Nouvelle Revue Française*)—that Sartre embodied at his peak (as Barthes did after him, though far more fragilely).

It is significant that this brief history of the social sciences opens, with Sartre, on what these sciences have continually doubted: the dignity of engaging thought in matters of form, what Francis Ponge has called "the rage for expression." Because what matters is not whether the act of writing, with its motives and destination—around which Sartre wove his definition of literature ever more sovereignly—is more elegant or more personal, but whether it is more true. And it is precisely this rage for expression we encounter today in the sincerity with which historians, anthropologists, and sociologists not only ask how to go about writing their science but engage with the purpose that literature and the social sciences have in common: namely, an unyielding description of reality. This is the meaning at the heart of the *engagement* that Sartre demanded of prose: to ensure that nobody could claim ignorance of the world, and that all be answerable for it.

Marielle Macé

Jean-Paul Sartre, *Situations II* (Paris: Gallimard, 1948). Republished by Gallimard, 2012.

1949

THE MEDITERRANEAN AND THE MEDITERRANEAN WORLD IN THE AGE OF PHILIP II: BRAUDEL'S INTERLOCKING DURATIONS

Between 1940 and 1945, while in a German prison camp, Fernand Braudel (1902–1985) put the finishing touches to the definitive architecture of his thesis, started twenty years earlier, about the Mediterranean in the time of King Philip II of Spain. He chose to dissect his study into various planes, or tiers, distinguishing between three time frames structuring his analysis. The first is that of the *longue durée*: a "virtually motionless," "almost timeless history," corresponding to the Mediterranean climate and environment, geomorphological relief and stability, and an expanded Mediterranean linked to the Sahara, northern Europe, Russia, and the Atlantic Ocean. The second part examines the conjuncture of the sixteenth century and its economic oscillations; this corresponds to a "slow rhythmed" "social" history, describing price cycles, trade flows, the stratification of societies, and the various forms of warfare. Then comes the third part, devoted to events and politics, the more "traditional" part, as Braudel observes, presenting the rapid movement of battles pitting Spain against the Ottomans, diplomatic talks and treaties, and including the famous pages about the death of Philip II.

Braudel wanted *La Méditerranée* (*The Mediterranean*) to function as a manifesto for a new way of writing and doing history now that the war was over. This approach, with the institutional backing provided by the founding of the new economics and social science section in 1947 at the École pratique des hautes études (EPHE), carried forward the type of social and economic history associated with the *Annales*. Although the book finally contained little in the way of figures and measurements, it sought to establish a dialogue with economic history and sociology. Nevertheless, among its mosaic of descriptions and bountiful metaphors, what readers mainly took from the book was the layered conception of sociohistorical times. It was only later, though, that Braudel radicalized his historiographical positions on this subject: In his famous article in the *Annales* on the *longue durée* (1958), he invited the social sciences as a whole, in the face of structuralism, to integrate the long-term effects of geography and the environment in analyzing and understanding social facts, thus giving the historical discipline a predominant place in the unity of the "human sciences."

"I have restarted *La Méditerranée* I don't know how many times," he explained in 1977. In fact, while writing the first volume (1967–1979) of *Civilisation matérielle, économie et capitalisme* (*Civilization and Capitalism*), Braudel also prepared a second, substantially reworked and influential edition, whose American translation (1972) brought him international recognition. On the strength of his position at *Annales*, at the EPHE, and at the Collège de France, he was now surrounded by what Jack Hexter ironically dubbed the "Braudelian world," an entire extended network of students, correspondents, and associates contributing to works published by the newly formed Centre de recherches historiques in the "Affaires et gens d'affaires" (Trade and traders) and "Ports, routes, trafics" (Ports, roads, traffic) series. Their work supplemented *The Mediterranean* with notes, maps, and new data about the Italian lands in the sixteenth century or the Atlantic. Together, they confirmed one of the main theses of the book—namely, that the political importance and economic prosperity of the Mediterranean were maintained through to the mid-seventeenth century and beyond even. Braudel, who had drawn on a mass of documentation gathered in Spain, France, Italy, and Dubrovnik, nevertheless came to realize that the renewal of studies on the Mediterranean in the early modern period necessarily entailed better knowledge of Turkish archives and the Ottoman world. As full of intuitions and suggestions as ever, *La Méditerranée* continued to feed into new avenues of inquiry, such as environmental history, merchant networks and behavior, migrations and personal mobility, the forms taken by maritime trade traffic in coastal societies, and bonded labor.

Braudel's way of thinking about space and time, as set out in *La Méditerranée*, has substantially fueled thought over the past forty years on how scales and durations interlock. Additionally, as shown by philosophers (first among them, Paul Ricœur), Braudel remains essential reading for anyone interested in the plotting of historical narratives. For example, the passages on the 1571 Battle of Lepanto contain counterfactual propositions, showing that Braudel was also a historian of the possibilities and discontinuities within historical processes. Braudel's style of geohistory has also been applied to other "Mediterraneans" around the world—for example, Southeast Asia, the Indian Ocean, the Caribbean, and the Baltic Sea. Even "global" historians trace a lineage back to Braudel, despite there being the occasional misunderstanding here, for in his instance the "globality" has less to do with a scale encompassing the whole world than with a way of "systematically going beyond the limits" of a historical problem.

La Méditerranée obviously contains dated passages, such as those about the backwardness of "Islamic civilizations," which bear the mark of the colonial then developmentalist context in which it was written, leading Braudel to neglect the simultaneity and reciprocity of borrowings between Western Europe and Islam in the early modern period. The book has also been criticized for its Eurocentric "Mediterraneanism." In the wake of Braudel, the uncertain field of "Mediterranean studies" has continually debated the forms of unity, fragmentation, and fracture affecting the Mediterranean world. Nowadays, the Mediterranean is no longer thought of as an "exceptional" figure but as a very lively laboratory for research in history and the social sciences—a laboratory whose foundations were undeniably laid by Fernand Braudel's masterpiece.

Guillaume Calafat

Fernand Braudel, *La Méditerranée et le monde méditerranéen à l'époque de Philippe II*, 3 vols. (Paris: Armand Colin, 1949). Republished by Armand Colin, 2017. Translated into English by Siân Reynolds as *The Mediterranean and the Mediterranean World in the Age of Philip II* (New York: Harper & Row, 1972–1973).

1949

THE ELEMENTARY STRUCTURES OF KINSHIP: LÉVI-STRAUSS FOUNDS KINSHIP ON MATRIMONIAL EXCHANGE

On reading the *thèse d'État* defended by Claude Lévi-Strauss (1908–2009) at the Sorbonne after several years of exile in the United States, the American anthropologist Robert Lowie laconically described it as being "in the grand style." If Lévi-Strauss's secondary thesis on *La vie familiale et sociale des Indiens Nambikwara* (*Family and Social Life of the Nambikwara Indians*) is highly classical, the primary thesis—*Les structures élémentaires de la parenté* (*The Elementary Structures of Kinship*)—stands out starkly for the ambition of its project, style, and method. Its great achievement is to present a synthetic theory of a set of facts that had already been extensively debated but hitherto envisaged separately: How are we to explain both the universality of the incest prohibition (it is *a minima* a forbidden form of marriage in all places) and the extreme variability with which it is applied (with the circle of prohibited people varying considerably from one society to another)? Why are kinship groups exogamous? How are we to explain the occurrence of privileged unions between certain cousins, the children of a brother and a sister (cross-cousins) and not between children of two sisters or two brothers (parallel cousins)? How are we to interpret the emergence of kinship systems from the viewpoint of social evolution? In answering these questions, Lévi-Strauss puts forward a series of answers whose originality announces a method—structural analysis—inspired by the linguistics of Ferdinand de Saussure and Roman Jakobson.

In the same way as the phonemes of a language have no intrinsic but only positional meaning, so kinship groups do not exist independently of one another. In the field of kinship, the relationship that takes precedence over the terms is marriage. Marriage, which cannot be reduced to a private contract between two people, is a form of exchange in which two family groups enter into an alliance in which each cedes one of its members. Taking exchange as the prime reason for kinship systems (building on work by Mauss) presents two advantages. It makes it possible to solve the question of where the incest prohibition comes from. Matrimonial exchange contains the logical implication of this prohibition, in that it imposes marrying outside one's own circle of relatives. Since it is impossible for a man to marry his sister or daughter, he is compelled to marry the sister or daughter of another man, who in turn renounces marrying his own close relatives. There is thus no need to speculate on the origin of the incest prohibition. Exogamy and incest prohibition are just the two faces—one negative, one positive—of a same imperative of exchange between family units otherwise condemned to isolation. This structural theory of kinship is also an evolutionist scenario, for it is henceforth impossible to imagine the existence of family units prior to the emergence of the incest prohibition. The idea of the family is not posterior to the emergence of culture, it is the most manifest concomitant expression thereof.

The second advantage of such an analysis is that it explains the apparently arbitrary principles relating to marriage between cross-cousins. Lévi-Strauss distinguishes between *elementary structures*, in which matrimonial alliances are regulated by prohibitions but especially by injunctions to marry such and such a relative, and *complex structures* in which the circle of prohibited relatives is identified, though without laying down any guidelines about the choice of spouse.

Based on comparative work encompassing Australia, southern India, China, and even Siberia, Lévi-Strauss teases out two formulas for exchange: *restricted exchange*, bilateral marriage in which two men exchange their sisters; and *generalized exchange*, associated with the asymmetry of matrilateral marriage, based on cycles in which at least three groups point toward each other (A gives to B who gives to C who gives to A). The third formula, that of patrilateral marriage, comes somewhere between the other two and is assimilated to a *deferred* restricted exchange, with reciprocity being delayed to the following generation, but also to asymmetric marriage, giving rise to shorter and less integrative cycles. Unlike bilateral marriage, exemplified by practices in Australia, and unlike matrilateral marriage, whose existence was observed by Marcel Granet in China and by the Dutch school in Indonesia, patrilateral marriage is more consistent with the model than with empirical observation. The transformational analysis advocated by Lévi-Strauss—and subsequently fined-tuned by his vast comparative undertaking on Amerindian myth—turned each kinship system studied into a variant of all the others. The book was translated into English by Rodney Needham in 1969, but Lévi-Strauss's formalism seemed too abstract and speculative for the British empirical tradition, as evidenced in the famous debate with Edmund Leach about the generalized exchange of the Kachin of Burma. Lévi-Strauss's intuitions nevertheless bore fruit in southern India, thanks to work by Louis Dumont, then in Amazonia, after ethnographic research took off into this part of the world.

The severest criticisms have been directed toward the idea of exchange: either in disputing, from a feminist perspective, the subordinate position of women as objects of exchange between groups of men, or by questioning the universality of exchange, in the light of societies that privilege endogenous unions (between the children of two brothers) or those that afford only marginal recognition to marriage (the Na of China). But Lévi-Strauss stood by his theory, refuting feminist criticisms by inverting the terms (women could just as well exchange men without altering any aspect of the model) and by arguing for the universality of exchange as a necessary condition for kinship systems. Nearly seventy years after it was first published, *Les structures élémentaires* remains a unique work that is both deeply inspiring and profoundly disconcerting. It enjoys the rare privilege of still being contested and celebrated with a force equaling the power of its propositions.

Laurent Gabail

Claude Lévi-Strauss, *Les structures élémentaires de la parenté* (Paris: Presses universitaires de France ["Bibliothèque de philosophie contemporaine"], 1949). Republished by Éditions de l'EHESS, 2017. Translated into English by James Harle Bell, John Richard von Sturmer, and Rodney Needham as *The Elementary Structures of Kinship* (Boston: Beacon Press, 1969).

1949

MALE AND FEMALE: MEAD DENATURALIZES THE DIFFERENCE BETWEEN THE SEXES

In the same year that Simone de Beauvoir published *Le deuxième sexe* (*The Second Sex*), Margaret Mead (1901–1978) examined the construction of male and female identities, comparing the ontogenesis of the relations between the sexes in eight societies she had already studied in Polynesia (*Coming of Age in Samoa*, 1928), Indonesia (*Balinese Character*, 1942, written with anthropologist Gregory Bateson, her third husband), the United States (*And Keep Your Powder Dry*, 1942), and Melanesia (*Growing up in New Guinea*, 1930; *Sex and Temperament in Three Primitive Societies*, 1935).

A pupil of Franz Boas and Ruth Benedict at Columbia, Mead adhered to culturalism, which stresses the variability of behaviors acquired through the socialization and enculturation of young children and by the communication and acculturation of traditions among adults. As of the 1920s, psychology and psychoanalysis fed into the thought of these anthropologists who, though often refuting the Freudian doxa, particularly the Oedipus complex, sought what, in addition to language, is "unconscious" within societies and transmitted from one generation to the next.

Mead focuses on parent/child relations to identify the conditions in which men and women acquire aptitudes to carry out such and such an activity, to behave in such and such a manner, from one culture to another. Her approach is driven by two key ideas: The fixing of male and female roles derives from functional and anatomical differences between the sexes linked to the reproduction of the species yet without being determined by these (what Françoise Héritier went on to call the "differential valence of the sexes"); this acquisition of sex-related attributes takes place within the relational dynamics at work in childhood and adolescence, based around the differentiated usage of bodily orifices (the mouth and anus) and the genital organs (the vulva and penis).

This is where the subtlety of Mead's theory, underpinned by Bateson's work on "schismogenesis," has often been misunderstood: The biological invariants of sexuated bodies listed by the sciences may seem to be innate predispositions; but they are in fact only actualized, or replaced, reinforced, or inhibited, through complimentary symmetrical or reciprocal relations deployed between men and women. For example, the secretion of large quantities of testosterone may lead to attitudes of dominance, but such behavior by men also triggers an opposed attitude of submission among women, retroactively reinforcing the interdependence of these gendered attributes ("complimentary schismogenesis"), to the extent that it will be imitated and reproduced by these women and thus mutually exacerbated in either sex, hence engendering two equivalent genders ("symmetrical schismogenesis"). Only the principle of reciprocity is capable of stabilizing these complementarily or symmetrically adjusted behaviors either, in the first case, by the alternating permutation of a form of domination and submission in the two sexes or, in the second case, by the concomitant abandonment of radicalized forms of dominance behaviors.

For Mead, the construction of male and female identities thus occurs on the immanent plane of relational dynamics between the sexes and owes nothing to bodily biology, even though the latter may condition certain virtual complementarities, present from the stage of parent/infant interaction (with the passive receptiveness or active prehension of the encouraged/ discouraged mouth during breastfeeding or the elimination *versus* retention of fecal matter by encouraging sphincter control or not).

This theoretical framework for apprehending what is innate and what is acquired in the differentiation of sexuated behaviors paradoxically makes it possible to defend essentialist and existentialist positions at one and the same time. For Mead, one is not born but rather becomes a woman—through menstruation, childbirth, and the menopause, marking the irreversible stages absent in the life of men, consequently obliged to define their masculinity on the basis of activities forbidden to women. Despite this, the instinctive nature of maternal behavior is refuted by the diversity of forms of childbirth, even if "women may be said to be mothers unless they are taught to deny their child-bearing qualities." And civilizational decline threatens whenever the conduct of complex activities (government, science, art, religion, industry) is the preserve of a single sex. The lack of interaction precludes stimulation of the creativity and inventiveness of mutually adjusted behaviors: "is not the danger for a society to deny its girls the right to use their minds or their bodies in some way that is permitted to boys?"

While Mead takes note of studies showing that activity rhythms are sex-related (men alternating violent effort and compensatory rest, with women practicing monotonous and continuous work in tune with their biological rhythm), it is better to emphasize that in fact this innatist fiction only transpires among the Iatmul. In Samoa, the rhythms are the same for the two sexes and determined by rank and age; among the Arapesh, men and women alternate between these two rhythmic styles; the Balinese know nothing of sudden bursts of work; and middle-class American women are caught in a double bind (though educated to freely choose their spouse and employment, upon marrying they are assigned monotonous tasks not recognized as labor).

While Mead's empirical descriptions and accounts are often persuasive, her ethnography and generalizations have come in for criticism, given the extent to which the societies described seem to have been "warped." Arapesh men and women appear similarly gentle and sensitive, Mundugumor men and women similarly violent and aggressive, and Chambouli men and women inversely distinct from Americans. But the key point of her demonstration remains intact: Irrespective of the attributes a society confers on men and women, these are independent of the biological substratum, and sexual roles—what we today call gender—vary greatly from one culture to another; that is the lesson the social sciences and feminists have taken from this work, which was instrumental in liberalizing customs in the United States.

Laurent Berger

Margaret Mead, *Male and Female: A Study of Sexes in a Changing World* (New York: Morrow, 1949).

1949

SOCIAL THEORY AND SOCIAL STRUCTURE: MERTON SUGGESTS A CODE OF CONDUCT FOR SOCIOLOGY

Though feted as one of the great classics of twentieth-century sociology, *Social Theory and Social Structure* by Robert K. Merton (1910–2003) is not a book in the ordinary meaning of the term but a collation of texts written at different periods on various subjects. Its kaleidoscopic nature may seem disconcerting, but one should not be misled by this appearance: Whether analyzing the structures of individual action or the action of social structures on individuals, examining the dynamic of groups and organizations or the elementary mechanisms of social life, it deploys a very coherent theoretical matrix. As the chapters progress, Merton lays down the groundwork for, if not an overall theory of society, then at least a general framework for sociological inquiry. This framework was tirelessly reworked, supplemented, and explained by its author over the course of the book's many subsequent editions (the 1968 edition, the most widely used today, runs to 702 pages, compared with the 423 pages of the 1949 edition). But from its first edition, the book contained the main points in Merton's ideas about sociology, revealing the originality of his approach. It is open to Karl Mannheim's sociology of knowledge and certain contributions of the Chicago school (particularly William Thomas), putting forward a new vision of functionalism that stood apart from the then-dominant structural-functional school, instituted by the sociologist who had been Merton's mentor at Harvard in the 1930s, Talcott Parsons.

From the outset, Merton stated his refusal to indulge in the abstractions of social philosophy typical of the period. To his mind, it was important that sociological theories be empirically verifiable and based on rigorous investigation methods. One could even say that this is the programmatic intent lending his work its coherence: that of "regulating" the practice of inquiry and especially of linking up theory and empirical inquiry in a satisfactory manner. In this respect, the approach is meant to be inseparably analytical and normative: Merton seeks to establish a sort of "code of conduct" for the profession of sociology—a profession he was ceaselessly involved in organizing from the chair he held at the University of Colombia from 1941 to 1979.

What does this code of conduct entail? First, Merton calls for the development of middle-range theories, illustrating their benefits by examples. By encouraging these local theories focused on a defined aspect of social reality (for example, the theory of reference groups or that of social mobility and stratification), he seeks to break both with atheoretical sociography and with general theory disconnected from inquiry. As an optimist, he thought that this more modest bottom-up approach would eventually generate gains in knowledge.

On this basis, the various "paradigm-essays" composing the book present investigation protocols, along with operatory concepts for inquiry. Their specificity is that they encapsulate a theoretical viewpoint (such as the famous notions of serendipity, the effect of making a scientific discovery or technical invention without having sought to do so, or a self-realizing prophesy, a prediction that comes true by its modifying actors' behavior). The chapter about "functional analysis in sociology" exemplifies this strategy, which systematically includes thinking about the limits of the reasoning submitted to the reader. Merton, seeking to introduce some order in the usage of the tricky notion of "function," which was inspiring most of his American colleagues in the late 1940s, took the opportunity to lay down a framework for analysis that he deemed more robust, although still to be tested in future research. Though useful, perhaps not all his classificatory work is conclusive: For example, the distinction between manifest function and latent function did not produce the hoped-for results and was not really taken up. But for Merton, the fact that a proposition failed to convince was a result in itself because verifying it entails setting to one side theoretical options that turn out to be disappointing. Thus, in the chapter on "Social

17   *Merton Suggests a Code of Conduct for Sociology*

Structure and Anomie" (1938), he sets out a structural approach to the social and cultural origins of deviant behavior, which led to major developments in sociology and criminology—until the paradigm dried up.

By gathering articles in *Social Theory and Social Structure* that had already been copiously cited, Merton knew he would increase the profile of his book. Indeed, it is his best-known work, more so than *On the Shoulders of Giants* (1965), which he considered to be his masterwork. Chapters are given as assigned reading in courses on method or introductory modules to the history of social theory. This is what he expected, and he was used to sharing his initial ideas with students before consolidating them in his essays. Still, the influence of the ideas in *Social Theory and Social Structure* has not been universal. Though extensively read in Italy and Eastern Europe, Merton is less studied in France. While Henri Mendras's 1953 translation into French (*Éléments de méthode sociologique*) met with some success, Merton's contribution in France remained limited to matters of theory and method, thus occluding his many empirical insights. Nevertheless, Merton's book is a classic that has exerted a lasting effect on research and is useful to re-consult, taking as one's example the attitude its author recommended when reading classical theory: without fetishism or reverence, and with a constant concern for critical revision and actualization.

Arnaud Saint-Martin

Robert K. Merton, *Social Theory and Social Structure* (New York: Free Press, 1949).

1950

SOCIOLOGIE ET ANTHROPOLOGIE: MAUSS AND THE CONSECRATION OF THE SOCIAL UNCONSCIOUS

Sociologie et anthropologie (Sociology and anthropology) is based on a misunderstanding. The postwar intellectual renaissance was in need of an anthology of the main texts by Marcel Mauss (1872–1950), Émile Durkheim's nephew, to revitalize his legacy. This was an opportunity to rediscover "Essai sur le don" ("The Gift," 1923) and "Les techniques du corps" ("Techniques of the body," 1934) and appreciate that the nephew's genius ended up rivaling that of his founding ancestor. The volume includes other texts—namely, "Esquisse d'une théorie générale de la magie" ("A General Theory of Magic," 1902), "Rapports réels et pratiques de la psychologie et de la sociologie" ("Real and practical relations between psychology and sociology," 1924), "Effet physique chez l'individu de l'idée de mort suggérée par la collectivité" ("The physical effect on the individual of the idea of death suggested by the collectivity," 1926), and "La notion de personne" ("The Category of the Person," 1938). Over the course of the revised editions, the publisher ended up including "Essai sur les variations saisonnières des sociétés eskimos" ("Seasonal variations of the Eskimo," 1904), written with Henri Beuchat. The addition of this text, which anticipated the developments of American cultural ecology fifty years later, rebalances the anthology toward anthropology, undeniably making it a better book.

Independent of being a collection of texts, the book displays Mauss's dazzling theoretical imagination to the full, while also exhibiting his vast curiosity, versatility, and ability to turn his hand to virtually anything. This may be seen in the themes discussed—and the historical periods and cultures on which his arguments draw—as well as in the methods followed: While "Essai sur le don" is of proto-structuralist persuasion, and "La notion de personne" is profoundly marked by a nicely judged evolutionism (pertaining to the moral order), "Les techniques du corps" is a culturalist gem. Hence the tendency to distinguish between two Mausses: the Mauss who takes hold of an object or field (reciprocity, the body, seasonality), invents it in the strong meaning of the term, and seems to exhaust all potential analysis from the outset; and the Mauss who inquired into the preoccupations of his contemporaries, addressing magic (that is, the irrational) and the relationship between the individual and the collective (that is, how psychology relates to sociology) or advocating dialogue with personalist philosophy, which was very much in vogue just before the war. Both Mausses figure in this collection, but it is obviously the contributions of the former, however imperfect or approximate they may have been said to be, that still have the power to stun us by the power and audacity of their theory.

Georges Gurvitch, the guardian of the temple, had entrusted Lévi-Strauss with writing the preface. This was a serious mistake. The misunderstanding could not have been greater. He no doubt expected the young anthropologist, just back from a long period of exile in the United States, to diligently emphasize the filiation with Durkheim and laud the good pupil of the French school of sociology. Lévi-Strauss pursued the exact opposite line. In his lengthy text with its feverish style and marked philosophical tones, punctuated with hard-hitting formulations ("Mauss still believes it possible to erect a social theory of symbolism, whereas it is quite clear that one must instead look for a symbolic origin for society"; "the ethnological problem is thus ultimately a problem of communication"; "the universe started signifying well before we started knowing what it was signifying"), he delivers a reading of Mauss that strips him bare, in which praise and criticism are equipoised; he also takes the opportunity to clear the ground for his own benefit. Lévi-Strauss had just published *Les structures élémentaires de la parenté* (*The Elementary Structures of Kinship*), for which "Essai sur le don" was the main source of inspiration; he claimed to be a follower of Jakobson and was starting a dialogue with Lacan, which would soon be cut short. His two watchwords at the time were *language* and *unconscious*.

Concerning "Essai sur le don" in particular, Lévi-Strauss recognizes his predecessor's great merit in transcending our ordinary categories and in placing goods, statuses, and people on the same plane in a mechanics of a reciprocity. But he reproaches him with not having seen the principle of exchange underpinning that of reciprocity, lying at a deeper level, that of a general and social unconscious specific to human culture. There is no similarity in cultural behaviors, notably pertaining to the balanced circulation of goods; but there is a common foundation to all human cultures, residing in exchange (of women). Lévi-Strauss's criticism is even severer concerning categories. Although Mauss understands their cultural nature and entrusts anthropology with drawing up their inventory through cultural diversities, he does not appreciate that they issue directly from language and are necessarily embedded in systems of meaning. Nevertheless, to the extent that signification (in other words, the cognitive capacity to generate signifiers) always exceeds knowledge, all increases in the latter imply a readjusting of categories. This idea resurfaced in *La pensée sauvage* (*The Savage Mind*), in inflected form, for that matter. Another dazzling idea: The *hau* and the *mana* need to be thought of as "floating signifiers," or as zero signifiers devoid of any specific signified, as adjustment variables for gaps between categories. This idea reemerged much later (at the end of *Mythologiques*) in Lévi-Strauss's theory of the ritual as a space of non-signification, precisely because it was interstitial space that, unlike myth, was saturated in meaning.

This book opened up a space between Mauss and Lévi-Strauss, between the former's faculty for observation and common sense taken to the point of incandescence—for, ultimately, it is *almost* a matter of common sense that reciprocity creates social ties or that bodily postures respond to codes laid down by culture—and the latter's ambition to subject the data given by reality to transmutation, which, by virtue of the model offered by the structures of language, opened up greater potential for interpretation. And it is most definitely within this space that, over the past seventy years, the main debates of the social sciences have taken place, turning their back resolutely on any naturalist temptation.

Emmanuel Désveaux

Marcel Mauss, *Sociologie et anthropologie* (Paris: Presses universitaires de France ["Bibliothèque de sociologie contemporaine"], 1950), with a preface by Claude Lévi-Strauss. Republished by PUF, 2010. Most of the collection has been translated into English as separate publications (*A General Theory of Magic* translated by Robert Brain [London: Routledge and Kegan Paul, 1972]; *The Gift: The Form and Reason for Exchange in Archaic Societies* translated by W. D. Halls [New York: W. W. Norton & Company, 1990]; and *Sociology and Psychology: Essays*, translated by Ben Brewster [London: Routledge and Kegan Paul, 1979]).

1951

THE ORIGINS OF TOTALITARIANISM: ARENDT AND THE RADICAL NOVELTY OF TOTALITARIANISM

Over sixty years after it first came out, it is not really a matter of "rereading" *The Origins of Totalitarianism*, for this book has never ceased being read, studied, and taught in many languages around the world. It was published in New York in February 1951 as a single volume, divided into three parts: "Antisemitism," "Imperialism," and "Totalitarianism." However, it opened with an introduction that was cut from the second edition, in 1958, and never replaced, though as of the third edition, in 1966, Hannah Arendt (1906–1975) opted to insert prefaces to each of the three parts (one of which poses the three questions guiding her work: What happened? Why did it happen? How is it possible?). But above all, *The Origins of Totalitarianism* finished with brief "Concluding Remarks," which she deemed sufficiently "inconclusive" to cut in 1958 and replace with a text that considerably shaped the book's subsequent destiny.

Another point of note is a concise entry found in Arendt's notebooks that is most informative about a question never explicitly raised in the book itself: "Method in the historical sciences: forget all causality. Instead: analyze elements in the event. The central event is that in which events suddenly crystallize. Title of my book fundamentally wrong; it should have been called *The Elements of Totalitarianism*." This entry is dated June 1951, just a few months after her book came out. But it only had one direct effect—namely, the title of its translation into German, by Arendt herself, which was published in 1955: *Elemente und Ursprünge totaler Herrschaft*.

This brief note and other documents show that Arendt soon reached two realizations: The first was the risk that her book, whose intellectual workmanship and style were that of "monumental" history, might give the feeling that anti-Semitism (linked to the decline of the nation-state) plus imperialism (bound up with the increasing prevalence of racial theories) led inexorably to totalitarian domination; second, she had not managed to capture the radical novelty of a type of regime that was not wholly explicable in terms of its past or conceivable in the classical or more recent categories of tyranny, despotism, and authoritarianism.

As it stood, her thesis was that while all known political regimes had functioned to maintain stability in human affairs, the two totalitarianisms rested alike on the "laws of movement," which she resumed as follows: "People are threatened by Communist propaganda with missing the train of history, with remaining hopelessly behind their time, with spending their lives uselessly, just as they were threatened by the Nazis with living against the eternal rules of nature and life, with an irreparable and mysterious deterioration of their blood." More empirically, totalitarian regimes were characterized by, among other factors, the monopoly one party exerted over organizing the masses, the importance of propaganda, and the decisive role played by the secret police. As for the more opaque phenomenon of concentration camps and extermination, it could only be approached keeping David Rousset's formula in mind that "ordinary people do not know that everything is possible."

This is all a considerable achievement and would no doubt have sufficed to establish *The Origins of Totalitarianism* amid the landscape of its period and subsequent periods—despite the first part being thrown slightly off balance by the desire to overturn the vision that Jews supposedly had of themselves as eternal victims of history, despite the notion of imperialism seeming to be lifted straight from the agenda of historians, and despite the analyses of Nazi and communist societies being thrown into disarray by the flood of previously unreleased archives and the use of new models. But almost as soon as her book came out, Arendt was certain it needed a "supplement," the intuition of which was encapsulated in a few words jotted down in March 1952: "ideology = logic of an idea." This was the starting point for a text completed in just a few weeks and on which *The Origins of Totalitarianism* closed as of its German translation in 1955 and its second

American edition in 1958: in the space of twenty-five or so pages, "Ideology and Terror" remarshals all the material with incomparable force, isolating the two major components to the totalitarian phenomenon.

We have already noted the aspects of this book to have aged, for reasons in no way attributable to its author. But one major point remains undimmed: Who still reads Carl J. Friedrich's *Totalitarianism* (1954) or Friedrich and Zbigniew Brzezinski's *Totalitarian Dictatorship and Autocracy* (1965), not to mention the thousands of pages devoted to discussions of the criteria of totalitarianism(s)? Arendt and the most eminent representatives of the American social sciences might have maintained a wary distance from each other, but the facts of the matter are simple and cruel: An "academic" literature in tune with its epoch has lost its sheen, while this heterodox book continues to sit atop what one may call what one likes, but why not the "social sciences"? As for the pairing of ideology and terror, who would deny its use in rendering recent phenomena intelligible; hence why not also designate them "totalitarian"? One of the lessons of *The Origins of Totalitarianism* is that one of the specificities of great concepts is that they remain available for periods after their invention, productive in disciplines other than that of their creator, and applicable to objects other than those for which they were forged.

Pierre Bouretz

Hannah Arendt, *The Origins of Totalitarianism* (New York: Harcourt, Brace, 1951).

1952

KNOWLEDGE OF LIFE: CANGUILHEM REDEFINES THE PRINCIPLE OF LIFE

Though this masterwork by Georges Canguilhem (1904–1995) looks like a disparate set of lectures and journal articles, its unity is nevertheless real. After an introduction about "Thought and the Living," there are three parts about experimentation in animal biology, cell theory, and several correlated themes: "Aspects of Vitalism," "Machine and Organism," "The Living and Its Milieu," and "The Normal and the Pathological." A chapter about "Monstrosity and the Monstrous" was added for the 1965 second edition. The appendix—composed of notes on fibrillar theory and cell theory and an extract on the anatomy of the brain—confirms that this book, with its at times dry style of writing, is not to be read as a systematic treaty, even though it works toward a single objective: determining the properties of "life" while explaining how thought may understand a protean phenomenon transpiring in numerous beings in a state of continuous evolution—that is, "the living."

A first line of inquiry examines the phenomenon of life by looking at the organism: its composition, dysfunctions, development, and interactions with the environment. The second is more gnoseological: Canguilhem asks why the theoretical options of vitalism and mechanism have lasted so long and what ideas further our knowledge of life or, on the contrary, impede it. He shows that the history of science is fundamental for mapping out the field of theoretical possibilities, within which the human mind pursues its quest for intelligibility (hence the study of cell theory to apprehend the constitution of living bodies brings out an oscillation between the hypothesis of a continuous plastic substance and that of a composition of heterogeneous parts).

Through inquiry into how the whole may be linked to its parts, Canguilhem considers the system of relations established both within organisms and between organisms and their environment. Rather than seeking a universal essentialist definition of life, it is better to envisage it "as an order of properties"—that is, "an organization of powers and a hierarchy of functions whose stability is necessarily precarious." The goal is to follow how numerous internal and external interactions fashion living beings. Drawing on various domains (physiology, pathology, embryology, and teratology), he demonstrates the benefits of a two-stage intellectual operation of identifying elements then connecting them to higher levels of organization. Following in the wake of Claude Bernard, Canguilhem shows that decomposing living beings into organs and functions is only pertinent if the organism is initially addressed as a *whole*: It is thanks to the discovery of the regulation of glycemia within the body that it was possible to assign a function to the pancreas. More broadly, the functions of an organism depend on its relations with its environment. In this respect, illness is not a state whose abnormality may be quantitatively measured; rather, it a modification of capacities for action, "a pace of life regulated by norms that are vitally inferior." Works in embryology and teratology point toward a similar conclusion, for what seems monstrous at a given moment is the norm at another stage of evolution.

The notion of milieu thus holds a central place. Drawing on discoveries in ethology (Jakob von Uexküll) and in pathology (Kurt Goldstein), Canguilhem states that "it is characteristic of the living that it makes its milieu for itself, that it composes its milieu." This invitation to abandon conceptions that treat the organism as a being adapting to external constraints has two implications, one epistemological and the other anthropological. Instead of explaining how life appears within a physical-chemical universe, we need to envisage each living being as a sensory-motor, metabolic center from which the environment is perceived and organized. Vitalism properly understood is a constant attempt to understand the movement by which organisms transform themselves and transform their milieu by inventing new functions and ways of being in the world. Contrary to a metaphysical vitalism postulating a vital principle present in all bodies, this approach implies observing the diversity of singular organizations manifest in each living individual. Mechanism is thus critiqued, and analogies between living beings and designed artifacts are denounced as outright epistemological obstacles.

To forge authentically biological concepts, it is essential to decenter our perspective and not study life purely from our human experience of it. Yet it is in the pragmatic relation to the world that all knowledge of life originates. The implications of this reversal in the relations between the living and its milieu are thus also anthropological. André Leroi-Gourhan's work is mentioned to point out that within evolution, human techniques (medicine, domestication) may be viewed as ways of transforming the milieu. There is never any immediate knowledge of life but only knowledge mediated by technical processes (be these material, intellectual, or scientific), thanks to which humans try to act on vital processes while seeking to render them intelligible.

By identifying an impassable pragmatic horizon for exploring life, Canguilhem's work puts forward an original way of connecting *technè* and *épistémè*, paving the way for approaches that go far beyond traditional history of science or any epistemology of Bachelardian inspiration. By emphasizing the need to contextualize knowledge of—and power over—life, it offers profound inspiration for all anthropological approaches that, in the wake of Foucault, examine biopolitics or forms of life.

Perig Pitrou

Georges Canguilhem, *La connaissance de la vie* (Paris: Vrin, 1952). Republished by Vrin, 1965. Translated into English by Stefanos Geroulanos and Daniela Ginsburg as *Knowledge of Life* (New York: Fordham University Press, 2008).

1953

COMBATS POUR L'HISTOIRE: FEBVRE ANNOUNCES HISTORY'S FUTURE

Combats pour l'histoire (Combats for history) is a compilation of texts whose purpose is to construct history as a social science. The collection is composed of Lucien Febvre's programmatic articles, book reviews, reminiscences about scholars, and memories about the experience of men of his generation. One cannot avoid situating the texts in the periods when they were written, as he would no doubt have done himself. They reveal the sensibilities forged from the run-up to the Great War through to the aftermath of the Second World War. The most moving instance of this is his invocation of Marc Bloch. *Combats pour l'histoire* was compiled three years after the posthumous publication of Bloch's *Apologie pour l'histoire* (*The Historian's Craft*) by Armand Colin, the same publishing house that brought out *Annales*, the review that Bloch and Febvre had founded together in 1929. Febvre (1878–1956) was a historian of Franche-Comté at the time of Philip II, of the Reformation, of the "appearance of the book," and of the time of Rabelais and Marguerite de Navarre. He also viewed himself as a historian of his time and demanded that his colleagues be likewise.

The thread connecting these thirty-three texts is his view of history as a science still undergoing gestation and whose birth has only been announced. One may identify three phases: the future of an emergent discipline, present combats to usher it forth, and a past with a style steeped in nineteenth-century literary essays. One is inevitably struck by the distance that has opened up between Febvre and where we now stand. His pages are as much swashbuckling intervention as they are reflection. To mention but one instance, his writing, with its use of the vocative and second-person address, resonates with the spoken word. Indeed, many of these texts started off as lectures given by a professor who did not seek to conceal the role eloquence played in their composition. And yet, the feeling of distance generated by the style needs to be understood as stemming from the history separating the present-day reader from the author of these pages.

It would be unfair to retain solely Lucien Febvre's dated and dramatic mode of address. He attacks yet rarely disparages the most firmly held ideas in the intellectual and academic setting of his period: the agreed narrative of literary history; the isolation of intellectual history from all consideration of the social conditions in which texts are produced and received; the narrow field of vision focusing on national space, taken as central, and a rigid, linear way of thinking of the passage of time. These are but a few of the shortcomings he flags. What strikes us today—the contrast being so pronounced—is the role Febvre advocated for the reviews that mattered in his life, the *Revue de synthèse* and the *Annales*, along with others such as the *Revue de métaphysique et de morale*. He views these scholarly publications as places of expression, polemic, and even intervention in contemporary events. He might not erase the distinction between scholarly journals and periodicals of essays and opinions, nor does he confine academic journals to mere erudition.

Taking part in public discussion in no way means converting beliefs into slogans. For the correct method consists in "complicating what seems too simple." This critical exploration is turned toward the future of intellectual work. But anticipation, Febvre writes almost apologetically, should not dress itself up as prophecy. On the contrary, the correct approach consists in allowing experimentation to take its course. Hence, organizing or reorganizing history as a discipline requires firm discussion and a resolute approach. Febvre does battle on a great number of fronts, pulling in his wake the agenda of historians in dialogue with historical linguistics, social psychology, geography, literary studies, sociology in the Durkheimian tradition, and even ethnology. The attraction to social science does not exclude pursuing research on the cultural similarities of places and periods. In *Combats pour l'histoire*, Febvre, like Lévi-Strauss, is quick to raise the alarm that cultural legacies risk being eroded then conflated on a worldwide scale.

30   *Combats pour l'histoire*

However, history's future is not defined solely by its openness to other disciplines. After all, claiming a discipline has become closed is often a specter one raises to better set oneself apart, rather than a practice doing observable harm to intellectual life. The history Febvre announces was to be a collective exercise in research. This point is made in several chapters of the book. It is the main thesis running through the work. Calls to copy a life or earth sciences laboratory are bravely assumed. The collective work builds and combines a very large volume of data in order to move beyond individual cases (at best) and anecdote (at worse) and to relate different specialisms and issues to throw light on a conjointly defined historical problem.

Febvre not only sets himself up as the person to order these methods and techniques of investigation, but he also wishes to be involved in the issues of the day. That is why some of the questions he raises speak to us today. He rejects a definition of "being French" in terms of "race," holding "Blacks, Arabs, and Indochinese" living in mainland France to be "authentic Frenchmen." He also asserts that "in France there is no hostility toward foreigners, except perhaps if they bring their country with them and return with it unchanged at the end of their stay." Are not the terms of the debate still valid today?

Jean-Frédéric Schaub

Lucien Febvre, *Combats pour l'histoire* (Paris: Armand Colin ["Économies, sociétés, civilisations"], 1953). Republished by Bouquins, 2009.

1954

POLITICAL SYSTEMS OF HIGHLAND BURMA: LEACH EXPLODES THE STABILITY OF SOCIAL STRUCTURE

Political Systems of Highland Burma was written by Edmund Leach (1910–1989) under highly unusual circumstances, illustrative of how World War II affected the social sciences. The work of one of the preeminent figures in British anthropology, and the fruit of fieldwork in Burma from October 1939 to June 1940, the book had to be entirely rewritten after the war, based on memories and historical documents, for Leach's notes, photographs, and field sketches had been destroyed during the Japanese invasion.

The book is about two ethnic groups, the Kachin and the Shan, living in the valleys and mountainous regions of northern Burma. It contains previously unknown ethnographic data and interprets them in an ambitious and innovative theoretical framework.

Leach argues primarily that social structures are essentially unstable, upending the convictions of the most illustrious representatives of the functionalist school (Alfred Radcliffe-Brown, Meyer Fortes), who considered social roles and statuses as being mutually reinforcing to ensure the stability of a social structure (the "mechanical" or "organic" equilibrium). Change was possible within such a framework but limited to a transitory state between two balanced hence static structures. Leach was one of the first to refute this model, showing the dynamics of transformation inherent to the functioning of all social structures (dynamic equilibrium). To his mind, these dynamics derived from the conceptualizations that social actors have of roles and statuses, which are always ambiguous because of the power relations pitting them against each other.

The starting point for his analysis is the existence of a paradoxical situation among the Kachin, who have a dual political organization comprising two antagonistic forms: *gumlao* and *gumsa*. The former, described by Leach as "democratic," is a headless system only found up to the level of the village, in which authority is spread equitably between all the representatives of lineages without any distinction of rank. The second is "autocratic" and corresponds to the chiefdom model, that is, a centralized system marked by a distinction into "noble" and "common" lineages, and a pyramidal structure linking village communities, each led by a hereditary noble chief directly subordinate to a paramount chief. The historical reconstitution Leach conducts for the regional level reveals that certain currently *gumlao* or *gumsa* Kachin villages were in the past organized on the opposite political model. Drawing on ethnographic, linguistic, and historiographic data, Leach argues that the *gumsa* system owes its existence to certain Kachin chiefs having sought to imitate the behavior of the Shan princes, whose political allies they were, and emulate the hierarchical organization of the Shan "principalities." On this basis he erects a general theory of social change in the form of an oscillatory model, drawing his inspiration from Vilfredo Pareto's concept of moving equilibrium: Over the course of history, Kachin tribes perpetually oscillate between the two opposed poles of the *gumsa* and *gumlao* systems, without ever embodying either in lasting fashion, for structural reasons. The contrast between these two political types pertains to the ideal rather than the empirical plane, for in practice protagonists perceive them as two possible orientations for an overall system in motion that accommodates the complexity of relations between the populations in the irrigated rice-growing valleys and those on the cleared hills. Leach points out, in passing, the distance which necessarily exists between these ideal models (those of the ethnologist, those of the society studied) and the empirical reality that analysis seeks to describe.

The book is thus one of the earliest attempts to deconstruct the "primordialist" conception of ethnicity that prevailed at the time. Unlike his predecessors, Leach does not start from the idea that the Kachin and Shan are two populations with distinct origins whose convergent migratory movements merely united in one place. Nor does he hold that their respective cultures form discrete independent units; rather, the boundaries between the two are porous and interdependent. He thereby prefigures the works on ethnicity undertaken fifteen years later by one of his most brilliant pupils, Fredrik Barth.

And so, *Political Systems of Highland Burma* marks a turning point, demonstrating that in the stead of a classical anthropological monograph about an ethnic group envisaged synchronically, it is appropriate to follow an interethnic and multicentered approach conducted from a diachronic perspective. The various peoples in the "region of the Kachin hills" might well display many cultural differences: The Shan speak a Tai language, are Buddhist, engage in irrigated rice cultivation, use buffalo and plows, and live in states headed by a hereditary prince with authority over military garrisons protecting trade routes. The Kachin, on the contrary, speak several distinct Tibeto-Burman languages, are animist, use hoes to cultivate cleared land, live in tribes in the mountains, and so on. Nevertheless, they are economically and politically entwined and communicate with each other using a shared ritual language. This language, performed through simple "ritual acts" understood by all, "says something," Leach explains, about the social relations of the populations in terms of status. It consequently justifies taking the region, not the ethnic group, as the most appropriate unit of analysis.

This deliberately polemical book made Leach's name and introduced him to the general public. Ever since it was published, it has inspired generations of social scientists working in such varied fields as politics, ethnicity, kinship, ritual, myth, and social models in general.

Pascal Bouchery

Edmund Leach, *Political Systems of Highland Burma: A Study of Kachin Social Structure* (Cambridge, MA: Harvard University Press, 1954).

1955

MEANING IN THE VISUAL ARTS: PANOFSKY REPLACES BEAUTY WITH MEANING

As an introduction to the "iconology" that won him acclaim, Erwin Panofsky (1892–1968) used a trivial example: Let us imagine, he says, that a man raises his hat as he sees us in the street. Our perception and practical experience allow us at first to give this little event and ordinary object a basic meaning. We identify the forms and an expressive intent. If we know the relevant cultural codes, our understanding then takes over: We may reach a second level and interpret the gesture as a polite greeting. From this "conventional meaning," we could proceed to an "intrinsic meaning, or content"—in this instance, a moral portrait of the man, provided we place this isolated act in a set of more general information about his person, environment, social belonging, prior behavior, and so on. Equally, a work of art may be analyzed in three phases. During the first "pre-iconographic" phase, we identify pure forms making up the "patterns"; in the second iconographic phrase, we detect the broader "themes," "embodied in images, stories, and allegories"; and during the third and specifically iconological phase, we seek to grasp "the underlying principles which reveal the basic attitude of a nation, a period, a class, a religious or philosophical persuasion" as particularized in a single work.

The three operations—describing what we see, identifying the theme represented, and looking for intrinsic meaning—are distinct yet connected. The task Panofsky assigns to art historians and theoreticians is to conduct the first two in order to reach the third. This tripartite scheme, which he first conceived in the 1920s but subsequently reworked several times, is now viewed with a certain weariness, but it was sensational in 1955 in the United States, when encountered in the opening pages of *Meaning in the Visual Arts*, then in 1969 in the French microcosm when Bernard Teyssèdre referred to it in his foreword to the French translation.

What was so new about these proposals by a German scholar, a former professor at the University of Hamburg, a disciple of Ernst Cassirer and Aby Warburg, who, after being banned from teaching by the Nazis in 1933, found refuge at Princeton, New Jersey? Not only were they "one of the finest challenges ever directed against positivism" (in the words of Bourdieu, who introduced Panofsky to France), but they also provided, in an erudition tainted with humor, the theoretical bases for the history of art, thereby setting the discipline on new footings. For exploring the "meanings of a work of art" meant re-creating it historically, steering clear both of the emotive excesses of aesthetes and of the formalism of Heinrich Wölfflin, guilty of separating content from form. More specifically, the aim was to replace the beholder's sensibility with rationality, replacing the issue of beauty with that of meaning. This was to be carried out by a "humanist discipline," taking its place among the human and social sciences—namely, iconology, whose ambition was and is to be a science of interpretation and history of the human mind as manifested in artworks. This is neither a semiotics of the image nor a theory of visual language issuing from verbal linguistics, but the branch of a science of culture capable of apprehending overall meaning in the arts.

Meaning in the Visual Arts provides dazzling illustrations of how to move beyond iconographic description to reach an incomparably more demanding iconology that is capable of reconstituting the world of symbolic values. Panofsky's methodological exposé would never have had such impact had it not been validated by a series of erudite yet surprising analyses: on the theory of human bodily proportions, on the Gothic as seen by the Italian Renaissance, on mannerism in architecture, on the relation between Dürer and antiquity—and above all, on Titian's *Allegory of Prudence* and on the theme of *Et in Arcadia ego* in the work of Guercino, Poussin, and Fragonard.

This final text, of remarkable clarity and subtlety, reveals better than any other the scope and limits of Panofsky's method. Its impact is evident not only in the author's great earlier and later books (including *Perspective as Symbolic Form*, *Renaissance and Renascences in Western Art*, and *Saturn and Melancholy*) but also among the historians of art he inspired, such as Edgar Wind and William Heckscher. As for its limits, they have been traced over recent decades by such varied authors as Michael Baxandall (*Painting and Experience in Fifteenth-Century Italy*, 1972), Svetlana Alpers (*The Art of Describing*, 1983), and especially Georges Didi-Huberman (*Devant l'image* [*Confronting Images*], 1990), with the main objections being that Panofsky remains too Hegelian in his use of the notions of *Zeitgeist* and *Volksgeist*, as if all the productions of a period belonged to the same "organic unity"; that in building his intellectual constructs he neglects the signifying function of plastic patterns; and that in considering the work of art as discourse for the historian to decipher, he exaggerates literary knowledge and represses the worrying, violent, or dark aspects an image may have. Like the shepherds in the painting by Poussin, he seems more fascinated by the inscription *Et in Arcadia ego* on a sarcophagus than by the skull above. Nowadays, many specialists (and would-be specialists) prefer Aby Warburg to Panofsky. Many of us wonder whether works of art may not contain "more than meaning." Nevertheless, the author of *Meaning in the Visual Arts* has indeed drastically renewed our understanding of the Renaissance and the Middle Ages: hats off!

Yves Hersant

Erwin Panofsky, *Meaning in the Visual Arts* (Chicago: University of Chicago Press, 1955).

1955

THE SOCIOLOGY OF BLACK AFRICA: BALANDIER SOCIOLOGIZES AFRICA

On arriving in French Equatorial Africa in 1948, Georges Balandier (1920–2016) traveled around the colonies of Gabon and Congo. The considerable material thus gathered form the basis for his *thèse d'État* defended in June 1954 at the Sorbonne. The primary and secondary theses were published simultaneously the following year under the respective titles *Sociologie actuelle de l'Afrique noire* (Present-day sociology of Black Africa) and *Sociologie des Brazzavilles noires* (Sociology of Black Brazzavilles). Balandier supplemented these with his lively memoirs of his time as a traveler and ethnosociologist in *Afrique ambiguë* (Ambiguous Africa), published in 1957 in the "Terre Humaine" collection.

In French ethnology of the early 1950s, Balandier was atypical. After studying classical ethnology at the Musée de l'Homme in the early 1940s, he went on to discover sociology, particularly through the work of Georges Gurvitch. Above all, he plunged into reading British and American anthropologists, enthusiastically learning how, for nearly a quarter-century, they had worked to renew the issues of acculturation, social change, and modernization in colonized and colonial societies, particularly in Africa. In addition, he frequented French and African intellectual circles on the Rive Gauche, particularly the anti-colonialist movement based around the journal *Présence africaine*. These combined influences materialize in "La situation coloniale: notion théorique" (The colonial situation: A theoretical notion), an article published in 1951 in *Cahiers internationaux de sociologie*. This text, which became famous, sets out the main argument in the issue to which he henceforth devoted his energies, appearing unchanged as the first chapter of *Sociologie actuelle*. It is remarkable that the notion of "situation," on which his thoughts are based, traces its ancestry back not only to the ideas of the anthropologist of South African origin, Max Gluckman, but also to those of the Parisian intellectual Jean-Paul Sartre who had used it (in the plural) as the rousing title for his collection of articles published in 1947.

Balandier sets out the work derived from his thesis as "sociology," intended to signal the more than symbolic break with typical research into African societies. Yet *Sociologie actuelle* comes across as a fairly classical ethnological monograph, with over half the text being a comparative study of the Fang people in Gabon and the Bakongo people in Congo, in which he describes and analyzes at length their histories of settlement, their habitat and kinship structures, and their symbolic beliefs. It is true that this ethnology is intended primarily as an ethnology of the *present moment*—of the specific moment of the mid-twentieth century. Balandier thus resolutely situates his analysis within the perspective of ongoing cultural and social change and of the demographic, religious, and political crises and reactions triggered by the present-day colonial "situation." This approach allows him to apprehend certain phenomena as "revealing" the social structure and, consequently, the past and present historical dynamics giving rise to this structure. Thus, the messianic and prophetic movements that appeared during the colonial period are not only an expression of cultural malaise but an attempt to "take back the initiative," as Balandier notes. He takes this a step further, putting forward the innovative hypothesis that resistance to the violent and structuring effects of repressive colonial administrative and economic oversight transpires especially in religious forms, whose content and manifestations are soon revealed in their political dimension and powerful critique of the established order. In other terms, these new religions, which are fundamentally syncretic, since issuing from a combination of traditional beliefs and new Christian seeds, need to be analyzed as anti-colonial movements.

One of the sizable changes taking place was of course the development of towns. Balandier even devoted an entire work to this subject, drawn from his secondary thesis, examining all the individual and collective facets of these new forms of social demographic grouping. In a methodological innovation, he compares two African districts in Brazzaville, leaving the white town to one side. This forerunner to urban anthropology produced little impact in the years immediately following its publication, despite a glowing review by Claude Lévi-Strauss in the *Revue française de science politique*. Indeed, *Sociologie actuelle* met almost the same fate. For Balandier's ambivalent use of the terms "ethnology," "sociology," and "anthropology" sat ill with how the disciplines were officially organized at the time: Ethnology still predominated for "primitive" societies, while sociology paid scant attention to places outside the Western world. It was only gradually—as Balandier came to hold positions within academia and research institutions, first in the economic and social science section at the École pratique des hautes études (EPHE) in 1954, where he founded a Centre d'études africaines in 1957; then as professor at the Sorbonne in 1962 and as head of human sciences at the Office de la recherche scientifique et technique outre-mer (Orstom) at the same period, while heading teams and supervising doctoral students—that his approach was taken up by African studies. And it was only really in the mid-1960s and especially the 1970s that he saw his "current situation" and anthropology of towns take off and inspire, while not a school in the formal sense, a multidisciplinary thematic and analytic current that he described as "dynamist" and "critical."

Jean Copans

Georges Balandier, *Sociologie actuelle de l'Afrique noire: Changements sociaux au Gabon et au Congo* (Paris: Presses universitaires de France ["Bibliothèque de sociologie contemporaine"], 1955). Republished PUF, 1982. Translated into English by Douglas Garman as *The Sociology of Black Africa: Social Dynamics in Central Africa* (New York: Praeger, 1970).

1956

THE POWER ELITE: MILLS AND THE CONFISCATION OF POWER

Charles Wright Mills (1916–1962), a professor at Columbia University in New York and a prominent figure in postwar sociology, often came across as an intellectual troublemaker. At the height of the Cold War, he called for East–West dialogue, supported the Cuban revolution, and denounced the decline of American democracy—alienating most of the leading specialists in his discipline. Even today, his caustic, politically committed writing rarely leaves readers indifferent. *The Power Elite*, published under the presidency of Dwight D. Eisenhower, is no doubt the most discussed of his various works. It is the third in a trilogy, coming after *The New Men of Power* (1948), a portrait of US union leaders, and *White Collars* (1951), a description of the salaried middle classes. It analyzes the entanglement of political, economic, and military interests. Mills states that a minority, composed of individuals with similar backgrounds, education, and lifestyle, has confiscated power and has the single-handed capacity to make decisions likely to affect the population as a whole.

As a pacifist, Mills was worried by the militarization of US society since the Second World War. One book left a lasting imprint on him: *Behemoth* by Franz Neumann (1942). The structure of power in Nazi Germany was organized around four institutional orders: capitalist monopolies, the Nazi party, the state bureaucracy, and the armed forces. A permanent war economy bound the whole together. Without amalgamating the Third Reich and Franklin Roosevelt's America, Mills detects a similar tendency toward the entwining of powers. It was also during the war that he started a close intellectual association with Hans H. Gerth (1908–1978), an exile who introduced him to German sociology. Together they wrote a treatise on social psychology that provided the theoretical basis for most of Mills's subsequent works. Called *Character and Social Structure* (1953), the treatise draws on the works of two main pairs of authors: Sigmund Freud and George Mead, on the one hand, and Karl Marx and Max Weber, on the other. The first pair shows how individual actors and their psychology are linked to institutions such as the family, while the second pair provides a way of thinking about social structures from a comparative and historical perspective. Gerth and Mills explain that developed societies have five main institutional orders: the political order, economic order, military order, religious order, and kinship order. At each period, a specific type of relationship is built up between them, thus composing the social structure. In their contemporary world, the two sociologists considered it was "coordination" that prevailed: a handful of individuals circulated between the powerful institutional orders and ensured that their interests worked in concert.

The Power Elite describes how this mode of integration took hold in the United States. It draws on very diverse sources: works by historians, press articles, quantitative analysis of dictionaries of notables, and so on. The theoretical background to the work is partly removed, for Mills wanted to reach the widest audience. The initial chapter, "The Higher Circles," sets out the central thesis: The United States is said to have gone through a progressive centralization of power, after the monopolization of the tools of policing, production, and communication had marginalized family and religion to the advantage of business, the army, and the state. Mills then presents the components of the power elite, the "corporate chieftains," "warlords," and the "political directorate," before attacking the "thesis of equilibrium" defended by theoreticians of pluralism, for to his mind, America was in fact run by a "power triangle."

The tone is deliberately polemical. But Mills's way of thinking of the elite is original. He rejects Italian neo-Machiavellian theoreticians (Gaetano Mosca and Vilfredo Pareto), whom he views as too imprecise and inclined to consider the powerful as the main actors of history. Inspired by Weber, he also refuses to speak of a "ruling class," reserving the term "class" for an

42   *The Power Elite*

economic approach to social stratification and positing that political and military determinations are equally important in the management of public affairs. They are even so entwined in the economy that the state should not be reduced to a repressive instrument of the bourgeoisie. The elite is defined first and foremost as a "status group" owing its prestige and power of persuasion to the institutional positions held by its members. It also constitutes a cohesive group formed by a set of interconnected "cliques."

The Power Elite has received extensive commentary. Mills divided these critiques into three categories: "liberal," "radical," and "intellectual." He was accused of giving too unitary ("monist") a vision of power, of insufficiently emphasizing the political weight of big business, and of not being interested in the concrete conditions of decision making. The work thus triggered debates that marked political science in the 1960s and 1970s. Its publication also brought about a shift in Mills's career, turning him into an international figure. His thought was subsequently taken up by the British New Left. He also had to respond to attacks sparked by his virulent accusations. In *The Sociological Imagination* (1959), he applied his model to sociologists themselves: under the effect of the centralization of power, they were submitting to bureaucratic command or taking refuge in highly abstract theory, rather than serving the public—as the "politics of truth" Mills advocated would have demanded that they do.

François Denord

Charles Wright Mills, *The Power Elite* (Oxford: Oxford University Press, 1956).

1957

THE USES OF LITERACY: HOGGART FINALLY CASTS LIGHT ON WORKING-CLASS CULTURES

When *The Uses of Literacy* came out in 1957, an article in the *Daily Herald* declared that Richard Hoggart (1918–2014) was no doubt an "angry young man," like the authors and playwrights associated with the New Left who had broken with traditional elitism. Like them, Hoggart came from a modest background—more specifically, from the working class whose culture he sought to depict in this unclassifiable work, which has become a classic in the social sciences.

Though *The Uses of Literacy* is read as one of the founding texts of the Centre for Contemporary Cultural Studies (CCCS) founded in 1964 in Birmingham, it is both an extension of and a break with the thinkers of his period. When he wrote *The Uses of Literacy*, Hoggart was a professor of literature. In the context marked by the industrialization of cultural products, the rapid expansion of mass consumption, and the evolution of the working classes, he shared the worries most notably voiced by the Leavises—F. R. Leavis was professor of English literature at Cambridge while his wife Q. D. Leavis was a literary critic—in the very influential review *Scrutiny*. Mass culture, particularly print culture subject to commercial imperatives (the subtitle of Hoggart's book is *Aspects of Working-Class Life with Special Reference to Publications and Entertainments*), was distressingly poor, not only in comparison to the legitimate canon but also to "traditional" popular culture, which, if no longer authentic, was at least aligned with the values held by this class. This depiction brooked no appeal, and the tone in the second part of the book about these mass-market cultural products is very pessimistic, veering at times toward the rhetoric and value judgments of cultural declinism.

But as Stuart Hall pointed out, "genealogy is not destiny." Hoggart, a former scholarship boy, did not work at a prestigious university for the upper middle classes; instead, he taught evening courses for adults at the University of Hull, where many of his pupils were former workers who had resumed their studies. Here lay the fundamental break with the Leavises, leading him to establish another intellectual family at the CCCS, which included Raymond Williams, E. P. Thompson, and Stuart Hall. Where the Leavises went wrong, to his mind, was on focusing on textual study without ever taking individual reception into account. This is the entire thrust of the first part of the book, written after the second: It describes in great detail the lifestyle of the working class—their way of living, thinking, judging, and appreciating—so as to reposition the cultural products imposed on them within their way of life. The error was to suppose that individuals were like putty, in which the stereotypical messages of mass culture were imprinted. On the contrary, Hoggart argues, the new cultural products were linked in complex ways with the traditional values of this working class, who actively reinterpreted them to support new attitudes. Additionally, the second error of the declinist approach was to screen off or underestimate what individuals did with the cultural products that they admittedly consumed: Irony, skepticism, nonchalant consumption, oblique attention—all functioning as forms of resistance and distancing—are fundamental to understanding what actually happens when reading a tabloid or sensational magazine.

If Hoggart, who was forty years old when the book came out, was an angry young man, he was above all undisciplined, and the various forms of this indiscipline opened fruitful paths for research into culture, first by providing this term with a far larger definition, since it now encompassed ways of life and lifestyles. But the innovation also resided in his method, once again both breaking with and expanding on traditional practice. With his literary education, Hoggart drew on the tools of literary criticism but applied them to cultural products that were illegitimate since decidedly works of popular culture. Equally, he broke with the stance of the intellectual looking down from on high: His writing assumes the subjective dimension to the

45   *Hoggart Finally Casts Light on Working-Class Cultures*

production of knowledge, with the text combining ethnographic study and autobiographical passages. His writing draws abundantly on his memories as a young orphan brought up in a world of women in a household composed of a grandmother, two aunts, and a self-effacing uncle. Indeed, in answer to the accusation that he neglected the world of work and analysis of production relations, instead of focusing on the domestic sphere, he responded that his position as a scholarship boy had kept him even more firmly enclosed in this "feminine" world removed from traditional masculine values. Lastly, if it is such a pleasure to read *The Uses of Literacy*, it is no doubt because of his unflagging attention to detail, the ethnographic precision permeating everything he writes: the importance accorded to sensations, postures, gestures, and smells; the use of indirect free discourse causing the intellectual phrasing to be strewn with "common sense" expressions. All this allows us to hear the interior dialogues and to experience, almost sensorially, the nostalgia and at times the painful contradictions of a professor of literature who, having changed class, was now the eulogist of cultural studies.

For all these reasons, *The Uses of Literacy* is a pioneering book. It introduced new ways of thinking about culture, its effects, and its publics; it promoted multidisciplinarity and initiated the ongoing debate on ways to write the social sciences.

Christine Détrez

Richard Hoggart, *The Uses of Literacy: Aspects of Working-Class Life with Special Reference to Publications and Entertainments* (London: Chatto & Windus, 1957).

1957

MYTHOLOGIES: BARTHES DEPLOYS SEMIOLOGY TO DEMYSTIFY MYTH

Mythologies is still the book most often associated with Roland Barthes (1915–1980). Its success is counterintuitive. The 1957 volume is a collection of articles published in periodicals between 1954 and 1956, nearly all of which are about current affairs ("my current affairs" as Barthes states in his 1971 preface): the Dominici affair, the lionization of Abbé Pierre in the media, the irruption of Poujadism into politics, the launch of the Citroën DS 19, the way plastic was making its way into everyday life, Hollywood epics. On the face of it, nothing marked *Mythologies* out as a future classic, or as giving rise to a new type of research.

All consecrations are at least partly based on a misunderstanding. By the 1980s, there was no longer anything "current" about the "material" discussed by Barthes. Many of his references had become opaque. While not all the objects and events had fallen into oblivion, they were all sufficiently outdated to foster nostalgic interpretations: The DS 19 now transported readers back to earlier days, while the rare steak tasted of times past. *Mythologies* had acquired a retro charm. It was read, imitated, and singled out in sentimental terms; it had become "vintage." Barthes had foreseen this: on the final page he accuses himself of having endowed certain objects with a "surprising compactness which I savored with delight," but which was ill-suited to its critical and militant purpose.

To tell the truth, neither the enlisting of "little mythologies" for sentimental research into times past nor their insertion in a sumptuously illustrated edition (2010) can account for the shockwave they produced. To gauge just how powerful this was, we need to set the subsequent readings to one side and appreciate anew how fiercely novel an undertaking *Mythologies* was. In the dying days of the Fourth Republic, it came like a bolt out of a not-so-blue sky. In 1957, readers all experienced a sense of shock. Writing in *Le Monde*, Jean Lacroix spoke of "an extraordinary book" (in the strong meaning of the term: far from delighting in it as palatable, he held it, and perhaps its author, to be "profound and cruel"). Though *Mythologies* might make us smile, it alarmed its initial readers, and when Barthes appeared on the TV show *Lectures pour tous*, the show's host, Pierre Desgraupes, was visibly a bit startled.

The first shock, the first move that grabbed the reader, was the way in which Barthes made objects talk. According to a well-known anecdote about Jean-Paul Sartre, on returning from Berlin, where he had come across phenomenology, he explained to his friend Raymond Aron the revelation he had encountered: It is possible to philosophize about a glass of beer! The revelation of *Mythologies* was that it was possible to conduct social critique and political analysis concerning President René Coty's bottle of Daumesnil or a packet of washing powder. Better still, one could do it rigorously, scientifically even, using a method set out in the afterword.

"Myth today." Drawing on Saussure, Barthes authorizes himself to redefine myth as a "second-order semiological system"—"that which is sign in the first system" (the Saussurean "associative total of a concept and an image") becomes a "mere signifier" within the second level. Myth is thus said to be a "meta-language, because it is a second language, *in which* one speaks about the first." This attempt at formalization soon attracted fairly sharp criticism from linguistics (Georges Mounin), from nascent semiology (Umberto Eco)—and first and foremost from Barthes himself, who predicted his mythologist would encounter "some difficulties, if not of method, at least of feeling." For even supposing the overall scheme of mythology to be a "justified" subdiscipline of semiology, the mythologist remains a divided figure, covering an inherently political move with the cloak (Noah's cloak?) of scientific endeavor. He is thus even more seriously torn: He can only combat myths by distancing himself from the collectivity who "consume" them, and from whom, in working for them, he shuts himself off. He destroys the "collective language" for which he has nothing to substitute and remains on the sidelines of history, in whose name he investigates the mythological abuses of language. Barthes ends up comparing this pure agent of negativity to Saint-Just, declaring: "what constitutes the Republic is the total destruction of what opposes it."

This strange revolutionary reference places *Mythologies* in its true light—that of a political clarification operated through semiology. And the thing clarified is the very notion of *myth* as ceaselessly brandished for over half a century, from Georges Sorel and his "theory of social myths" to Georges Bataille and Roger Caillois, without forgetting Louis Aragon, André Breton, Jean-Richard Bloch, André Malraux, or Alfred Rosenberg. There is no need to point out that there are more than just nuances differentiating their conceptions of myth, and more than mere differences between their ideological positions. Nevertheless, all these versions stem to a greater or lesser extent from Sorel's vision of myth as irrefutable (it is not a truth judgment), as something one may take or leave (approve or disapprove), and as dynamic (it is a source of collective energy, a weapon to be deployed). By defining myth as "an utterance" that may be subject to "semiological" analysis, Barthes puts a definitive end to the interminable and (to his mind) pointless debate about whether myth is politically useful or harmful. Sartre had been the first, back in 1939, to decry intellectuals' obdurate circling around myth "to such an extent that I fear, to speak like these authors, that there is today a myth of myth, which should itself be the subject of a sociological study."

Back in 1957, *Mythologies* mapped out the path subsequently taken by semiology of the image, of political discourse analysis, and of advertising messages; the primacy accorded to language analysis paves the way for the linguistic turn—only its great achievement does not lie in radically demystifying any given minor French mythology, but myth itself, one of the great, most overused, and inoperative words in the philosophical and political logosphere.

Philippe Roger

Roland Barthes, *Mythologies* (Paris: Éditions du Seuil ["Pierres vives"], 1957). Illustrated facsimile edition of press articles, Éditions du Seuil, 2010. Republished by Points ("Essais"), 2014. Translated into English by Richard Howard and Annette Lavers as *Mythologies* (New York: Hill and Wang, 2012).

1957

THE KING'S TWO BODIES: KANTOROWICZ AND THE MYSTIQUE OF POLITICS

Ernst Kantorowicz (1895–1963), having lived in exile in the United States since 1939, published *The King's Two Bodies* six years after being appointed a faculty member at the Princeton Institute for Advanced Study. At Berkeley, in 1949, he had opposed Senator Joseph McCarthy's anti-communist purges, despite having participated as a young German Jew in the persecution of the communists in Munich thirty years earlier. Bolstered by his reputation as a champion of academic freedom, with the publication of this book, Kantorowicz became one of the most important medievalists of the twentieth century.

The King's Two Bodies analyzes the dualist principle underpinning political authority in the Middle Ages—the opposition between a natural, mortal, physical body and a supernatural, eternal, mystical body—a "man-made irreality" of which men had become "slaves." This book, which went on to exert great though delayed influence (only being translated into French in 1989, for example), was the outcome of several decades of research on medieval "political theologies" and how they related to early modern ideologies. Kantorowicz's study of medieval political theologies developed over a series of publications, starting in his 1927 biography of Emperor Frederick II and continuing in several penetrating essays, such as a famous one devoted to the formula "pro patria mori" (1951).

It is no easy task to define the object of research at the heart of *The King's Two Bodies*: The terms "ideas," "formulas," "beliefs," or "concepts" are both too reductive and too rigorous. Kantorowicz draws on learned treatises, illuminated manuscripts, frescoes, and compilations of law, as well as liturgy and the poetry of Dante and Shakespeare. The scope of his analysis suggests the ambitions of semiotics but remains on an intellectual plane rather than an anthropological one—this is one of the major differences between his approach to medieval royal power and Marc Bloch's in *Les rois thaumaturges* (*The Royal Touch*).

Kantorowicz starts from the English legal tradition of the Elizabethan period and works back through the genealogy of the dualist principle as applied to the body of the king (or queen, though he never addresses the problem of Elizabeth I being a woman). The King-judge, like the Christ, whose nature is both human and divine, conjoins two natures in a single person. From this principle follows a cascade of fundamental legal distinctions, working their way down from the summit of constitutional theory to the most humdrum property disputes. Secular authorities borrowed these images and metaphors from religious discourse, liturgy, and Christian theology and elaborated them before, in turn, lending them back to the Church. Without this exchange, without this mystical and Christological dimension, it would be impossible to understand the development of the idea of royalty and, by extension with it, the notion of political power in the West.

Admittedly, this dualism gives rise to a certain number of paradoxes and a bizarre physiology of power that the famous English historian of law, Frederic W. Maitland, found ridiculous but which Kantorowicz, on the contrary, takes seriously, demonstrating its crucial importance in building up an impersonal idea of state and of the law, transcending mortality. Having implicitly rejected the august English-speaking tradition of constitutional history, awash in common sense, Kantorowicz unveiled the religious kernel that persists even in American *Incs.*, those modern-day mystical bodies/corporations that likewise aspire to superhuman duration and power.

With *The King's Two Bodies*, Kantorowicz definitively turned his back on the historian he had been in the interwar period, when he had written his other great, strange book, *Kaiser Friedrich der Zweite*. Published in Berlin twenty years earlier, without footnotes, this book was influenced, even in its writing, by the dazzling figures the young Kantorowicz encountered among Frederick's lawmakers and even more by the prophecy and the encomiastic literature that had flourished around the emperor. By 1957, Kantorowicz wrote very differently, now in a new language, replacing the evocative and poetic power of his youthful work with a more amiable, more direct prose, leavened with humor. Frederick II had represented a Germanic myth and an ideal of state power founded on an identification between Prince and Law (an identification consciously assumed by the emperor, who defined himself as the "living law on Earth"). With *The King's Two Bodies*, Kantorowicz, on the contrary, renounced the biographical structure or any construction of myth; he thus abandoned Germanism in favor of a broader vision of Western civilization. From Frederick II, he retained the vision of the law embodied in the person of the emperor, the formula *lex animata in terris*, which reappears in *The King's Two Bodies*, alongside other theological-looking legal formulas: *Christus-fiscus* (Christ's purse) and *Dignitas non moritur* (the office does not die).

There remain a few traces of the man he had once been as a student in the reactionary and aestheticizing circle of the poet Stefan George. Certain of his colleagues, holding these traces to be a discreditable stain on his reputation, chided him for them after his death. The links between the mythopoetics practiced in the *George-Kreis* during the 1920s and Nazi ideology are clear to see, yet complicated, for Kantorowicz and these intellectual aesthetes, who viewed themselves virtually as a secret society, also cultivated their disdain for Hitler. Thirty years later, having fled persecution and lost family members in the camps, Kantorowicz remained a man of the "Old World," elitist perhaps, but doubtless no Nazi sympathizer. His intellectual legacy is far less problematic than that of the historian Percy Ernst Schramm, for example, or of the jurist Carl Schmitt. With *The King's Two Bodies*, in a transformed world, and addressing his new English-speaking readers with broadly liberal and democratic sentiments, Kantorowicz pointed out the mystical essence of politics and the great power the imagination exerts over human reality.

Serena Ferente

Ernst Kantorowicz, *The King's Two Bodies: A Study in Medieval Political Theology* (Princeton, NJ: Princeton University Press, 1957).

1958

THE AFFLUENT SOCIETY: GALBRAITH AND THE HERALDED END OF POVERTY

From the moment it was published, *The Affluent Society* by John Kenneth Galbraith (1908–2006) was a best seller. Although a very descriptive book introducing little in the way of methodological innovation, it was the first overview of the postwar productivist and consumerist model. Galbraith's literary talent (he did not hide his admiration for the prose of John Steinbeck) and his sense of formulation did the rest. Thereafter, every history book would employ the title of Galbraith's volume to summarize the postwar years in the United States and, more generally, the West through to the mid-1970s. Strong economic growth and its corollary, mass consumption, definitively chased away the specters of the 1929 Great Depression. Writing at the height of the Cold War, Galbraith, a Harvard professor of economics of Canadian origin, dissected the strengths of the US economic model and, like many intellectuals, described the emergence of a middle-class society bound together by shared consumerist values.

From the outset, the book's reception generated a lasting misunderstanding. For unlike many of his contemporaries, Galbraith did not adopt a triumphalist tone. He cast a deliberately critical eye over the process of modernization that many of his fellow economists wished to export around the world, particularly to newly independent nations. With the note of moralism that often characterized his writing, he returned to a topic raised at the dawn of the century by one of his spiritual mentors, Thorstein Veblen (1857–1929). In studying the shift from a culture of rarity to one of abundance and the emergence of a leisure class, Veblen worried about the social and cultural consequences of this "conspicuous consumption." Galbraith applied this line of questioning to the 1950s, worrying in turn about how social critique was buried beneath the weight of mass consumption. He particularly targeted economists who were increasingly turning away from critical discourse about inequality toward consensual, arid mathematical modeling.

This forms the starting point of the book, written at the request of the Carnegie Corporation. In the early 1950s, this philanthropic foundation wanted to know if the return of economic growth during the Second World War had reduced the number of people living in poverty. To answer this, Galbraith drew on the thesis of a Russian economist living in the United States: Simon Kuznets. Inequalities, Kuznets optimistically wrote in 1955, were about to disappear. With the wont for modeling that Galbraith deplored, Kuznets drew an upside-down U-shaped curve: A first phase of industrialization increased inequalities, which were stabilized in a second phase of state interventionism, before a final phase saw them inevitably decline. Over the course of his research, Galbraith embraced this optimism, even if he remained wary of its schematic presentation. Thanks to the wage, monetary, and fiscal policies implemented since the 1930s, the United States had entered the downswing of the curve, and poverty in the country was now "residual," limited to spheres of the traditional economy and handicapped people. Yet Galbraith wanted the US to remain vigilant for the country's "slate was not left cleaned." Being strongly influenced by psychology, he feared that a "preoccupation" (in the psychological meaning of the term) with the poor might disappear amid this affluent society—a warning that he issued to economists and the American public alike.

But from the moment the book was published, this warning was eclipsed by an exceptionalist view of US society. One year after the scare occasioned by Sputnik being put into orbit, the country reassured itself by reading about the economic and social success of its model as depicted by Galbraith's sharp pen. The reception was more reserved in intellectual and academic spheres: Economists were very skeptical about his use of psychology, reproaching him for the lack of theoretical modeling, going so far as to describe him as an "economist for non-economists," as one uncharitably noted. But above all, many intellectuals deplored his ambiguous position

54   *The Affluent Society*

toward productivist ideology, which he never called into question. Others accused him of underestimating the scale of poverty. In another best seller of the period, *The Other America* (1962), the Catholic intellectual Michael Harrington directly attacked Galbraith's analyses, regretting the statistical approximations in calculating the poverty threshold and the postulate that poverty was geographically limited. But it was a Swedish intellectual, Gunnar Myrdal, who put forward the sharpest repudiation of Galbraith. In *Challenge to Affluence*, published in 1963, Myrdal shows that poverty was not a residual phenomenon in the society of plenty but, on the contrary, a product of the age of affluence. The shift toward a post-Fordist economy would only increase the number of poor people in the United States, who Myrdal assimilated for the first time to an "underclass," a term destined to have a lasting impact on poverty studies. From Myrdal to Thomas Piketty, the evolutionist vision of equality has repeatedly come in for criticism. The affluent society bore the seed of many dangers other than the possibility of neglecting the social question. From environmental risks to productivist postulates and the requirement for growth, the social sciences have never ceased inquiring into the model described in *The Affluent Society*.

Romain Huret

John Kenneth Galbraith, *The Affluent Society* (New York: Houghton Mifflin, 1958).

1959

THE PRESENTATION OF SELF IN EVERYDAY LIFE: GOFFMAN TURNS DAILY LIFE INTO THEATER

The Presentation of Self in Everyday Life was first published in 1956 by a small Scottish publisher. Initially known only to a few, it became a classic on being republished in 1959 in the United States. Its great originality lies in taking "face-to-face interaction" as an object of legitimate scientific inquiry. The book considers that the gestures, words, and glances exchanged in ordinary life and everyday contact call for specific sociological investigation.

This intuition came to Erving Goffman (1922–1982) between 1949 and 1953, when preparing his PhD thesis in the Shetland Islands. Following in the footsteps of his supervisor, he had gone there to study a small semirural community but returned with a new object of sociological inquiry: "conversational interaction."

Goffman, a self-identified disciple of Émile Durkheim (and not a member of "symbolic interactionism," a movement with which he is sometimes wrongly associated), devised this new object, in tandem with the method to analyze it. To sociologically analyze conversational interactions (and face-to-face interactions more generally), they need to be considered as a system independent of the singularity of the individuals taking part. Goffman puts forward a holistic perspective, rather than an individualist or intersubjective way of viewing daily interactions, focusing on ordinary exchanges between individuals not for their content but for their form—that is, for the "structure of social encounters—the structure of those entities in social life that come into being whenever persons enter one another's immediate physical presence."

The purpose is to denaturalize all the little things making up everyday life. Pushing the metaphor of social life as a theater as far as it will go, Goffman produces a set of concepts for describing "face-to-face interactions" from a dramaturgical perspective. This shows us to be tireless actors placed on stage in front of a public, always worried about the quality of our performance, displaying a "face" we regard as appropriate and, with varying degrees of awareness and conscientiousness, coyly cloaking anything that might contradict our performance. We cannot fail to monitor, however slightly, the impressions others receive, while for our part, as spectators, remaining on the lookout for the slightest information emitted by the sheer bodily presence of other actors to properly define the situation—for Goffman, *everything is a signal.*

Admittedly, most of the time we reach a "temporary consensus," thus warding off the worst possible outcome: embarrassment. We thereby form "teams" that last for the duration of the interaction and follow certain shared rules: "circumspection" (the choice of the right teammates for the situation), "dramatic loyalty" (respecting the attitudes adopted by team members), and "discipline" (the capacity to master one's role). We draw on the resources offered by spatial organization, playing on the distinction between the "front region" (stage) and "back region" (wings).

But we are often caught in "contradictory roles." We then draw on teammates to get us out of awkward situations. Goffman gives the example of how business managers put a rapid end to a meeting with a client to prevent the latter losing "face" (a central concept in his work, applied to the social apparatus as a whole) "by teaching their secretary to come and interrupt them at the right moment on the right pretext."

While Goffman is interested in self-presentation, he seems to get even more pleasure out of describing how it can backfire. Such descriptions have two functions. The first is methodological, contrasting with what was holding the order of interaction together when it seemed to be flowing smoothly. The second is analytical: emphasizing the uncertainty weighing on interactions.

And indeed, all interactions exist in a state of tension: "While the likelihood of disruption will vary widely from interaction to interaction, and while the social importance of likely disruptions will vary widely from interaction to interaction, still it seems that there is no interaction in which the participants do not take an appreciable chance of being slightly embarrassed or a slight chance of being deeply humiliated."

This first book by Goffman played a major role in the renewal of sociology at a time when ethnomethodolgy was emerging (around the figure of Harold Garfinkel), along with the ethnography of communication (Dell Hymes) and conversational analysis (Harvey Sacks), though Goffman always maintained a certain distance from these currents. For the specific effect of *The Presentation of Self* on the social sciences was that it removed the analysis of individuals' "self" from the sole domain of psychology, instead proposing a fully sociological treatment: "In analyzing the self, then, we are drawn from its possessor, from the person who will profit or lose most by it, for he and his body merely provide the peg on which something of collaborative manufacture will be hung for a time. And the means for producing and maintaining selves do not reside inside the peg; in fact, these means are often bolted down in social establishments."

Goffman distanced himself from psychology even more directly in the response he gave to criticism of his work by two authorized representatives of symbolic interactionism.[1] In this controversy, Goffman was accused of practicing "structuralist" analysis that failed to take individuals' singularity into account. This provided Goffman with the opportunity to emphasize that as a reader of Durkheim and Alfred Radcliffe-Brown, ever since his thesis he had primarily endeavored to "rescue the term 'interaction'" from the grasp of social psychology by explaining "principled ways" observable in social life by which place is made, with varying degrees of success, for each of these singular stories.

Édouard Gardella

Erving Goffman, *The Presentation of Self in Everyday Life* (New York: Anchor Books, 1959).

---

[1] See Erving Goffman, "Review: A Reply to Denzin and Keller," *Contemporary Sociology* 10, no. 1 (January 1981): 60–68.

1960

CENTURIES OF CHILDHOOD: ARIÈS REDISCOVERS THE FEELING OF CHILDHOOD

Who would have thought that in postwar France, where the left dominated minds and publications, the renewal of a large branch of French historical scholarship would stem from a man who described himself, with sly humor, as a "true reactionary" hailing from the "traditional right"? Though on the margins of academia, Philippe Ariès (1914–1984) was an avid reader of the works of historians coalescing in the "new history" current; he ended up being accepted by them to the point of contributing an entire chapter to the volume published under this title by Jacques Le Goff, Roger Chartier, and Jacques Revel in 1978, the same year he joined the Centre de recherches historiques at the École des hautes études en sciences sociales (EHESS). His chapter was on "the history of mentalities," and it is under this slightly old-fashioned label that he is still known and appreciated today.

L'enfant et la vie familiale sous l'Ancien Régime (*Centuries of Childhood*) is part of the body of research in France relating to the family, viewed as the cradle of demographic decline and renewal, a cell reverberating with the ups and downs of economic life, and the crucible of individual and collective behavior. The impulse from a new and rapidly developing discipline, historical demography, considerably influenced the choices guiding Ariès's inquiry. But he gave a very personal interpretation of the changes affecting populations of earlier times, seeking to bring to light the unconscious structures dictating individual behavior. He had already trawled through parish registers, paying particular attention to fertility and its control; the book resulting from this archival research appeared in 1948, published by éditions

Self, under the title *Histoire des populations françaises et de leurs attitudes devant la vie depuis le XVIIIe siècle* (History of French populations and their attitudes toward life since the eighteenth century). He insisted clearly on his main point: the "cultural incidences of demography." This work attracted the attention of demographers working for the Institut national des études démographiques (INED) but did not circulate among academic circles.

L'enfant et la vie familiale sous l'Ancien Régime carries on directly from this earlier work. Ariès deciphers change within the seemingly most immobile societies, studying their resilience to external blows and their capacity to adapt. Born and brought up in a royalist and Vichyist milieu and attached to the ideas of *Action française* (an anti-Semitic, nationalist, and corporatist current) and the values of the Catholic tradition, Ariès never relinquished his distrust of the state and its incursions into the private sphere. Forearmed against the smothering of what he saw as the true underground forces of society, he nevertheless departed from the family legacy in the attention he paid to "collective consciousness of change." Though a traditionalist and an atypical member of the right-wing cavalry, he neither refused nor feared technological progress: This may be seen in his career in the tropical fruit trade, in which he introduced automatized then computerized procedures for documentation (his area of responsibility), while it also transpired in his wonder at the how progress opened up the world.

The banner he planted in the sleepy backwater of family history was perhaps that of the royalist old guard, but in his hands, it fluttered in a new breeze. The first edition of *L'enfant et la vie familiale* attracted the interest of historians, but without resounding more widely. Its translation into English (1962) introduced his ideas to a larger American readership, including sociologists and psychologists. But it was not until the 1973 republication by Seuil that he reached circles outside the historical profession in France.

The two main lines of his demonstration relate to the circumstances in which children were educated. In traditional societies, education was based on imitating what adults did. This learning meant young children were very quickly plunged into the adult world and thus became socialized. Admittedly, since the late Middle Ages, families represented infancy as a particular age, but the lack of precision in the terms referring to subsequent phases in child development clearly indicate the inability to represent childhood as a specific age. The second line of inquiry thus relates to the enclosing of children within the family, which, faced with an invasive state, closed in on itself and, as a corollary, developed educational institutions as of the seventeenth century. A substantial part of the book (one-half) is devoted to "school life," in which pupils were placed outside the adult world. This generated a firm demarcation between ages, causing adults to view children in a new way and re-center family affections around them, a phenomenon that, Ariès argues, was reinforced from the eighteenth through to the twentieth century.

Ariès's originality also lies in the sources he employs, drawing not only on demographic observations but also on literary texts, archives pertaining to the private realm, and especially images, which he studies with passion. This was his Achilles' heel for critics who accused him of "impressionism." Medievalists mocked his flattened vision of the medieval period that neglected the stages in the feeling of childhood, which was far richer and more varied than he thought—but their derision was to no avail because he cheerfully admitted this accusation. Demographic historians objected to the overly linear vision of the emergence of the nuclear family and revised his chronology. And the exclusively French focus of his analyses was also questioned. Nevertheless, his posterity, alert to his ambiguities and quick to make the relevant caveats, has been fruitful. Too fruitful? "God grant that [the history of the family] is not subject to the same inflation as [demographic history]," he breathed with a touch of vanity in 1973.

Christiane Klapisch-Zuber

Philippe Ariès, *L'enfant et la vie familiale sous l'Ancien Régime* (Paris: Plon, 1960). Republished by Éditions du Seuil ("L'Univers historique"), 1973. Republished by Points ("Histoire"), 2014. Translated into English by Robert Baldick as *Centuries of Childhood: A Social History of Family Life* (New York: Alfred A. Knopf, 1962).

1961

HISTORY OF MADNESS: FOUCAULT REENDOWS MADNESS WITH ITS DESTABILIZING POWER

In 1961, Plon published *Folie et déraison: Histoire de la folie à l'âge Classique* (*History of Madness*) in a collection edited by Philippe Ariès (the historian of the family and of "mentalities"). Its author was thirty-five-year-old Michel Foucault (1926–1984), who had studied philosophy at the elite École Normale Supérieure and also held a diploma in psychopathology. In itself, this publication promised to be a nonevent, since the book was taken from a doctoral thesis in philosophy, an academic format renowned for being highly codified and short on surprises. Yet this book (which was published again in 1972 by Gallimard) amounted to a genuine cultural shift. It was a largely unidentifiable literary object. It includes arduous speculative conceptual passages (on the relationship between the Same and the Other, and the dialectic of Reason and Madness), meticulous highly learned sections (on medical classifications, diverse internment practices, therapeutic arsenals, etc.), together with lyrical flights on Racine and Diderot, the whole conducted in a flamboyant and baroque style bound together by narrative impetus.

Histoire de la folie is a metaphysical drama and a political fable. The metaphysical drama is that of the exclusion of Madness by dogmatic and sovereign Reason; the political fable is the tale of how arrogant medicine slowly confiscated madness's powers of social and cultural destabilization. The demonstration is conducted in three main stages. The first, taken from the sixteenth century, is the sending of fools aboard boats. This was both a social practice and a literary theme (the "ship of fools"). The insane were handed over by municipal authorities to boat owners, who then sailed from town to town. For their part, poets penned poetic descriptions of these vessels filled with the witless. For Foucault, this image demonstrates how tolerant and how attentive even the Renaissance was toward voices of madness, capable of carrying messages from netherworlds. The skeptical wisdom of Montaigne even makes it possible to understand that madness is perhaps also a *margin* of reason, a place of respiration and fantasy.

The theatricality with which the book ventures into the classical age is historically determined. "A date can serve as a landmark: 1656, the decree that founded, in Paris, the Hospital General." Madness is no longer a poetic reverie, an occasion for philosophical musings on the relativity of reality and the reasonable. For the word "hospital" should not mislead us; we are dealing with places of confinement and sequestration. At first there was no medical purpose. Anything disrupting the streets of Paris—poverty, vice, madness—was locked up in the hospitals of Bicêtre and La Salpêtrière. Madness emerged primarily as an illness, as a public disturbance. The division into what makes sense and what is unreasonable coincided with that between good manners and impropriety, between conservatism and the transgressive.

The scene that opens the final act echoes, though in reverse, the classical act of exclusion: Philippe Pinel, an asylum doctor and former revolutionary, released the mad from their chains in 1793, restoring them to their humanity—for under the ancien régime, the mad could be enchained like beasts. This is the moment when madness was delivered from its guilty kinship with crime and vice and restored to its own truth: it became a mental illness, a pathological determinism.

Foucault thus builds up his tale through these three great succeeding sequences: In the Renaissance, madness was apprehended through a poetic imaginary that saw it as destabilizing boundaries; in the classical age, it was apprehended from a police perspective, which held it to be a social and political problem; in our modern era, it is apprehended by a diagnosis enclosing it within scientific definition. Admittedly, Foucault was aware that at least since the medicine of the ancient Greeks, madness had given rise to solicitude and specifically medical treatment. Humanity clearly did not await Pinel and the nineteenth-century asylum to consider madness as an illness. Yet the idea is to conduct an "archaeology" of psychiatric reason, which underpins the division into "normal" individuals and the "mad." Medical diagnosis was preceded by police discrimination. While philosophy traditionally defends the thesis of reason as integrating, conciliatory, and classificatory, Foucault's tale portrays the other face of rationality as that which excludes, condemns, and discriminates. This fine classical reason of which we are so proud perhaps carries within it an element of hidden violence. Psychiatry claims to have "saved" madmen, by making them "victims" of their pathology. But this medicalization comes at a cost: In being entirely objectivized, madness loses its powers to worry. Yet what if the "delirium" of de Sade, of Friedrich Hölderlin, of Antonin Artaud told us more about the reality of desire and the world than medical dissertations reducing them to the insignificance of a symptom?

Ten years after this 1961 book, the so-called anti-psychiatric current (for example, Ronald Laing and David Cooper, in its English strain) denounced the "myth" of mental illness. It is society that drives people mad, the anti-psychiatrists said, it is family norms that condemn the most fragile to insanity, either because they become mad in the stead of others or because they find delirium offers an escape from the fetters of the "reasonable." Foucault's thesis anticipated these radical inquiries. With its resolutely Nietzschean inspiration, it made it possible to raise the question of the secret, hidden link—which philosophy adamantly refuses to envisage—between rational knowledge and moralizing violence. And if, at root, madness is a point of collapse, an "absence of an œuvre," it is perhaps because the truth is vertiginous and unbearable.

Frédéric Gros

Michel Foucault, *Folie et déraison: Histoire de la folie à l'âge classique* (Paris: Plon, 1961). Republished by Gallimard ("Tel"), 1972. Translated into English by Jonathan Murphy and Jean Khalfa as *History of Madness* (London and New York: Routledge, 2009).

1962

HOW TO DO THINGS WITH WORDS: AUSTIN AND LANGUAGE AS ACTION

Published in 1962 after the death of John L. Austin (1911–1960), *How to Do Things with Words* reproduces twelve lectures that he gave in Harvard in 1955, based on Austin's own notes. The title encapsulates the thesis: Speaking is not so much a matter of representing the world as acting on it. In saying *I name this ship the Queen Elizabeth*, I am not attributing to myself the property of naming but am naming the ship; in saying *I promise to come*, I promise to do so; and in saying *the meeting is now open*, I open it. In his first lecture, Austin labeled such statements performatives, as opposed to constatives, which, in accordance with the traditional view of language, describe the world. In the other eleven lectures, Austin sought to define and characterize performatives, finally leading him to question the very existence of constatives and "to play Old Harry with two fetishes which I admit to an inclination to play Old Harry with"—namely, "(1) the true/false fetish and (2) the value/fact fetish."

So, whereas the tradition merely noted that the statement in the grammatical present *I promise to come* occurred at the same moment as the promise, Austin argues that it is "in saying" *I promise to come* that the promise occurs. The statements *I promise to come*, *I name this ship the Queen Elizabeth*, and *the meeting is now open* have the linguistic value of constituting promises, namings, and openings, even if, of course, like all actions, these openings, namings, and promises may fail. It is by drawing on conventions (Austin speaks of "felicity conditions") that language makes it possible to act, and if these conventions are not followed, the action does not take place. I may shout *the session is now open* until I am blue in the face, but parliament will not thereby start sitting. Language, as Austin describes it, is not magical. Using it does not suffice to act, but using it involves seeking to act.

Rhetoric had already studied the ways in which, by the means of discourse, one may move, persuade, or console, and so rhetoric likewise tied language to action. But the connection that Austin conceives of is stronger than that recognized by rhetoric. To formulate it, he proposes distinguishing between three types of speech act: "locutionary" acts, which consist in choosing sounds from a vocabulary, then producing and organizing them in accordance with a grammar; "illocutionary" acts, which are accomplished conventionally *in* saying; and "perlocutionary" acts, which are carried out *by the fact of* saying and are the effects produced by saying on someone else or on myself. Rhetoric was interested in perlocutionary acts; Austin discovered illocutionary acts. Even the speaker of the statement *the cat is on the mat* is performing an illocutionary act—an act that engages him to assert that the mat is under the cat and that will fail if there is no mat. Speaking always consists in acting, with or without success.

Austin died young and left only articles that were subsequently published in three collections: *Philosophical Papers* (1961), *Sense and Sensibilia* (1962), and *How to Do Things with Words* (1962). The third collection gave rise to much research and is the most famous. It has profoundly influenced all those—be they linguists, sociologists, or philosophers—who are interested in language and its role, either within society in general or in scientific practice in particular. The main question of debate concerns the boundary separating illocutionary from perlocutionary acts. For saying, using words in accordance with language rules, does not encompass all factual consequences of utterance, however commonplace they may be. But is it really possible to isolate the consequences of an utterance from the utterance itself? What is an order if it may not be obeyed? Can I congratulate someone who does not understand I am congratulating him?

The theory of illocutionary acts continues to be a topic of discussion, particularly with contemporary research into writing by anthropologists and historians. Who is acting when the utterance is written as a graffiti on a wall, without any signature? Is it in the same meaning of "acting" that a particular individual "acts" by saying *I promise to come*, and that a monarch "acts" as monarch in signing a letter with his seal? In linguistics, however, Austin's very innovative theory was watered down by John Searle's formulation of it. This associates within the meaning of an utterance a proposition, representing the world, and an illocutionary value, indicating primarily whether the speaker is guaranteeing the conformity of the proposition to the world (as is the case in statements), or if, on the contrary, the speaker is asking that the world change in such a way as to conform to the proposition (as is the case in orders). The illocutionary phenomenon being thus isolated, limited, and circumscribed, Austin's theory was readily accepted. Just as the tradition held that it could leave the study of imperatives and questions to one side and focus solely on studying statements, so many linguists, illogically and paradoxically, have solely paid attention to the proposition expressed, leaving to one side the question of its illocutionary value. Much of contemporary linguistics, together with the philosophy of language, has started paying renewed attention to the constitution of a proposition and its truth conditions: What role does the context play in completing it? What dating is carried out by grammatical tenses? Is it referring to the real world or only to a possible world? The "true/false fetish" is fighting back.

Marion Carel

John L. Austin, *How to Do Things with Words: The William James Lectures Delivered at Harvard University in 1955* (Oxford: Clarendon Press, 1962).

1962

THE STRUCTURAL TRANSFORMATION OF THE PUBLIC SPHERE: HABERMAS AND THE DECADENCE OF "PUBLICNESS"

Like all great books, *Strukturwandel der Öffentlichkeit* (*The Structural Transformation of the Public Sphere*) has at times been a victim of its own success. The choice of "public sphere" for the English translation of *Öffentlichkeit*, "publicness" as theoretical principle and realm of discursive practice, should not mislead us into viewing this as designating a public space (in French, the title of the book is "L'espace public") open to all, on the model of the public square. The book goes over changes to the public sphere from the late seventeenth century through to the twentieth century. Under the ancien régime, individuals were indissociable from their status, with political communication operating vertically to stage power in great monarchic rituals. This is what Jürgen Habermas (born 1929) calls the "public sphere structured by representation," a characteristic of absolutism and an order-based society. He opposes this to the "bourgeois public sphere," whose appearance and development during the eighteenth century and politicization in the wake of the French Revolution he describes at length. This bourgeois public sphere, favored by the development of economic exchange, was based on critical discussion and argument, thanks to the emergence of new forms of sociability at the intersection between the private and the public (masonic lodges, coffeehouses, clubs, and salons), together with the reading of newspapers. It was fueled by an ideal of free discussion between private individuals making "public use of reasoning" and thus capable of opposing power—that is, subjecting it to criticism. Finally, as of the nineteenth century, this public sphere was denatured by publishing capitalism, the culture industry, and political communication. The expansion of the public sphere in the days of mass culture paradoxically ruined the principle of the public that had endowed it with its critical strength. Hence, Habermas denounces the "refeudalization" of the public sphere: The idea of rational, horizontal, and critical discussion has been henceforth subverted by vertical communication by interest groups and by technologies seeking to control opinion. Publicness has given way to advertising, marketing, and the manufacture of opinion.

Despite—or because of—this narrative in terms of "rise and fall," the book has profoundly influenced many sectors in the social sciences, relaunching debates about the nature and role of public opinion in liberal democracies. The book's impact was particularly strong among historians of the eighteenth century, who, during the 1990s, in the context of the assertion of cultural history (the history of the book, of sociability, and of political cultures), took the "public sphere" as the dominant paradigm for interpreting the Enlightenment. Following this initial enthusiasm, historians questioned Habermas's linear accounts, put forward other publics (women, peoples), and nuanced many of his interpretations grounded in an outdated bibliography. But these revisions do not affect the heart of the book, whose intellectual project is neither historical nor sociological, in the classical sense of the term, but thoroughgoingly philosophical. Habermas seeks to reconstitute the ideal-type of the Enlightenment public sphere in order to extract the normative principle capable of guiding contemporary political critique. In this respect, the book remains faithful to the tradition of Habermas's masters at Frankfurt, who sought to establish the normative principles of a critical theory of ideologies. But unlike Adorno and Horkheimer, Habermas does not denounce the Enlightenment and its negative dialectic. On the contrary, he set out to apprehend publicness, shorn of its ensnarement in public opinion and taste, as a source capable of revitalizing democracy and critique. The bourgeois public sphere, conceived as the encouragement of the Kantian project of the *Aufklärung*, may provide a democratic model for civil society and remedy the pathologies of mass democracies.

Rereading his book today, one is struck by the ambition of its critique of representative democracy, drawing on certain elements from Marxist criticisms, while accommodating the liberating fertility of the principle of rational discussion inherited from the Enlightenment and liberal thought. In some respects, it is no doubt this ambition that endows the book with its topicality at a time when liberal democracies seem increasingly less steady on their foundations, threatened by neoliberalism, the transformation of the media, and the unexpected return of authoritarian religious traditionalism.

Hence the limits of the book in the eyes of a contemporary reader reside less in its historical simplifications than in its logocentrism and excessive rationalism, as if the processes by which society is instituted as a democracy and the critical virtues of the public sphere hang solely on the thread of rational argumentation. We are ever more aware that public space, both in the eighteenth century and in our days, is profoundly shaped by images, fed by passions, stimulated by curiosity, and rhythmed by media attention spans. These aesthetic and emotional inner workings of publicness may favor the "refeudalization of the public sphere" or else feed the critique of power and collective emancipation. And so arguably, what we urgently need to do today, in the age of new media and the digital revolution, is to think of how the cultural and political legacy of the Enlightenment invites us to face up to the inherent contradictions of publicness in its different dimensions, be these rational, aesthetic, or emotional.

Antoine Lilti

Jürgen Habermas, *Strukturwandel der Öffentlichkeit: Untersuchungen zu einer Kategorie der bürgerlichen Gesellschaft* (Frankfurt: Suhrkamp, 1962). Translated into English by Thomas Burger with Frederick Lawrence as *The Structural Transformation of the Public Sphere: An Inquiry into a Category of Bourgeois Society* (Cambridge, MA: MIT Press, 1989).

1962

THE STRUCTURE OF SCIENTIFIC REVOLUTIONS: KUHN CONCEIVES OF SCIENCE AS WORK COMMUNITIES

If *The Structure of Scientific Revolutions* is one of the most influential books of the second half of the twentieth century, and by far the most famous work of Thomas Kuhn (1922–1996), it is because it sparked memorable polemics throughout the 1960s and 1970s, particularly between philosophers, historians, and sociologists of science, and subsequently spread to many other fields of knowledge. At the heart of the book (and its success and the attacks it triggered) lies the notion of paradigm. Kuhn defines it as the disciplinary matrix uniting a group; as the concepts, ways of doing, and technical tools underpinning their undertaking; and as the set of ontologies and principles shared by the group. In the 1969 postscript, Kuhn recognizes that he loads the term with many different meanings and that he would have been better understood had he linked it more closely to the training of scientific communities and, particularly, the role of "exemplars"—namely, the repeated exercises and tasks that science students must perform and by which they are socialized in the milieu on the ways of doing science and knowing the "correct" ways of addressing problems and the tools that "work."

The notion of paradigm implies recurrent shifts from one to the next, what Kuhn calls "scientific revolutions." When habitual ways of addressing problems no longer work (such as at the origins of relativity and quantum mechanics, for example), conceptual revolutions occur, and new paradigmatic frameworks emerge. Kuhn thus conceptualizes the dynamic of science as a series of "normal" phases (moments when one paradigm reigns supreme) and moments of crisis (when contradictory representations coexist, the prototype being Bohr's 1913 model of the atom). He thus insists on the difficulty the old guard have in living in this new world and in appropriating, beyond the formal aspects, the deep physical meaning of these novelties. On this point Kuhn goes back to Max Planck, the father of the idea of quanta, who wrote that a theory never convinces anyone, but that one generation dies and another is born for whom the new theory is natural.

The main actor in science is thus not the solitary inquiring individual facing the world but the organized community of practitioners and the implicit dimension of their collective practices. Faithful to his master Alexandre Koyré, Kuhn insists on the impossibility of any knowledge devoid of a priori ideas—be they ontological or philosophical. Borrowing Michael Polanyi's idea of "tacit knowledge," he argues that the "incorporation of ways of doing," the creation of a second nature, is what underpins scholarly practice. And with Ludwig Wittgenstein, he emphasizes that the only way to fully assimilate the meaning of action and knowledge is through usage. In short, science too is a form of life.

One may thus appreciate the shock felt by philosophers and historians of science (more than by scientists, who often saw this book as reflecting their daily experience). Kuhn was read as "desacralizing" science, since he erases the issue of how it relates to truth, a point to which he returned at length in his defense. He was deemed to have paved the way to the relativity of knowledge, making scientific knowledge too dependent on the conditions of its production. And it was argued that paradigms, in their relative incommensurability, destroyed the cumulative nature of knowledge that philosophers of science held so dear—something that Kuhn disputed, calling for a less rigid reading of his work.

There is no denying that Kuhn departed radically from previous perspectives. But he was also very much a thinker of his time. Thinking in terms of *structure* was commonplace in the 1960s, and the notion of *paradigm* fit in easily with the social and historical sciences of the period, which were thinking in terms of long-time frames, stabilities, and the principles organizing the thought structures of an era. As for the term *revolution*, it is of course central to contemporary geopolitics and Marxism. As its usage peaked among many intellectuals, it flooded through history and the philosophy of science in the wake of Koyré's invention of the "scientific revolution" as the founding act of European modernity.

Kuhn was also very much of his time in a deeper way—namely, his tendency to analyze things on a single, "macro" scale. On this point his heirs, who went on to invent science studies, parted ways with his work. In tandem with history (through microhistory) and other social sciences (through Geertz's anthropology and Boltanski's sociology, for example), they turned their attention to in-depth analysis, giving a new place to agency and actors' reflexivity, while also dismantling the silo in which science tended to be placed, instead linking it to political dynamics and technical operations. In comparison to this, Kuhn's portrait of science is of an autonomous world of scholarly communities at work, operating in isolation and cut off from the world. That is not surprising when we think of the nature of the objects he was discussing, such as quantum mechanics. But it is surprising when we think of the type of science being ushered in by the Cold War. This was tightly bound up with the war effort, driven by military technology and social demands, and geared toward innovation and economic life. This takes us back to Kuhn's formative involvement in teaching history to young scientists in the *General Education in Science* program at Harvard. His task was to communicate to this broad public the principles driving science, and their internal functioning, and this was no doubt a factor in his setting aside the profound transformations affecting those working in science at that time. He thereby preserved a major myth, that of "Science"—that is, a body of knowledge that is essentially pure because living in accordance with its own rules, far removed from the tumult of ordinary life.

Dominique Pestre

Thomas S. Kuhn, *The Structure of Scientific Revolutions* (Chicago: University of Chicago Press, 1962).

1963

THE MAKING OF THE ENGLISH WORKING CLASS: THOMPSON RESTORES THE EXPERIENCE OF THE WORKING CLASS

In December 1963, Victor Gollancz, a London-based publisher with socialist leanings, brought out a book of over 800 pages, *The Making of the English Working Class*. While the object of study was classical, the book was unorthodox and provocative. The cover shows a miner from Middleton going back home, with one of the first steam engines for transporting coal to nearby Leeds in the background. Yet the book does not start with the industrial revolution; rather, it begins with the 1790s, when, echoing events in revolutionary France, England witnessed the rapid emergence of many working-class political associations. The study ends with the 1830s and 1840s, marked by the emergence of the Chartist movement that pushed for the democratization of the parliamentary political system. The book was an unexpected success with the public. It was republished five times over the following decade and translated into Italian (1969), Spanish (1977), German (1987), Portuguese (1987), and French (1988). Further translations continued to appear, with more recent ones in Chinese (2001 and 2013), Japanese (2003), and Turkish (2004).

Although educated at Cambridge University, Edward P. Thompson (1924–1993) was still on the margins of academia in 1963. He had been teaching at Leeds University since 1948, where he gave evening classes to adults, most of whom were workers from the old industrial region. An active member of the Communist Party since 1940, he left it in 1956 to defend his idea of humanist socialism by participating in the emergence of the New Left. He particularly objected to the simplifications of economic determinism and to the top-down organization of political movements. Instead, he campaigned for political action by ordinary people rooted in their own social experiences. By this date, Thompson had already written a large body of work on literature, politics, and history.

From the very first lines of the preface, the book presents itself as a manifesto for a new way of thinking and writing about social history. *The Making of the English Working Class* is "a study in an active process, which owes as much to agency as to conditioning. The working class did not rise like the sun at an appointed time. It was present at its own making." Thompson does not remain tied to the idea of a straightforward correspondence between the dynamics of the industrial revolution (technical transformations, the development of the manufacturing system, the appearance of factory workers, etc.) and the dynamics of social and cultural life. On the contrary, he demonstrates that qualified workers in traditional crafts, such as cobblers, weavers, saddlers, booksellers, and printers, working at home or in small workshops, played just as important a role in the making of the working class as factory workers, who were still in the minority in the 1830s and 1840s. Continuity with the cultural and political traditions of the craft world is, for Thompson, closely bound up with the awareness that these diverse groups had common interests, which guided their subsequent organization. Hence "the making of the working class [was] a fact of political and cultural, as much as of economic history."

In opposition to a history long focused on the development of labor movements, trade unions, and socialist ideas, Thompson grounds his approach in a diversified ethnography of the working class, paying equal attention to forms of work ("the curse of Adam"), workshop rituals, and trade festivals with their banners and dances as to political traditions, Methodist practices, anonymous threatening letters, farmers' account books, and workers' gardens. However, these practices took on new meanings during the political repression of the working class triggered across Europe by the French Revolution. The working class in England became inseparable from this specific context, combining innovations brought about by the French Revolution and the counterrevolutionary policies it provoked across Europe. It thus preceded the making of the manufacturing working class in the years

75 *Thompson Restores the Experience of the Working Class*

1790 to 1830, which saw the development of a unified class consciousness and thenceforth of solidly established forms of worker organization: "trade unions, friendly societies, educational and religious movements, political organizations, periodicals." These were instrumental in structuring a genuinely working-class mindset.

In the 1960s, the book did much to free historians of economic determinism, which was not the sole preserve of Marxists. By applying the methods of ethnography to work practices, family relations, and religious preaching, it gave a central place to sociocultural processes, with such novel notions as agency, experience, moral economy, and community, all of which could be applied on a scale exceeding industrial England and the discipline of history. The debates launched by the book, which was strongly opposed to the proposals of Louis Althusser and his disciples, led historians and sociologists to rethink such fundamental ideas as social class and working-class culture.

These proposals contributed to Bourdieu's ideas in the 1970s, as well as to the development of critical positions taken by the Subaltern Studies group in India, which rewrote a history of colonial domination by taking into account the realities of castes and religious practices. More recently, readings of Thompson have fueled reflection on the relations between history and literature, inspired by his writing practice that combined analysis and narration, while placing center stage figures whose lives had been reduced to silence.

Jean Boutier and Arundhati Virmani

Edward P. Thompson, *The Making of the English Working Class* (London: Victor Gollancz, 1963).

1964

GESTURE AND SPEECH: LEROI-GOURHAN LINKS UP GESTURE AND SPEECH

To trace the origins of humankind with paleontological and archaeological data is in itself a prehistoric inquiry of the first order; to further integrate a systematic reflection on the current conditions and future prospects of humankind bestows this undertaking with theoretical scope and philosophical repercussions of even grander magnitude. This is the main contribution of *Le geste et la parole* (*Gesture and Speech*), published over fifty years ago by André Leroi-Gourhan (1911–1986). By mastering the contributions of prehistory and exploring in depth both its biological and technological dimensions, this book provides the basis for a truly fundamental anthropology encompassing tools and language, machines and memory, species and society.

Without necessarily imposing any retrospective coherence, *Le geste et la parole* clearly represents the culmination of a series of long-running lines of research and empirical studies. In the early 1930s, while working under Paul Rivet in renewing the Musée de l'Homme (whose deputy director he was to become after the Second World War, alongside Claude Lévi-Strauss) and while discovering Orientalism at Langues O' (nowadays INALCO) and at the Musée Guimet, Leroi-Gourhan also roamed the paleontology gallery at the Muséum national d'histoire naturelle and approached human/animal relations from a jointly economic and iconographic perspective. He returned from an intensive mission in Japan from 1937 to 1939 with the material for his thesis on the *Archéologie du Pacifique-Nord* (Archaeology of the North Pacific, 1946), as well as the substance of the comparative technology that he then developed in the two volumes of *Évolution et techniques* (Evolution and techniques, 1943, 1945) around the key notions of *tendency, fact, borrowing, innovation*, and *technical milieu*. Lastly, while teaching colonial ethnology in Lyon starting in 1944, then as professor in general ethnology and prehistory at the Sorbonne in 1956, Leroi-Gourhan came into contact with Catholic intellectual circles and wrote several articles about the relation between techniques and society in animals and in humankind, texts that paved the way to the 1964 *Le geste et la parole*.

Such diverse influences result in an ambitious panorama brimming with ideas, whose narrative and interpretative substrate remain however anchored in biology. Leroi-Gourhan posits the *enchaînement* (interlinking) of animal forms from jellyfish through to reptiles and mammals, to the first Australanthropes and then to present-day humans, much like an evolutionary current "pointing in our direction." This approach, more Bergsonian than Darwinian in its orientation, allows him to present the human trajectory as a cumulative series of "emancipations" or, better still—given the historical connotations of the term—of "liberations." Thus, the hand, freed from tasks of locomotion by bipedalism, could be devoted to manipulation and toolmaking, in turn freeing the mandible from the need to grasp objects and thus enabling the face, now shortened, to make room for a larger brain, all of which quite naturally favored the emergence of articulated language.

In parallel to this diachronic systematics, Leroi-Gourhan also develops an original interest in "operational behavior" from a synchronic perspective. He thus distinguishes between "automatic" behavior, which is instinctive and generic to the species, and "machinal" (by rote) behavior, acquired through experience and education within the group, which may at times be suspended and overtaken by "lucid" behavior, in which language and the use of symbols dominate. This is the context in which the idea of the "*chaîne opératoire*" (operational chain), subsequently taken up by numerous researchers, first emerges: "Techniques involve both gestures and tools, organized in a chain by a syntax that simultaneously endows the operational sequence with fixity and flexibility." This new attention to effective material action unfolding between memory and milieu had, of course, psychological and linguistic implications. Beyond that, it served to address the distribution of resources and knowledge from a sociological perspective, similar to a theory developed by Leroi-Gourhan's teacher Marcel Mauss. Without there being any mention of historical materialism, or even the possibility that humans might be the actors of their own history, *Le geste et la parole* encouraged many of the anthropologists, archaeologists, and technologists who read it, such as Robert Cresswell, Maurice Godelier, and Pierre Lemonnier, to research a range of empirical and theoretical issues concerning the reciprocal relationship between techniques and society and involving modes of production, social organization, and material and ideal aspects of life.

In addition to these tangible concerns, other readers readily took up the speculative aspects of *Le geste et la parole*, particularly concerning the changing relationship between memory and symbols. The many different inscriptions of thought on various types of objects and media as documented by Leroi-Gourhan, from decorated caves to calculating machines, have served to put the episode of alphabetic writing into perspective, and notably for Jacques Derrida, to provide an antidote to Western logocentrism. As for Leroi-Gourhan's speculations on the future of humanity, it would seem that the process of successive exteriorizations that he mapped out threatens to become double-edged, with a welcome "liberation" from constraints now displaced by a more uncertain "dépassement" ("overtaking"). In comparison to the cumulative continuity that he claims from the first flintknappers to nineteenth-century craftsmen, the industrial revolution brought about a clean break, leading to the delegation of programs of action—and even of feelings—to artificial organs. As noted by readers such as Edgar Morin, Serge Moscovici, and Bernard Stiegler, Leroi-Gourhan's presciently raised the specter of a looming planetary ecological catastrophe, alongside that of an increasingly uncontrollable technical golem. This brings into question the role of humanity and the human subject, whose hand will soon be composed solely of an index finger to hit buttons or else, to update this image, to tap away at a smartphone like the Thumbelina of Michel Serres.

Nathan Schlanger

André Leroi-Gourhan, *Le geste et la parole*, vol. 1, *Technique et langage*, vol. 2, *La mémoire et les rythmes* (Paris: Albin Michel ["Sciences d'aujourd'hui"], 1964–1965). Republished by Albin Michel, 1991. Translated into English by Anna Bostock Berger as *Gesture and Speech* (Cambridge, MA: MIT Press, 1993).

1965

MYTH AND THOUGHT AMONG THE GREEKS: VERNANT AND THE EXPERIENCE OF THE GREEKS

Greece is not a model! The publication of *Mythe et pensée chez les Grecs* (*Myth and Thought among the Greeks*) ushered in a productive season for anthropology of the ancient world, marking a clean break with classical studies that had attributed a monopoly on rational thought to the Greeks. In a move of unprecedented scale, Jean-Pierre Vernant (1914–2007) placed ancient Greece at the heart of the social sciences, at the point of overlap between sociology, anthropology, psychology, and history, thus reviving the project of Fustel de Coulanges's *La cité antique* (*The Ancient City*) published in 1864. A philosopher and Hellenist, Vernant had studied historical psychology under Ignace Meyerson and sociology under the Hellenist Louis Gernet. Thus, it was not simply a matter of bringing the two disciplines into contact, as in Clyde Kluckhohn's *Anthropology and the Classics*, or of juxtaposing facts from distant societies. Unlike the "Cambridge ritualists," Vernant did not seek to portray the Greeks with a tinge of primitivism but rather to sound out "the inner man." The enthusiasm for rites and traces of a distant past, which had characterized the first half of the twentieth century, gave way to an interest in mythic language. And while Lévi-Strauss's structural analysis provided a model, it was Meyerson who provided the intellectual infrastructure.

This collection of thirteen studies in historical psychology was a great success, going through nine reprints in the space of twenty years, with two new expanded editions incorporating five additional articles and being translated into many languages. It was also a total work, embracing Greek society by studying the great frameworks of experience: spatial organization, the interplay of time frames, narrative logics (of myth, politics, medicine, law, and mathematics), the notion of work, how action relates to memory, resemblance phenomena (images and doubles, misleading appearances, imagination), and the problem of identity. These are the psychological "functions" studied by analyzing "works" (*oeuvres*), in Meyerson's meaning of the term—that is, "precise forms" into which a mindset is projected: texts, situations, and artifacts. The analysis thus examines Hesiod's mythical account of races by looking for an "intellectual code" specific to myth, investigates the religious expression of space and movement by comparing cultural data about two divine powers, Hestia and Hermes, and studies the *kolossoi*, artifacts serving as stand-in doubles, to better apprehend how the visible was presented and figured by the Greeks. These analyses marked their period, and not just among scholars of antiquity. If Vernant focuses on technical activities, it is not solely because of his interest in work, as product and activity, but primarily to examine how the secularization of Greek cities, in the fifth century BCE, affected technique. Vernant raises, in particularly acute form, the question of forms of rationality in the city. Since *Les origines de la pensée grecque* (*The Origins of Greek Thought*), he had been interested by the advent of rational knowledge in archaic Ionia, placing it within the context of modifications in the mythical and religious realm specific to democratic cities. In searching for changes to "mental activities," he sought to understand how the figure of the philosophers came to be distinguished from that of the *magi*. If the sixth century BCE saw the emergence of new discursive forms rooted in debate rather than the word of authority, it is because the fate of Greek reason was closely linked to the development of the city. Rational thought was brought into existence by the city.

But *Mythe et pensée* does not simply continue the historical project of sketching the development of the city and how thought freed itself from myth. It is the actual dialectical relationship between thought and myth that lies at the heart of the research program, paving the way for other works. One of these works appears in two volumes cowritten with Pierre Vidal-Naquet— *Mythe et tragédie en Grèce ancienne* (*Myth and Tragedy in Ancient Greece*), published in 1972 and 1986. The other was written with Marcel Detienne in 1974—*Les ruses de l'intelligence: La mètis des Grecs* (*Cunning Intelligence in Greek Culture and Society*). These works examine the threefold conjuncture

81   *Vernant and the Experience of the Greeks*

between myth and "what is not myth": rational positive thought, tragedy, and democracy. The case of Greece thus cast a different light on French debate in the 1970s, in which modern democracy did not seem conceivable without leaving religion behind (Marcel Gauchet). Through its institutions, such as sacrifice and divination, and the forms taken by figuration, Greek polytheism played a key role in structuring social relations in the city. Drawing on the structural analysis of Georges Dumézil and Claude Lévi-Strauss, Vernant proposes a change in paradigm for analyzing Greek myths and pantheons, leaving to one side the quest for essences and symbolic interpretations of mythic narratives to better objectify the system of relations between the gods specific to each narrated situation. This marks a break with the traditional approach to the history of Greek religion, laying the groundwork for a religious anthropology whose comparative program he clearly defined ten years later in his inaugural lecture at the Collège de France.

It is certain that the agendas of historical anthropology and psychology converged on this comparative project. In the twenty years between the first and last edition of *Mythe et pensée*, Vernant conducted intensive comparative research at the Centre de recherches comparées sur les sociétés anciennes, set up in 1964 as part of the economic and social sciences section at the École pratique des hautes études (EPHE): From *Problèmes de la guerre en Grèce ancienne* (*Problems of War in Ancient Greece*, 1969) to *Corps des dieux* (*Bodies of the Gods*, 1986), he and his fellow authors conducted many inquiries based on minute analysis of the specificities of each society studied. *Mythe et pensée* may thus be seen as a study awaiting comparison. Writing in 1989 in the journal *Métis*, Vernant noted that "it is only by comparison, in confrontation with other civilizations, that all the features characterizing Greek man, as a political animal, take on their full relief, come together in a relatively coherent picture, and acquire, from a comparative, not a normative point of view, their value as an intelligible model facing other models with a different general appearance."

Cléo Carastro

Jean-Pierre Vernant, *Mythe et pensée chez les Grecs: Études de psychologie historique* (Paris: Maspero, 1965). Republished by La Découverte-poche, 1998. Translated into English by Janet Lloyd with Jeff Fort as *Myth and Thought among the Greeks* (New York: Zone Books, 2006).

1965

READING CAPITAL: ALTHUSSER AND THE SILENCES OF CAPITAL

Lire Le Capital (*Reading Capital*) is the result of work conducted by Louis Althusser (1918–1990) and his pupils in a seminar at the École normale supérieure in 1964 and 1965. It is thus not surprising that the texts by Jacques Rancière, Pierre Macherey, Étienne Balibar, and Roger Establet (about critique, the mode of exposition, the key concepts, and the plan of *Capital*) issue, despite their theoretical originality, from the general framework erected by Althusser in his two texts forming the center of the work.

This framework is fundamentally a new theory about how to read, in response to a problem Althusser raised in his foreword to *Pour Marx* (*For Marx*)—namely, the deficiencies of French Marxist theory, bogged down in a humanist conception of Marx, society, and politics. Hence, *Lire Le Capital* pursues two objectives. The first is to place Marxist discussion on the field that *Capital* actually addresses—that is, the mode of capitalist production—and so extirpate it from that of the ahistorical anthropology of work established in the *Economic and Philosophical Manuscripts of 1844*. The second is to extract from *Capital* Marx's science of society so as to give Marxism adequate tools for understanding capitalist reality.

The first objective is fulfilled by the thesis of an "epistemological break" separating Marx's youthful writings from *Capital*, with the latter needing to be recognized as his truly scientific work. Scientific here means "non-ideological," for in *Capital*, Marx no longer allows his questions, concepts, and issues to be dictated by bourgeois philosophy and science but manages to transform them into "problems." The second objective is fulfilled by the theory of reading that Althusser and his coauthors build up around the concept of "symptomatic reading." This introduces a psychoanalytical method into philosophy and the social sciences more generally, for they argue that the only way to tease out the logic underpinning a text is to listen to its silences.

In accordance with Freudian principles, a text needs to be read with an ear to what it does not voice while nevertheless saying it through the replies given to questions it does not raise. This approach leads Althusser to a way of thinking about the production of theory, in which the field of science determines the questions that may be raised and the objects that a theory may "see" (that is, conceptualize). Thus, Marx is able to form the *concept* of surplus value, a *word* that already existed in the economic thought of David Ricardo, by raising the question of its production—in contradistinction to classical economic doctrine, which, starting from the principle that the exchange in the labor contract is fair, is unable to conceive exploitation and so leaves surplus value as a "word" it does not think through. Consequently, Althusser rejects the classical philosophical question of whether concepts correspond to real objects, which dissimulates the fact that all theoretical activity is a matter of autonomous production (theory is "theoretical practice"), dividing reality according to internal criteria. It is precisely this division that symptomatic reading brings out, pointing out what the field hides from view. This is one of the sources of Bourdieu's idea of the field, and Althusser's famous theoretical anti-humanism is rooted in this rejection of the actors' intentions in producing theory.

This reading principle also makes it possible to tease out the discordance of historical times: It is through absence that the historicity specific to each social practice intervenes in the history of other practices. Thus, Althusser is able to argue for Marx's theoretical anti-historicism. For example, the fact that the history of the economy does not coincide with that of law should not lead us to treat them as two independent historicities; rather, we perceive the effects of the relative independence of one history on the other. It is precisely the absence of regulations of the capitalist economy by a still-feudal body of law that defines the overall history of England, without the heterogeneity of historical logics being reducible to a single mindset. Lastly, symptomatic reading allows Althusser to develop his theory of society as the

84   *Reading Capital*

structure of structures: Each structure is only present in the other through the effects it has on it. Hence structures determine one another once again through absence. In classical thought about causality, an effect is linked to a cause that may be determined in its own reality. For Althusser, however, thinking social causality by seeking "causes" in reality is a wrong perspective. In social reality, no cause is discernible; all we can see are effects. That is why Althusser states there is causality through absence (structural or metonymic causality). Society continues to be perceived as an articulated totality, but without the principle of its order being reducible to a finality, subject, or mindset. Despite the thesis that it is ultimately the economy that determines structures, Althusser puts forward a theory of social differentiation that takes spheres of action to be both autonomous and united, without drawing on Durkheim's spiritual unity. Social anthropology (Emmanuel Terray, Claude Meillassoux) has been quicker to take up this intuition than sociology has.

The concepts and theories put forward in *Lire le Capital* were extensively debated in the 1960s and 1970s. Echoes may be found in the work of Foucault, Bourdieu, and certain currents of feminism (Judith Butler), but also negatively, in the zeal with which the second generation of the Frankfurt school defended the concept of the intention of the acting subject. The work of Althusser and his disciples thus succeeded in the operation it attributes to Marx: upending the field of philosophy in the social sciences by forcing them to transform their traditional questions into problems.

Julia Christ

Louis Althusser, Étienne Balibar, Roger Establet, Pierre Macherey, and Jacques Rancière, *Lire Le Capital* (Paris: Maspero ["Théorie"], 1965). Republished by Presses universitaires de France ("Quadrige"), 2014. Translated into English by Ben Brewster and David Fernbach as *Reading Capital: The Complete Edition* (London: Verso Press, 2015).

1966

PURITY AND DANGER: DOUGLAS USHERS CONTEST INTO THE HEART OF THE SYMBOLIC ORDER

Order is often the preferred target of anthropologists. A tradition dating back to Durkheim examines institutions for their categories of thought and the rules of human behavior, looking for the principles guaranteeing the coherence of the social and symbolic order. In such a context, it is far from obvious that marginal, unspoken elements such as pollution, defilement, and impurity, rather than signifying the decomposition of this order, may instead reveal how vigorous and robust it is. This allows us to gauge the full achievement of Mary Douglas (1921–2007) with the publication of *Purity and Danger* in 1966, voicing a strident challenge to the British functionalist school. As a seasoned field observer of the Lele of Kasai, a matrilineal society in Congo, Douglas wished to raise social anthropology above the particularities of ethnography. This paved the way to thinking with remarkable astuteness about what order owes to disorder in the fields of religion, the body, and social organization.

The first stage was to cleanse savages of an accusation. Mary Douglas deconstructs the myth of a primitive mentality, so patent in the writings of James George Frazer and Lucien Lévy-Bruhl, and examines afresh the question of the effectiveness of symbols and rites. There is not scientific thought, on the one hand, then a magical way of thinking submitted to the arbitrary work of the emotions, on the other; rather, there is a single human experience grounded in a universal classificatory way of thinking. The reason Douglas insists on the continuity between profane "dirt" and ritual "defilement" is to signify this profound unity of human experience, concealed by the sheer multiplicity of taboos. She takes this as her laboratory of analysis, generalizing her comparison between societies displaying complex political forms and those that are simpler. The argument entails going back to the sources of the misunderstanding, following the path opened up by the historian of Judaism, Franz Steiner, in his posthumous work *Taboo* (1956). Are there truly people who conflate dirt and the sacred, as Frazer thought? Whence springs disgust of bleeding women, prohibited foods, and deviant or unclassifiable beings? How are we to account for the manifest contingency of taboos? Each society banishes bodily substances and unclassifiable beings. It would be wrong to see this as a matter of hygiene or morality. Defilement results from the specifically human faculty of perceiving the world through classificatory schemes organized into a system. A subtle game of inclusion and exclusion is brought to light. If social perception of a being is the product of cognitive classificatory work based on selection and memory, then ambiguous beings, with certain features belonging simultaneously to distinct categories, awaken feelings of disquiet, disgust, a feeling of discordance to the extent that they are imperfect members of their class or that their class defies the overall scheme of the universe.

Exhibiting the schematic nature of perception, a move inspired by Gestalt theory, grounds the analysis of religion in the most intimate experience. The goal is to base analysis of rites on a social theory of knowledge rather than a mere theory of action. While the prohibition of foods, inspired by the Book of Leviticus, stems from the Hebraic code for classifying animals, defilement (the loss of holiness, which is to say, of exchange with God) is a meditation on divine oneness and plenitude. In a dialectical reversal, human reflection on abominations also includes the liturgical act of recognizing God, with defilement and interdict being the two structural faces of the ultimate symbolic order. This transforms the definition of what a rite is: Its purpose is to establish a framework for experience by hedging off prohibitions. The body thus becomes the object of a semiosis, reflecting a social situation. This analogy turns pollution into the symbolic operator defining the internal and external boundaries of a group, revealing, in negative form, the immanent values grounding their existence. Indian societies offer a paradigm, since they view the body as a besieged town: All ingress and egress are placed under surveillance, for spies and traitors are feared. The anxiety the caste feels about excrement, saliva, and bodily margins expresses the danger imperiling the survival of the group. But because this survival is always associated with power, defilement may also guarantee a renewal of the social and symbolic order. The taxonomic anomaly of the pangolin makes it an ideal candidate for being included as a "royal victim" in Lele fertility rates. The rite thus recognizes the potentials of disorder, in Douglas's admirably precise analysis opening up functionalism to new philosophical horizons.

Its subtlety extends to pointing out the contradictions issuing from a system "at war with itself." Behavioral norms may, on occasions, contradict each other. Proof of this is the ambiguity of ritual dangers relating to sexuality, stemming from a contradiction between the desire to treat women simultaneously as persons and as currency in transactions between men. The paradox of purity is that it constrains experience to enter the logic of non-contradiction; conversely, defilement—wholly unexpectedly and through a subtle game of transformation—becomes the scheme constituting norms and power. In the wake of works by Edmund Leach and Rodney Needham, this book illustrates the success of structuralism in Britain. Its originality resides in ushering contest into the heart of the symbolic order. Nor did Douglas's ideas fall on barren ground, for the book left a profound mark on anthropological debate on symbolism and exclusion and became the starting point for critical thinking about the ideas of risk and ecological disaster. Its magisterial demonstration—that pollution is not solely the work of human beings but of a power inherent to the structure of ideas—has lost none of its force or relevance.

Andréa-Luz Gutierrez Choquevilca

Mary Douglas, *Purity and Danger: An Analysis of the Concepts of Pollution and Taboo* (London: Routledge, 1966).

1966

PROBLEMS IN GENERAL LINGUISTICS: BENVENISTE MOVES BEYOND STRUCTURALISM

While the fifteen or so books about the comparative grammar of Indo-European languages previously published by Émile Benveniste (1902–1976) had never reached a public beyond a small circle of specialists, *Problèmes de linguistique Générale* (*Problems in General Linguistics*), a collection of articles brought out by Gallimard in 1966, went on to become the best-selling French book on general linguistics, with 130,000 copies sold so far.

Benveniste had held a chair in comparative grammar at the Collège de France since 1937 and was an internationally respected Indo-Europeanist. By 1966, out of the hundreds of articles he had written, he had only devoted thirty or so brief studies to general linguistics, and it is these, initially published between 1939 and 1964, that are gathered in *Problèmes de linguistique générale*. It would be an understatement to say that this collection played a role in the intellectual deployment of his work. In the three years between this publication and the stroke that put an end to all his activity, he published a certain number of articles about general linguistics and a major book, *Le vocabulaire des institutions indo-européennes* (*Dictionary of Indo-European Concepts and Society*, 1969), which was far removed from any issues in theoretical linguistics. However, *Problèmes de linguistique générale* played a decisive role in the sudden dissemination of his research.

In the 1960s, the label "general linguistics" was the shibboleth of modernity in the human sciences. Promoted in Ferdinand de Saussure's famous *Cours de linguistique générale* (*Course in General Linguistics*), which had become a classic of high-brow culture in France, the term was adopted by André Martinet who, in 1955, spectacularly had the Sorbonne chair in linguistics renamed the chair in general linguistics, going on to use it for his *Éléments de linguistique générale* (*Elements of General Linguistics*, 1960), soon relayed by Roland Barthes's *Éléments de sémiologie* (*Elements of Semiology*, 1965). Taking advantage of this publishing wave, Nicolas Ruwet translated eleven articles by Roman Jakobson and published them, with much interest, under the title *Essais de linguistique générale* (Essays in general linguistics, 1963). Benveniste chose to call one of his two 1963 lectures at the Collège de France "Problems in general linguistics," and Nicolas Ruwet, who attended, soon suggested publishing his corresponding works under the same name. The staggering success of *Problèmes de linguistique générale* was due to a perfect sociological feeling for the context—that is, the wave of generalized structuralism.

The enthusiasm for structuralism, initiated in 1958 by Claude Lévi-Strauss's *Anthropologie structural* (*Structural Anthropology*), was based on the famous assertion that "phonology cannot fail to play the same role in renovating the social sciences as, for example, nuclear physics has played in the physical sciences." Researchers in the social sciences, seizing on this sentence, started devouring *Cours de linguistique générale*, together with the works of Martinet and Jakobson, ushering in a long decade of structuralism *à la française*, as evidenced not only in the work of Lévi-Strauss but also that of Barthes, Lacan, Althusser, and, to a lesser extent, Foucault and Bourdieu, soon followed by others working across all disciplines.

Benveniste's work, perfectly fitting this context, contains, in the first half of the book, articles published for a larger and more diverse readership than just linguists, paving the way for two presentations of linguistics that are exemplarily nontechnical, one taken from *Journal de psychologie* (1954) and the other a paper presented at the Académie des Inscriptions et Belles-Lettres (1962). These are followed by more difficult texts written for sociologists, psychoanalysts, and philosophers, alternating with articles about linguistics proper to underwrite Benveniste's scholarly legitimacy. And so, this book, despite not being particularly structuralist, became obligatory reading in the social sciences in France for a season or two, with its reassuring articles wholly unrelated to phonology about such matters as "categories of thought and categories of language," "the nature of pronouns," and "the correlations of tense in the French verb."

While the success of *Problèmes de linguistique générale* stemmed in part from a masterful publishing strategy, it was also due to a surprising decision by its author: "I deliberately abstained from any retrospective intervention in either the presentations or the conclusions." "How can one not regret this decision, towards which nothing compelled him," Tzvetan Todorov, his former pupil, noted a few years later, lamenting that he never got round to "a long-term work [in general linguistics] to crown his research over several decades" and made do with "these scattered studies, with dazzling insights, but fragmentary and repetitive." Yet this is no doubt the reason the book was such a success. It has no central unifying theme, no synthesis, nothing on which to found a theory or a school; instead, it reveals a linguist whose mind roams freely, in no way hemmed in by a rigid structuralism. He emphasizes the need to examine not just language but discourse too, to build a semantics (which he does not differentiate from a pragmatics), and to embrace John L. Austin's contribution about performatives, without forgetting subjectivity in language. And he raises in passing the decisive question of *énonciation* (utterance) while paying attention to the typology of languages and the role language plays in psychoanalysis. Out of sync with the immediate concerns of his discipline, Benveniste clearly picked up on fundamental yet neglected themes that resurfaced a few decades later on the West Coast of the United States.

It was only to be expected that the remarkable insights and anticipations of *Problèmes de linguistique générale* would have little influence on linguistics in 1966, which was evolving toward formalization. But it played a crucial role in renewing the adjacent human sciences in France.

Pierre Encrevé

Émile Benveniste, *Problèmes de linguistique générale* (Paris: Gallimard ["Bibliothèque des sciences humaines"], 1966). Republished by Gallimard ("Tel"), 2 vols., 1976 and 1980. Volume 1 translated into English by Mary Elizabeth Meek as *Problems in General Linguistics: An Expanded Edition, Volume 1* (London: HAU Books, 2021).

1966

THE SOCIAL CONSTRUCTION OF REALITY: BERGER AND LUCKMANN LAY THE BASES OF CONSTRUCTIVISM

Despite being wholly unknown to the general public, *The Social Construction of Reality* has exerted considerable influence on sociologists (so much so that it ranked fifth in the International Sociological Association's 1997 survey of the most important books in the discipline). This short treatise owes its prestige within the profession to having initiated what is today one of the most prominent approaches in the social sciences: social constructivism, based on the principle that all reality, whether it be deemed physical or social—colors, the figure of Bill Gates, quarks, pleurisy, motherly love, or the public deficit—are socially produced.

In setting out the theoretical basis for this approach, Peter Berger (1929–2017) and Thomas Luckmann (1927–2016), two young researchers from central Europe, certainly did not imagine revolutionizing sociology. They were simply reacting to the tendency toward objectivism in the structural functionalist sociology then dominant in the United States and reasserting the legacy of European sociology for which the discipline, to be fit for purpose, had to think reflexively about its own social foundations. As the subtitle emphasizes (*A Treatise in the Sociology of Knowledge*), it was by referring to the "sociology of knowledge" of fellow Austro-Hungarian Karl Mannheim that they sought to remind the profession of the need for reflexivity: a reminder they issued even more assertively in their call for a phenomenology of ordinary knowledge, following in the footsteps of their former teacher Alfred Schütz (1899–1959), an Austrian who, like them, had taken American citizenship.

Schütz's contribution was decisive. He taught Berger and Luckmann that daily reality has a "sovereign" status, that all theoretical knowledge of the social world is grounded in ordinary knowledge, that ordinary thought likewise "constructs" its objects and, better still, likewise uses the Weberian method of ideal-types—that it too "typifies." From Schütz's legacy, an initial sense of the idea of "social construction" emerges, assimilating it to the "ordinary" construction of reality (as opposed to "theoretical construction").

Marxist thought, as channeled by Mannheim, was their other major source of inspiration. From the earlier Marx they borrowed the idea that "while it is possible to say that man has a nature, it is more significant to say that man constructs his own nature, or more simply, that man produces himself." There is thus no point in looking for any strict determinism between the biological order and the social order: Man is an animal who cannot fail to produce his own conditions of existence himself (that is, collectively). This leads to a second complementary sense of the "social construction" of reality, opposing it this time to the idea of a human reality entirely given to man by his biological nature.

But if the indubitable objectivity of the social order is not provided by the biological constitution of humans, then where does it come from? This is the central problem that Berger and Luckmann identified at the heart of any sociological theory. Their own response consists in devising a conception of the self-producing processes of the human order, which, for purposes of analysis, they break down into three phases: exteriorization (*praxis*), objectivation (reification of the institution), and interiorization (socialization). By privileging *praxis* as its point of entry, this model wages combat against two inherent tendencies within sociology that all too often cause it to go into a spin: first, "intellectualocentrism," against which is reaffirmed the primacy of practical knowledge over theoretical knowledge; second, the reification of social structures and institutions, against which they emphasize that the social order has no objectivity without human objectivation practices, nor is there any "function" within this order without social interpretive endeavor because it is a given that "logic does not reside in the institutions and their external functionalities, but in the way these are treated in reflection about them."

93 *Berger and Luckmann Lay the Bases of Constructivism*

Although social constructivism flourished on American campuses as of the 1970s, it was only twenty years later that *The Social Construction of Reality* was translated into French. It is true that in the meantime, the constructivist approach had become the central perspective within French sociology, with Bourdieu redefining his approach as "structuralist constructivism," the sociology of social professional groups associated with Luc Boltanski, Laurent Thévenot, and Alain Desrosières, the sociohistory of Gérard Noiriel and Michel Offerlé, and Bruno Latour's and Michel Callon's anthropology of science and techniques.

Not even the intense debates in the United States and the philosophy of science, particularly around the works of John Searle (*The Construction of Social Reality*, 1995) and Ian Hacking (*The Social Construction of What?*, 1999), managed to dislodge constructivism because it is not merely a theoretical and an epistemological position. Rather, it preemptively militates against any enterprise, whether in society or in the social sciences, to naturalize the social order, and thus indissociably constitutes a political stance. In that respect, even though scholars who present themselves as social constructivists may at times vacate the ground of sociology (to indulge in the excesses of "ontological slicing and dicing" or derealizing practices), structuralism is no doubt a *consequential* sociological practice—that is, as Berger and Luckmann wished, one that implies reflexive analysis of its social foundations.

Cyril Lemieux

Peter L. Berger and Thomas Luckmann, *The Social Construction of Reality: A Treatise in the Sociology of Knowledge* (New York: Anchor Books, 1966).

1967

OF GRAMMATOLOGY: DERRIDA INVENTS A WRITING PRECEDING SIGNS

Few books symbolize the moment when one phase in the history of thought ends and another begins. Yet rightly or wrongly, for several generations, particularly outside France, *De la grammatologie* (*Of Grammatology*) represented the passage from "structuralism" to "post-structuralism" and even, more broadly, from "modernism" to "postmodernism." Of the various works Jacques Derrida (1930–2004) published that year, *La voix et le phénomène* (*Voice and Phenomenon*) was more restricted in scope (on the phenomenology of Edmund Husserl) and *L'écriture et la différence* (*Writing and Difference*) was a collection of articles; hence, *De la grammatologie* became the classic of the moment.

Yet the book harbored greater ambitions: Its task was nothing less than diagnosing an event enclosing 3,000 years of history—a history that was none other than that of "Western rationality," for which Derrida, in the wake of Husserl, put forward as a new concept. This history, Derrida argues, is based on a dual movement: first, a normative devaluation of writing (which, it was claimed, had to be anchored in speaking) and, second, a liberation from its effects (particularly through mathematics). This epoch announced its end through two events. One is cybernetics, which is the generalization of *putting the world into writing* through computing (with Derrida heralding this process), and the other is structuralism, in which *De la grammatologie* recognizes the name of its present, putting forward one of the great philosophical interpretations of it, alongside other major works of the period: Foucault's *Les mots et les choses* (*The Order of Things*, 1966), Deleuze's *Logique du sens* (*Logic of Sense*, 1968) and *Différence et répétition* (*Difference and*

Repetition, 1969), and Lyotard's *Discours, figure* (*Discourse, Figure*, 1971). Whereas the phenomenological tradition sought to ground rationality in evidence (defined by the undeviating presence of "things themselves," instead of evoking them from a distance), Derrida stated that this presence was itself conditioned by a certain regime of signs—more specifically, by writing.

The book is made up of two parts. The first seems to be a general reflection on the issues of a future (though impossible) science that Derrida calls "grammatology"; the second "illustrates" these general problems using a "case," that of Rousseau. In fact, the whole book is a "deconstruction" of structuralism in two phases, the first starting from linguistics, more specifically Saussure, and the second from anthropology, more specifically Lévi-Strauss (via Rousseau). The overall drive of the book consists in arguing that structuralism allows us to think something that it refuses to think, and this is because it marks a limit in the history of rationality, being both inside and outside metaphysics. Throughout the book Derrida repeats an operation that became characteristic of "deconstruction": bringing out the prime or original character of what is supposed to be derived or secondary or supplementary. While (phonetic) writing is meant to be a representation of the spoken word, which is itself a representation of something else (of the world or of thought), Derrida shows that all language is based on the very possibility of writing (not necessarily phonetic writing).

He does this, for example, by summoning Saussure, who, while repeating the age-old condemnation of writing and calling for linguists to study solely the spoken word, was unable to explain what a linguistic sign as differential entity was without drawing on the model of writing. More generally, if writing is a sign of the sign, and the great discovery of structuralism was to have shown that signs are not grounded in relation to any transcendent reality but in their lateral (or immanent) relation to each other within a differential system, then one may see that the lesson of structuralism is to have generalized the concept of writing.

But in that case, how are we to think of this arche-writing, which is the precondition for language, meaning, and so on? It cannot be a simple object, since it is the source whence objectivity derives its very condition. It thus seems to constitute one of those empirical-transcendental pairings of which Foucault speaks in *Les mots et les choses*. And in fact, the issue is the same: rethinking philosophy in a context where the opposition between fundamental and experimental, transcendental and empirical, is disturbed by the project of the humanities, particularly in their structuralist form, which take meaning, consciousness, rationality, science, ideality, and so on as objects in a new sense.

The reception of *De la grammatologie* is caught up with that of Derrida's work as a whole. Initially the book was seen as an internal radicalization of structuralism, particularly in the United States, because of the famous and lengthy foreword by its translator, Gayatri Spivak, a specialist in comparative literature who went on to become an eminent figure in gender and postcolonial studies. The book also played a key role in media studies and in reflection on technologies, particularly through the work of Friedrich Kittler (*Grammophon, Film, Typewriter*, 1986), Bernard Stiegler (*La technique et le temps* [*Technics and Time*], 1994), and Brian Rotman (*Signifying Nothing*, 1987), but also in a certain way for science studies, through the work of Bruno Latour.

This exceptional posterity also explains why it ended up symbolizing a period with which to break. Various figures in the contemporary return to metaphysics (particularly "speculative realism") viewed *De la grammatologie* as the very model of the operation to *derealize* the world into signs of signs and the *hypercritical* intoxication that they reject. Nevertheless, Derrida's work continues to inspire research in anthropology and the history of writing, on which it drew extensively, as illustrated by Pierre Déléage's recent *Lettres mortes* (2017). We may wager that when the polemics surrounding structuralism and post-structuralism have died down, we will be able to return to the fundamental question lying at the heart of *De la grammatologie*: What are the philosophical issues in the major events grouped under the label of "structuralism"?

Patrice Maniglier

Jacques Derrida, *De la grammatologie* (Paris: Minuit ["Critique"], 1967). Republished by Minuit, 1992. Translated into English by Gayatri Chakravorty Spivak as *Of Grammatology* (Baltimore: Johns Hopkins Press, 1976, rev. 2016).

1967

STUDIES IN ETHNOMETHODOLOGY: GARFINKEL AND THE PHENOMENOLOGY OF THE SOCIAL

When *Studies in Ethnomethodology* was published, it seemed to hail from a different sociological planet. Given the research it presents, the approach it uses, the program it sketches out, and the vocabulary it employs—which seems to come straight out of nowhere, starting with the term "ethnomethodology"—this impression was not unjustified. Yet Harold Garfinkel (1917–2011) had as his purpose to continue the work of Durkheim. He set out to give new content to Durkheim's aphorism that "the objective reality of social facts is sociology's fundamental phenomenon," showing how this objective reality is produced in the course of social life through the ordinary activities and practices of its "members." He thus took up a central tenet of Durkheim and used it as the cornerstone for an explanation of the endogenous production of the social order: Social reality is first and foremost a moral reality, with its two dimensions of obligation and desirability. But he placed this Durkheimian legacy within a framework taken from Husserl's phenomenology, using the works of Aron Gurwitsch and Alfred Schütz, and later of Maurice Merleau-Ponty, with which he was familiar.

Studies in Ethnomethodology sets out to develop a phenomenological sociology. Garfinkel never deviated from this phenomenological approach, even though he had a very personal way of reading the authors from this tradition. He chose to treat their concepts as indicating phenomena to be found, observed, and described, rather than taking them as they stood to figure out in abstract terms how reality, analyzed through them, might be ordered. Garfinkel sought these phenomena in "natural" situations and occurrences, sometimes at the cost of interventions seeking to disturb their habitual course, as chapter 2 of his book shows. Such is the case, for example, with the idea of "natural attitude," examined by studying situations and mechanisms that are capable of showing precisely what this natural attitude is and how it is "automatically" preserved by members.

The phenomenological approach may also be seen in Garfinkel's concern with giving social facts their concrete physiognomy and perceptible nature as "organizational things" (that is, of discovering the methodical living work) conducted progressively, together and in situation, without explicit reference to rules or models—through which these facts are dynamically organized into objective reality. The fact that social activities and situations are ordered by members' concerted operations, of which they are not aware, does not prevent them from appearing to be independent of what they accomplish and achieve. For they display a standardized, regular, anonymous, typical character and are reproducible by anybody, thus transcending their authors and circumstances. This contributes to their accountability—that is, the possibility of recognizing them as intelligible, rational, and justifiable, as socially approved and conforming to society's norms and values.

It is this methodical work conducted in concert by "members" that should be taken as the "precedent" for sociological analysis, rather than the corpus of theoretical texts by authoritative thinkers in the social sciences. This work remains unseen not only by "members" but also by sociologists. Rather than presenting a single method, *Studies in Ethnomethodology* thus provides widely varying exploratory exercises to make this work visible and to identify its main articulations.

The book, published when Garfinkel was fifty years old, contains texts written at different periods, some of which had already appeared separately. Of the eight chapters, only chapters 5 (the famous "Agnes case"), 6, and 7 were new publications. In a way, the final chapter presents Garfinkel's starting point, while the first sets out his endpoint. There is real continuity yet profound discontinuity between these two chapters. The final chapter starts from Schütz's perspective, according to which rationality as conceived by the practitioners of scientific disciplines (primarily rationality as means fitting ends) is at considerable remove from the manner, likewise rational in its own fashion, in which events, situations, people, and so on are treated by members going about their daily activities. Apprehending how these activities are provided with their properties of being clear, distinct, coherent, and meaningful, *from within their being carried out*, is precisely the program that Garfinkel assigns to ethnomethodology in the first chapter of the book, thus introducing a new conceptual approach.

In the 1960s and 1970s, ethnomethodology came in for sharp criticism from orthodox sociology, which accused it of being linked to the hippie movement, of being a sociology without society, or else of being a form of situationism. It is true that ethnomethodologies lay themselves open to this type of attack by arguing that mainstream sociology is incapable of seizing the real dynamic of social phenomena, essentially because its first move is to replace them with "reasoning beings" so as to then implement the conceptual method of "formal analysis." But at the same time, the blindness of sociologists as charged is striking, particularly their inability to see how Garfinkel's perspective takes up within sociology, in its own specific way, an intellectual move that is virtually axiomatic for those familiar with phenomenology, pragmatism, or quite simply Pierre Bourdieu's *Sens pratique* (*The Logic of Practice*).

Louis Quéré

Harold Garfinkel, *Studies in Ethnomethodology* (Englewood Cliffs, NJ: Prentice-Hall, 1967).

1968

MYTHE ET ÉPOPÉE: DUMÉZIL VIEWS MYTH AS EXPRESSING SOCIAL ORGANIZATION

The first volume of *Mythe et épopée* (Myth and epic poetry) came out in May 1968, but it bears the traces of another spring, that of 1938, when Georges Dumézil (1898–1986), as he explains in his preface, after much groping around, made a sudden discovery: The most ancient Romans, the Umbrians, displayed a conception of society that was also known to the Indo-Iranians and that underpinned the social order of the Indians. This conception was characterized by a tripartite functional division into priests, warriors, and producers. After having compared all the ancients who spoke so-called Indo-European languages, from Latin to Scandinavian tongues, from Greek to Ossetian, Dumézil gave his "literary assessment of the ideology of the three functions"—that is, the synthesis of three decades of research unearthing the traces that this scheme had left in the oldest literature produced by these cultures, be it lyrical, narrative, elegiac, or epic.

This first volume provides in-depth analysis of the *Mahābhārata*, of elegies by Propertius, of Virgil's *Aeneid*, then of legends of the Ossetians and Scythians, with an incursion in part four into the sort of thematic comparison (particularly the motif of choice, from Paris to Solomon), which he addressed in the two subsequent volumes that were brought out in 1971 and 1973. Throughout, his hypothesis is that these ancient narratives display "the transposition of the most ancient theology and mythology into epic poetry." The *Mahābhārata*, whose characters are incarnations of the gods, fits this hypothesis particularly well. Tirelessly following the meanders of this narrative material, Dumézil notes the traces left by a tripartite conception, such as the subtle motifs making it possible to distribute the five Pândava brothers—even though they are all warriors—into each of "the three fundamental functions whose harmony ensures the normal happy life of a society." These motifs may thus be read as traces of the differential oppositions existing between the gods they embody.

Using this seemingly simple hypothesis, Dumézil profoundly modified the way philology and social thought had been connected since the nineteenth century. Comparative mythology was placed on a new footing: It was no longer to be interpreted as if its meaning lay outside it, in historical or cosmic events recorded in distorted form or else in the operations of the intellect or plays of language of which it was the projection. While Dumézil worked within the perimeter established by comparative grammar since the nineteenth century, that of the affinities between the so-called Indo-European languages, it was no longer a matter of studying the linguistic facts themselves, be these syntactic particularities or onomastic echoes, to look for a "minimal level of shared civilization" implied by such a "language community." Rather, what explained the affinities found throughout the area conquered by these people "in the two last millennia before our era" was their shared form of primitive social organization, acting as the matrix for a shared "conception of the world, of the invisible and the visible." Philology set itself free from linguistics and shifted toward sociology.

Though echoing a revolution in thought dating from 1938, the publication of *Mythe et épopée* thirty years later coincided somewhat awkwardly with the peak of structuralism. Admittedly, it had paved the way in making the quest for regularity in oppositions and differences the key to comparative study. Yet, in respecting the perimeter laid down by the comparative grammar of Indo-European languages, it limited exploration and explanation of transformations to structures, a central component to Lévi-Strauss's anthropology. Additionally, archaeologists have subsequently put forward many objections to the material existence of an Indo-European civilization predating "dispersal," particularly Jean-Paul Demoule in *Mais où sont passés les Indo-Européens?* (2014).

With hindsight, though, we may better appreciate the significance of *Mythe et épopée* for all research linking philology and the social sciences.

In reading myth as an expression of social organization, Dumézil takes Durkheim's sociology of religion far further than he realizes, albeit with one major alteration, due to his having received Durkheim's legacy through the work of Marcel Granet—meaning that, to his mind, the "tripartite ideology" could subsist or do without the existence of any real tripartite division. Such a division was only to be found in the case of India, and the social division was thus "no more than one application among many others" of a structure relating to representation and revealing the primacy of the intellect.

One could also argue that Dumézil inherited from Marcel Granet his greater indifference to the boundary between the natural and the social than that detectable in Durkheim's and Mauss's study of primitive classifications. This indifference allowed him to move beyond rites as the heart of the social and take a greater range of practices—from combat techniques to livestock rearing, from the gathering of forest plants to palace life—as the motifs for recognizing the moments in a text where the social structure broke through to the surface. Dumézil thus proposed a way of experiencing the text in which the wealth of sociological results flows directly from the philologist's skill in the art of reading. This legacy will survive, even were one to decide to dissolve the Indo-European perimeter into a field of universal comparisons and to open up the combination of social functions beyond the tripartite scheme.

Arnaud Macé

Georges Dumézil, *Mythe et épopée*, vol. 1, *L'idéologie des trois fonctions dans les épopées des peuples indo-européens* (Paris: Gallimard ["Bibliothèque des sciences humaines"], 1968). Republished by Gallimard ("Quarto"), 1995.

1969

THE POST-INDUSTRIAL SOCIETY: TOURAINE AND THE ONSET OF A NEW TYPE OF SOCIETY

In the aftermath of the May 1968 movement, the French intelligentsia was ever more firmly in the grip of structuralism, often in tune with the prevailing leftism, and sociology largely adhered to the categories of "reproduction" and "habitus." Such is intellectual life. At a time of formidable social and cultural change, many wished to view this as merely the implacable play of structures, apparatuses, and authorities and so chased out the subject, sometimes even calling for its death.

Yet interest in social movements, ideas of freedom, creativity, and hence the subject (even though the term did not enjoy the success it does today) were not sidelined for all that. The wind of May 1968 was still blowing, flagging what was emerging, being built, and transformed in France and around the world. It was the components of this "renewed modernity"—others went on to speak of a "second modernity"—that Alain Touraine (born 1925) tackled head-on in *La société post-industrielle: Naissance d'une société* (*The Post-Industrial Society*), published in 1969.

Let us start by settling a matter of paternity. Even though Daniel Bell's *The Coming of Post-Industrial Society: A Venture in Social Forecasting* came out in 1973, he was the first to speak of "post-industrial society," as Touraine readily acknowledged. But where Bell saw a sort of development of industrial society, Touraine considered it to be the "birth" of another society.

In 1968, before the dust had even settled, Touraine published *Le mouvement de Mai ou le communisme utopique* (*The May Movement*), in which the themes of his next book already transpired. He argues that the student movement heralded the advent of a new society in which the central conflict could no longer be that between workers and labor masters. *La société post-industrielle* addresses this new type of society, analyzes it, and proposes the sociological tools for understanding it.

What form does historical action now take? It is not because the labor movement is no longer the main protagonist that social domination disappears. Instead, it acquires new forms, no longer limited to exploiting workers but operating in domains other than industry, including communication, consumption, and, according to Touraine, the imperialism of large organizations. It is a matter of alienation, of manipulating needs, of intrusion into private life. Under these circumstances, scholarly knowledge becomes a crucial issue, and the university emerges as a decisive institution.

This new society requires a new sociology. Touraine sides with those who replace the sociology of principles with that of decisions and policies (such as Michel Crozier, for instance), against the "old functionalism" and a way of thinking he calls "neoliberal." He places the study of "new social movements" at the heart of social analysis (the expression went on to enjoy great success). His program was to understand how collective action is formed, in which "consumers become producers, actors in their society and culture," to study "the production of history, the grip of power, the contradictions of dependent participation and inventing the future."

Touraine thus envisaged the "destruction" of "class society" (or industrial society) in favor of "new classes" and "new conflicts" in which those protesting against "programmed society" (another name for this new type of society) oppose technocratic power. He suggested distinguishing between reactions to a crisis (by university institutions, for example) and building a social movement (a student movement questioning the general direction taken by collective life, for instance). He calls for a new approach to leisure and to business at its various levels of operation, ultimately asking: "What is the point of sociologists?" His main response is that "only sociology makes it possible to move beyond the contradictions of technocracy and revolt in the name of personal and collective creativity [. . . and] rediscover the political reality of our society, to bring forth the social power lying behind the impersonal grip, and the social movements behind the revolt."

These two books, on the May 1968 movement and post-industrial society, were the decisive moment in Touraine's career when the method of "sociological intervention" came into being. As is known, this consists in linking the production of sociological knowledge to the empowerment of actors, inviting the latter to reflect. This reflection, focusing on these actors' own way of interpreting the social world, transforms their capacity to act on it. As of the 1970s, this approach gave rise to a proliferation of research on such varied themes as student movements, the antinuclear movement, regionalism, transformations in the labor world, and race—all conceived as facets of the emergent "new society." They were produced especially by a team of researchers—including François Dubet, Zsuzsa Hegedus, and myself, joined later by Nilüfer Göle, Farhad Khosrokhavar, Philippe Bataille, and many others—who worked alongside Touraine at the Centre d'études des mouvements sociaux, then, as of 1981, at the Centre d'analyse et d'intervention sociologiques.

These and other current developments, particularly relating to the construction of subjectivity and globalization, prove that nearly fifty years after its publication, and despite having inevitably aged in places, *La société post-industrielle* still trains its sights on the right targets. For we are not yet done with the birth of this society, which we still do not know how to name, other than to say that it comes after the previous one—that it is "post."

Michel Wieviorka

Alain Touraine, *La société post-industrielle: Naissance d'une société* (Paris: Denoël, 1969). Translated into English by Leonard F. X. Mayhew as *The Post-Industrial Society: Tomorrow's Social History: Classes, Conflicts and Culture in the Programmed Society* (New York: Random House, 1971).

1969

THE COURT SOCIETY: ELIAS DEFINES COURT SOCIETY AS THE CRUCIBLE FOR THE CIVILIZING PROCESS

When Luchterhand published *Die höfische Gesellschaft* (*The Court Society*), its author, Norbert Elias (1897–1990), was seventy-two years old. His only other book, *Über den Prozess der Zivilisation* (*The Civilizing Process*), published thirty years earlier in Basel, had been written in exile after leaving Nazi Germany in spring 1933, when he moved to Paris before settling in London in 1935.

The 1939 book had been forgotten in the tumultuous years of war and in Elias's career. In 1954, he became a lecturer at the University of Leicester, and it was not until 1969 that the book reappeared on the German intellectual scene with its first reprint by the Bern-based A. G. Francke publishing house. In the same year, Elias decided to revise and publish the Frankfurt University habilitation thesis that he had completed in 1933, though without being able to defend it. While the appearance of these two books drew attention to Elias's work, it was only when they came out as Suhrkamp paperbacks (in 1976 for *The Civilizing Process* and 1983 for *The Court Society*) that they became classics in the German social sciences.

For Elias, "court society" needs to be understood in two ways. First, the court is considered as a society—that is, as a social formation or configuration (Elias calls it a "figuration") in which individuals are linked by reciprocal dependencies imposing specific codes of conduct and behavioral control. Second, "court society" is understood as a society endowed with a court that is an essential element in maintaining a state of equilibrium in the tensions between socially dominant groups and thereby in the construction and reproduction of the power of the absolute sovereign who plays on the rivalry between the various elites. The seventeenth-century French court, to which Elias devotes most of his attention (even though the book sketches out comparisons on several occasions with feudal courts, Asian court societies, and the English and German courts), shows that it was an essential institution allowing the king both to control the traditional aristocracy, thus warding off princely rivalry, and to protect it, using it as a counterweight to the power of the officers of justice and of finance in charge of administering the kingdom.

Court society is based on three paradoxical principles. First, the greatest social difference was experienced within the greatest spatial proximity: At court, the absolute and sacred king asserted the distance separating him from his nobility by living among them at every moment. Hence private existence, that of the king and of the courtiers, was always on public display. Second, in court society, the social identity of the individual is determined by the credit granted or refused to his or her self-representation. The king is master of this performance and may give or withdraw his favor or modify the order of the ranks in the court ceremonial. Hence the bitter rivalry about the ranks in the hierarchy of etiquette, taken as the benchmark of social power. Third, at court, asserting social superiority presupposes submission. It is only by accepting to be domesticated by the sovereign that the aristocracy may display the distance separating it from officers of justice. Nor did the king escape this mechanism, since it was by submitting to the etiquette he imposed on his courtiers that he was able to dominate them.

The court played an essential role in building the absolutist state, which attributed a dual monopoly to the king, over taxation and over the legitimate use of violence, thus stripping the aristocracy of the ancient foundations of its power. It also played a central part in what Elias calls "the civilizing process." Court society imposed rigorous control over feelings and emotions, thus compelling individuals to interiorize stable, binding mechanisms of self-constraint to censor their impulses, to prohibit violent behavior, and to dissimulate feelings. Court life required special psychological properties of those participating in it: the art of observing others to detect their purposes, the capacity to observe oneself in order to master one's passions, and the interiorization of disciplines regulating the laws of court civility. "Court rationality," imposed and practiced in this way, defined a new "structure of personality," a new "psychic economy," that Elias refers to using the old word "habitus."

The first part of Elias's major book *Uber den Prozess der Zivilisation* (*The Civilizing Process*) was translated into French in 1973 (as *La civilisation des mœurs*) before being translated into English in 1978 as *The History of Manners*. The second part of the book was published in French in 1975 (as *La dynamique de l'Occident*) and in English in 1982 as *State Formation and Civilization*. The French translation of *Die höfische Gesellschaft* was published between the two parts of *Uber den Prozess der Zivilisation*. In English, it was published in 1983, one year after the second part. The separation of the two parts of the 1939 text, both in English and in French, and the fact that *Die höfische Gesellschaft*, though written earlier than *Uber den Prozess der Zivili-sation*, was in fact translated later, obfuscated the fundamental originality of Elias's perspective, which associated transformations in the exercise of power, changes to social structures, and modifications to the psychic economy over the lengthy course of Western societies, from the Middle Ages to the nine-teenth century. The building of absolutist states, the formation of court society, and the civilizing process were thus inseparably bound together. On reading the book today, one needs to situate it in its time to appreciate where it stands in Elias's work as a whole and to confront it with the many works that, over the past half-century, have either rejected or taken inspiration from its theses.

Roger Chartier

Norbert Elias, *Die höfische Gesellschaft: Untersuchungen zur Soziologie des Königtums und der höfischen Aristokratie mit einer Einleitung: Soziologie und Geschichtswissenschaft* (Neuwied: Luch-terhand, 1969). Translated into English by Edmund Jephcott as *The Court Society* (Oxford: Black-well, 1983).

1969

ETHNIC GROUPS AND BOUNDARIES: BARTH DESUBSTANTIALIZES THE IDEA OF ETHNIC GROUPS

The only name to have remained associated with the 1969 publication of *Ethnic Groups and Boundaries* is that of Fredrik Barth (1928–2016), though the book in fact presents seven studies, each by a different Scandinavian anthropologist, on such varied fields as Sudan, Ethiopia, Norway, Mexico, and (by Barth himself) Afghanistan. But it is true that the substance of the book is contained in the thirty or so pages of its introduction, in which Barth sets out theoretical propositions that went on to revolutionize how ethnic phenomena were approached. The central idea is that ethnicity is fundamentally a matter of social organization and only secondarily one of culture. Ethnic groups only exist in their relations to one another and are distinguished from one another by a set of (cultural) features that differ depending on the cases. What the ethnologist thus needs to consider is not the sum of the objective differences and similarities but what the actors themselves take to be significant. Viewed thus, culture does not transpire as an essence but as a repertoire of markers.

Barth's theory is built primarily around the question of boundaries (taken, of course, in the social, not territorial, meaning of the term). What is fundamental for the continuity and persistence of an ethnic group is maintaining its boundary—or boundaries, if in contact with several other groups. Research concerning ethnicity thus needs to examine the processes implemented by either side to maintain, alter, or possibly abolish boundaries.

The boundary is defined using linguistic or other types of cultural markers, making it possible to assign an individual to a given group. "Phenotypical" characteristics may also come into play, where the apprehension of these physical characteristics is of course itself cultural. As any boundary has two sides, assigning an individual to a determined group (that is, their *ascription*) is an indissociably internal and external affair. In other words, ethnic identity is both assigned by *others* and validated by *one's own*. This identity is binding, imposing axiological and behavioral norms on individuals. But these norms may undergo overall change without redrawing the boundary line (ethnic identity may change content without modifying the outline). This arises when a new context or situation makes them awkward or unbearable for the group as a whole. If, on the other hand, only a single individual is concerned, that person may seek to solve the difficulty by "crossing the line"—that is, by changing group (where this may result from a choice made in the hope of gaining advantages independently even of a specific problem: Barth adheres to methodological individualism). And what is true for individuals is also true for groups, be they families or other types of unit.

It is no exaggeration to say that the publication of *Ethnic Groups and Boundaries* led to a "takeoff" in anthropological research on ethnicity. Western ethnologists had long paid little (theoretical) interest to the eponymous object of their discipline. Ethnicity had primarily been taken as a *given*, defining and circumscribing their field of study. This was not the case in the East, where Russian and Soviet ethnographers, inspired by the quantitative and qualitative diversity of the "ethnic groups" present on their state territory—ranging from great Caucasian groups through to minor Siberian peoples—had developed a sui generis theory of ethnos. Focusing mainly on matters of ethnogenesis, this theory was based on a great—and closed—evolutionist scheme in which the generic concept of *ethnos* encompassed *tribes* from the primitive period alongside *ethnic groups* (or *peoples*) from the days of slavery and feudalism, together with the *nations* of the capitalist and socialist phases.

The West's indifference to theory lasted through to the great comparative undertakings of the 1950s (the most emblematic being George Peter Murdock's *Outline of World Cultures*). These required precise and universal definitions of the units making up the corpus—that is, the "ethnic groups" (or the "cultures") empirically provided by the field. There were many attempts

111   *Barth Desubstantializes the Idea of Ethnic Groups*

at definition based on selecting supposedly pertinent defining features (e.g., language and/or economic system and/or territory and/or religion), as was the case for the ethnos of Russian scholarship. This led to a theoretical dead end in which there were diverse rival definitions. Barth's "Copernican revolution" unblocked the situation by emptying the idea of ethnic group of its substance and unhitching it from that of culture, thus banishing great "transcultural" schema to the graveyard of epistemological illusions.

It therefore paved the way for an entire body of empirical research on ethnicity in action—that is, on the processes of ascription and "boundary" maintenance. However, while it might today appear inconceivable to return to purely substantialist conceptions, the debate continues about the nature and reality of ethnic phenomena. In particular, the question of the *emic* signification of this type of classification is still very much open. The fact that ethnicity is a social construct does not prevent this construct from being experienced as an essential reality, what a cognitivist approach would call the *primordialism* of actors—which may, of course, include "public authorities" and "populations."

Jean-François Gossiaux

Fredrik Barth, ed., *Ethnic Groups and Boundaries: The Social Organization of Culture Difference* (Oslo: Universitetsforlaget, 1969).

1970

EXIT, VOICE, AND LOYALTY: HIRSCHMAN THEORIZES THE EXPRESSION OF DISCONTENT

In 1970, Albert Hirschman (1915–2012) was a well-regarded specialist in development economics, a field in which he had already published several books and become a leading authority on Latin American countries. However, the publication of *Exit, Voice, and Loyalty* marked a turning point in his career. With this book, Hirschman—an economist by training—definitively joined the category of unclassifiable authors whose scholarship transcends disciplinary barriers and feeds into work right across the social sciences. Indeed, such is the book's ambition. In raising the very general question of the forms of action available to agents when their satisfaction with a service drops, or when they are disappointed with their involvement in some joint undertaking, Hirschman's purpose is to forge concepts for embracing problems relating to several disciplines and to construct a model that applies equally well to consumers dissatisfied with a good they have acquired, users unhappy with a public service, and activists disappointed by an organization to which they belong.

So, what may one do when a service, company, or organization is deemed wanting? The originality of Hirschman's answer lies largely in its simplicity. He states that in such situations, two strategies may be envisaged. Either users (citizens, consumers, etc.) may choose to defect (exit)—that is, leave the relation they had established to enter another relation, by invoking competition—or they may choose to speak out (*voice*) to express their dissatisfaction, with the aim of improving the relation in question. Of course, these two strategies are not always available. For example, in the case of a monopoly, the exit strategy is not really feasible, and so the only way of expressing discontent is to speak out. In other circumstances, it is speaking out that is impossible, or too costly, or too dangerous—under authoritarian regimes, for instance—in which case it is exit that will be privileged, perhaps in the form of emigration. Other factors may guide this choice, such as loyalty toward a firm or organization, which may delay defection and, in certain cases, encourage people to speak out while giving greater weight to their voice because of the threat of defection. According to Hirschman, one of the mistakes managers and leaders often make is to consider that if clients or users do not exit or use their voice, it is probably because they are satisfied. But it is possible that they are merely being loyal, though profoundly discontent. In this case, should the conditions become more favorable to defection or speaking out, their sudden departure or abrupt protest will not fail to catch unawares those in charge.

The interest of this approach is that rather than limiting defection to the economic sphere and speaking out to political action, it shows that the antinomy may apply to most social realms, and thus it helps us to think about very varied situations, some of which relate to the "macro" scale, such as spatial mobility, while others relate to the "micro" scale, such as the management of marital disputes. The great merit of the model also lies in its suggestiveness: It invites us to think of the range of possible interactions between defection and speaking out and particularly to analyze the way in which these two types of action may, depending on the situation, either attenuate or reinforce one another. The simplicity of the conceptual pair is also conducive to being enriched, critiqued, or extended in many different ways, which in fact many economists, sociologists, and political scientists have subsequently done. This has resulted in many stimulating complexifications, such as the distinction between vertical speaking, directly addressing the authorities, and horizontal speaking, enabling individuals to share demands and create the conditions for collective action.

"I believe it is important to present situations in a polarized way, perhaps even to exaggerate components of knowledge and observations that attenuate these oppositions," Hirschman once observed. "This is the reason why I usually introduce, in the first part of my writings, some schema which is then exposed to critiques, pointing out its limitations, in the second part." And, true to this propensity to self-subversion, Hirschman kept returning to his model to redefine its central concepts and modify them to respond to certain objections or take new situations into account, such as the collapse of the Berlin Wall, which led him to reexamine possible ways of combining defection and speaking out.

After this book, Hirschman produced others about the genealogy of the idea of interest, about the role of disappointment in engagement dynamics, and about reactionary rhetorical figures, all of which were as successful as *Exit, Voice, and Loyalty*. This is perhaps at least partly due to his particular style of writing, based, one might say, on a sort of systematic commitment to clarity. Thus, the concepts that Hirschman chose in building his models are always disarmingly simple, and it is precisely this simplicity that, paradoxically, endows them with such great operating capacity and analytical depth. For it is this simplicity that allows them to "travel," to encourage generalization, and to get as close as possible to the Hirschman's long-cherished dream—that of the unity of the social sciences.

Yannick Barthe

Albert O. Hirschman, *Exit, Voice, and Loyalty: Responses to Decline in Firms, Organizations, and States* (Cambridge, MA: Harvard University Press, 1970).

1971

THE VISION OF THE VANQUISHED: WACHTEL SWITCHES PERSPECTIVE ON THE SPANISH CONQUEST

La vision des vaincus (*The Vision of the Vanquished*) has long held a central place in American ethnohistorical studies. In this pioneering work, Nathan Wachtel (born 1935) helped alter how we view the Spanish conquest, its effects, and how Indian societies responded to the trauma of the "encounter." If the book has produced such an impact on generations of researchers, it is not solely for paying new, resolutely anti-Eurocentric attention to the reactions of Indian societies, thus offering an original analysis of the "other side of conquest"; it is also because it sets out a new way of thinking about the paths to follow in accounting for the history and historicity regimes of so-called primitive peoples "without history" or "without writing." Additionally, taking its place within contemporary debate about the relationship between structures and empirical reality, on the one hand, and structures and historical time, on the other, the book provided concrete proof that it was possible to apprehend a structural rationality independent of time.

While studying destructuring and restructuring within the context of colonial domination, *La vision des vaincus* seeks primarily to apprehend Indian praxis. By analyzing the practice of the dominated, this book, written at a period marked by nativist and third-worldist movements, reendowed Indian populations with some of their agency. No, acculturation has not always been synonymous with conversion or necessarily experienced as the abandonment of native tradition. Yes, through revolts, millenarian movements, and wars, Indians sought to regain control over their history. And though the pre-Hispanic social system collapsed, and though the Spaniards altered the course of American history to their advantage, certain "traditional" structures nevertheless continued to exist.

It is precisely on this point that Wachtel extricates these societies from a vision confining them to their archaic fate. First, he shows that even today, the trauma of conquest is interpreted and re-signified through native folklore, which provides a constantly renewed vision of the past. Second, he insists on the fact that resistance and revolt do not mean perpetuating some fixed and timeless tradition. By exploring the praxis of Indians from Peru and the northerly and southerly limits of the Spanish empire, he shows how acculturation, taken as a process, often informs a refusal of domination and shows that Indian societies, through borrowings, innovations, and creations, have cultivated their specificity while at the same time transforming themselves. Here, Indian resistance does not correlate to some purely negative operation to preserve and return to pre-Hispanic traditions and modes of social organization. Nor does it take place in a sort of "structural no man's land."

Being careful to break with any essentialism and to make the Indians the active though circumscribed agents of their new history, *La vision des vaincus* examines the meaning of revolts and resistance in so-called border zones. The passages about the history of contact between the Spanish and the Chichimeca, and the Spanish and the Mapuche, reveal the existence of a certain number of technical innovations, borrowings, and creations among the groups studied. Presentation of the cases of the Chichimeca and the Mapuche further and conversely explain why the conquistadores succeeded in conquering the Inca and Aztec empires. The Spanish failure in the border zones at either tip of Iberian America is largely (though not solely) attributable to the nature of the societies encountered: They were often nomadic, organized into a large number of independent sociopolitical units, and their members were not used to producing a surplus and paying a tribute. The notion of acculturation, designating "all the phenomena of interaction resulting from contact between two cultures," thus occupies a key role in the analysis. Lying at a strategic point in the human sciences, it provides a way of laying the foundations for an ethnological and ethnohistorical theory of sociocultural change. Here, Wachtel uses a distinction between two types of acculturation: one which is imposed, one which is spontaneous. The first, associated with situations of managed contact, designates the process by which indigenous culture moves toward Western culture. The second, occurring in contexts of non-managed contact, relates to the integration of Western components in indigenous culture.

La vision des vaincus considerably altered the course of research into populations in the colonial Americas. Through critical comparison of the representations of the past detectable in "conquest dances" and the folklore of Amerindian populations in present-day Peru, Guatemala, and Mexico, the book inaugurated a historical method (regressive history), together with an innovative approach for studying native historicity regimes. In apprehending folklore as a language, a collective and anonymous creation from which formal logics may be deduced, it perpetuated the structural analysis of Lévi-Strauss while taking up the legacy of collective psychology. Hence, the progressive and structural history initiated in *La vision des vaincus*—which reached full maturity in *Le retour des ancêtres* (*The Return of the Ancestors*, 1990)—is a central moment in the cooperation of all the human sciences (history, anthropology, and sociology).

Guillaume Boccara

Nathan Wachtel, *La vision des vaincus: Les Indiens du Pérou devant la conquête espagnole, 1530–1570* (Paris: Gallimard ["Bibliothèque des histoires"], 1971). Republished by Gallimard ("Folio"), 1992. Translated into English by Ben and Siân Reynolds as *The Vision of the Vanquished: The Spanish Conquest of Peru through Indian Eyes, 1530–1570* (Hassocks: Harvester Press, 1977).

1972

LANGUAGE IN THE INNER CITY: LABOV DEFENDS A UNIFIED THEORY OF LANGUAGE AND ITS SOCIAL USES

In 1972, when William Labov (born 1927) published *Language in the Inner City: Studies in the Black English Vernacular*, generative grammar was triumphant. The object of linguistics was henceforth the idiolect of the ideal speaker-listener, belonging to a homogenous community. Noam Chomsky's program introduced a convenient division of labor between those whose purpose was to explain linguistic competence and those who, following on from structural dialectology and linguistic anthropology, contributed to the study of performance through descriptions based on surveys of the social uses of language. This disastrous division—strengthened by the tenacious prejudice that competence and performance, "internal language" and "external language"—formed two radically separate fields of study. Social variation observable in language practice was, from this perspective, merely an epiphenomenon. This completed the rupture with the social sciences, particularly with anthropology, the chosen field of linguistics since Franz Boas and Edward Sapir, in favor of its exclusive attachment to psychology and biology

Language in the Inner City was one of the rare works of linguistics in the 1970s to have given grounds for hope to linguists unable to resign themselves to this division of labor. It may be read as the demonstration, about a precise case, of three fundamental propositions: Sociolinguistics is a linguistics in its own right; variation is just as much a fact of language as invariance; a formal system to account for this may be built. As a practical consequence, although the study of the social heterogeneity of language formed an integral part of the program of linguistics, the discipline's autonomy was only relative, and greater cooperation with new currents in sociology and anthropology was required.

Carrying on from earlier research, the monograph presented the results of a survey conducted in Harlem from 1965 to 1968 on the Black American vernacular (later called Afro-American English). Labov shows that this vernacular is only one dialect among others in American English and that its specific coherence was ignored by school programs for the Black community. The ambition was all the greater given that it lay on the very field of explanatory adequacy held by Chomsky and his disciples. Analysis in terms of variable rules satisfy the epistemological requirements for constructing a formal model (for example, in terms of assessing the number of rules) seeking to demonstrate the competence of speaking subjects. Thus, syntax rules governing the erasure of the copula *be* (*he fast*) and those of negative concord (*It ain't no cat can't get in no coop*) in Afro-American vernacular English are presented with all the requisite formal rigor, with the place of these rules being discussed within a pan-dialectal grammar of American English. The same is true of two other types of adequacy as defined by Chomsky, descriptive and observational, which seem to be better attained. Labov demonstrates the impossibility of using questionnaires to obtain judgments about the grammaticality of the vernacular. As soon as one is dealing with a dominated dialect, the survey relationship destroys the very object it is seeking to grasp. Linguists must adopt an ethnographic approach in order to overcome the "observer paradox" if they wish to have recordings within the peer group without their being subjected to the legitimate norm by the linguist's very presence.

Like Chomsky, Labov gives a central place to syntax and phonology but also to pragmatics, with analyses of the narrative syntax of accounts of personal experience and the sequential structure of verbal duels. In very concrete terms, the book seeks to promote a unified theory of language and its social uses. Surveys make it possible to specify the relationship between communicative competence and the social field where it is deployed. Studying the networks of sociability is indispensable for understanding linguistic variation internal to the group, which turns out to be correlated to the

120   *Language in the Inner City*

degree of integration (and loyalty) of its members (unlike the "lames" who frequent other groups and are in greater contact with adults). Labov thus documents an activity that plays a central role in relations between the members of adolescent gangs and other gangs sparring to control territory— namely, the exchange of *ritual insults*. In moving from the grammatical to the interactional, Labov contributes directly to the analysis of conversation and the ethnography of communication, a move he repeated in *Therapeutic Discourse* (1977).

What became of this book? It was largely ignored by the Chomskyan current but helped structure a current of variationist sociolinguistics in the United States and Canada, as well as other countries such as France, where, under the aegis Pierre Encrevé, it acquired an original form through its combination with the sociology of Pierre Bourdieu.

In the United States, the book gave rise to a debate between specialists of Afro-American vernacular English, which resulted in clarifying its status as a dialect of English. The thesis of a Creole origin followed by the slow process of "decreolization" and gradual assimilation to English was especially emphasized. While accepting this approach, which supposes a long-term convergence with varieties of American English, Labov, drawing on surveys in several cities, argued that a process of dialectal divergence was also at work, owing to the urban and social segregation affecting Black communities in the United States.

Michel de Fornel

William Labov, *Language in the Inner City: Studies in the Black English Vernacular* (Philadelphia: University of Pennsylvania Press, 1972).

1972

STONE AGE ECONOMICS: SAHLINS OVERTHROWS THE PRODUCTIVIST HYPOTHESIS

When *Stone Age Economics* came out, Marxist-inspired anthropology was developing strongly in the United States and in Europe. The anthropology put forward by Marshall Sahlins (born 1930) draws on this theoretical horizon, combined with perspectives taken from the American neo-evolutionist current, in the wake of Julian Steward and Leslie White. But amid the controversy opposing supporters of the "formalist" approach and those of the "substantivist" school, Sahlins proposed a most unorthodox and voluntarily iconoclastic form of Marxism shorn of dogmatism.

The book contains six essays written over the ten previous years, two of which were first published in France in 1968, when Sahlins was a visiting professor at the Université de Nanterre and living through the social upheaval of that unusual year. One of these essays, "The Original Affluent Society," had rapidly won Sahlins a reputation for originality, both within the anthropological community and more widely, and logically enough, it is on this idea that the book starts. Initially published in *Les Temps modernes* in the aftermath of the 1968 events, this text, strikingly in tune with the radical questionings of the period, conducted a disconcerting detour through hunter-gatherer societies—no doubt rather hastily assimilating those of the Paleolithic and those of the present day—to draw up a pitiless critique of the "consumer society" reviled by the youthful protesters. Sahlins explains that scarcity should not be conflated with poverty; the latter results from social inequality in the relationship between the ends pursued and the means available. True affluence, Sahlins argues, does not conceive of limitless economic needs that we seek to satisfy with increasingly developed yet forever impotent means; true abundance starts with limited needs that even rudimentary technical means may satisfy for everyone, and by very little daily work. This second philosophy, described as the "Zen path," was the option taken by hunter-gatherers. The former, on the contrary, is the philosophy gripping industrial societies, which chase after productivism, at the end of which insufficiency cannot but give way to frustration.

In another essay about "the spirit of the gift," Sahlins revisits one of anthropology's favorite topics, brought to light by Marcel Mauss in the 1920s and placed in a new perspective by Claude Lévi-Strauss in the introduction he wrote to Mauss's work. Taking up and discussing the primary sources (the Maori material on which Mauss had built his interpretation of the obligation to give in return, no doubt the Achilles' heel of his theory), Sahlins added his voice to a passionate debate that had energized anthropology for over half a century: the alchemy that generates the social order from material goods together with the obligation to start from a stance of exhibited disinterest. Or, put another way, how material goods shape ties, via the inner workings of a moral debt, exempt from subtraction or addition, which generates society above and beyond material needs.

Expanding on the theme of gifts, two other essays address the question of exchange in "primitive" societies, drawing on a view heavily inspired by the theoretical suggestions of Karl Polanyi. Sahlins examines forms of (generalized, balanced, and negative) reciprocity—a topic also found in the work of his friend and colleague Elman Service—providing a salutary demonstration that reciprocity, which is not a principle, should not be confused either with symmetry between the exchanging partners or with the equivalence of the terms exchanged. Without yielding to an angelic vision of social relations, Sahlins puts forward the system of gifts as an antidote to that of the market, while bringing into sharp relief how debt can act as a powerful lever for interdependence between social actors.

But there can be no exchange without prior production: That is what occupies Sahlins throughout two essays placed back-to-back about the "domestic mode of production," a Marxist concept adapted to the economic and social configuration of "tribal" (i.e., sedimentary) societies, a concept and adaptation that subsequently generated at times convoluted debates. Backed up by tables, he defends the idea of a tendency toward underproduction, said to be the economic corollary of the dispersal of social units translating the state of political "anarchy." This is "Chayanov's rule," according to which in a system of domestic production, intensity of work is inversely proportional to the productive capacity of the unit of production. For Sahlins, it is the emergence of a centralized power with ambitions for conspicuous prodigality, in which the principle of redistribution replaces that of reciprocity (once again, there are clear tones of Polanyi here), that is alone capable of dynamizing production capacities. In such a social system, unlike what happens in a capitalist economy, control of the producers induces control of the fruits of production. By presenting politics as that which determines economics, the classic Marxist schema is surreptitiously being inverted.

In throwing new light on fundamental matters in economic anthropology, as well as on many other issues, *Stone Age Economics* became a benchmark work and helped place Sahlins within the restricted circle of major figures in anthropology worldwide.

Francis Dupuy

Marshall Sahlins, *Stone Age Economics* (Chicago: Aldine-Atherton, 1972).

1973

THE LEGEND OF BOUVINES: DUBY DOES BATTLE WITH EVENTS-BASED HISTORY

"In the year 1214, 27 July fell on a Sunday." Thus opens *Le dimanche de Bouvines* (*The Legend of Bouvines*), one the most famous works of medieval historical scholarship. This book by Georges Duby (1919–1996) is often held to be the starting point for a reappraisal of events-based history after several decades of disgrace ushered in by criticisms from Marc Bloch, Lucien Febvre, and then Fernand Braudel. Duby partook in this vision of his book in his intellectual autobiography, *L'histoire continue*, published in 1991. Referring to the commission he received from Gérard Walter in 1968 for a volume in the collection "Les trente journées qui ont fait la France," Duby wrote: "I had accepted, to the great surprise, and perhaps indignation of my friends. They were amazed to see me write about an event, a battle."

This reminiscence already takes a certain distance from the original volume published in 1973, in which the tone was different. From the outset, events are criticized as the "spume of history"; the idea privileged is that of "traces" that "alone confer existence. Apart from them, events are nothing." Indeed, the subject matter of the book is not the battle but what it reveals about its epoch by the ways it has been remembered and transmitted to the contemporary period. The first section, fittingly called "The Event," is in fact sidestepped by Duby who, after a rapid "Stage Setting" chapter, confides the entire narrative of "The Day" to the chronicler Guillaume le Breton. This makes it clear that Duby's investigation is not going to focus on the reality of the episode but on its representation. The second part, "Commentary," proposes a first methodological innovation, now become a standard scholarly move, by plucking from the event a structural reading of the world in which it took place—the feudal society of the thirteenth century. The exceptional nature of the battle, reinforced by the fact that it took place on a Sunday, the Lord's Day, provides an opportunity to display the seigneurial order at work, its rituals of peace and war, its intertwining of violent conflict with the social, symbolic, and religious rules delineating a coherent universe, that of a military aristocracy not yet brought to heel by the monarchy. Lastly, the third section, "Legendary," proposes a further interpretive shift by demonstrating the magnitude of the memory-building about this victory, which eventually became a symbol of the Capetian monarchy, then of the French nation.

Thus, in 1973, *Le dimanche de Bouvines* presented itself as an anti-positivist manifesto, a critique of a way of doing history focusing on battles, the nation, and events. How the battle unfolded is screened off. Duby reaches the ultimate stage in the dissolution of the event, which exists solely through dovetailing accounts, with Duby's new plotting of it being merely an additional variant. It met with instantaneous success, leading Bernard Guenée to observe in a review published in 1974 in *Annales* "that it is almost too late to speak of this book." Guenée emphasizes the narrative form, praising how effective it is, rather than inquiring into its epistemological significance, noting especially the scale of its study of the memory and historiography about the battle, which strikes him as the most innovative aspect. Writing in 1975 in the *Bibliothèque de l'École des chartes*, Robert Fossier instead insists on its critique of positivist history and on the care with which the text circumvents any account of the battle, announcing his preference for the interpretation of feudal warrior society rather than the "Legendary" section, to which he pays scant attention. These two reviews defined from the outset the dominant reception, together with its ambivalences.

In *Dialogues avec Georges Duby*, published by Guy Lardreau in 1980, Duby is still very clear about the importance he attaches to writing, to traces, and to subjectivity. He says that with *Le dimanche de Bouvines*, he wanted to show that "the past has always been fiddled with, caught up in networks of discourse woven to ensnare the adversary or as a means of protection in combats where power is at stake." And it is in just such a manner, as a reflection on historiographical narrative and historical reality, that Eric Hobsbawm

126   *The Legend of Bouvines*

referred to Duby's book in the controversy with Lawrence Stone about narrative in history, published in 1980 by the journal *Past and Present*, and that the American medievalist Gabrielle Spiegel used *Le dimanche de Bouvines* in speaking of "Forging the Past" during the 1980s.

But at the same time, a project to adapt the book for film led Duby, as historical consultant, to pay greater interest to the factual aspects of the battle and thereby to the event itself. The 1984 new edition showed signs of this change, which also bore traces of the shift in the circumstances of French historiography toward a phase when events, actors, and politics were making their "comeback." Duby seemed to espouse this retrospective description of his work, in feedback revelatory of how historical scholarly discourse is manufactured. Thus, since the 1980s, the canonization of *Le dimanche de Bouvines* has paradoxically been conducted through an interpretation of it as an "event" and a celebration of Duby's style. The experimental aspects of this narrative, which are both reflexive and aesthetic, are pushed into the background, despite raising questions about the preconditions for historical knowledge and its transmission—questions that have lost none of their urgency. Admittedly, this reading is perhaps, today, only another discussion of the publishing event of 1973; the greatness of such books is that they allow several successive, at times contradictory presents to recognize themselves in it in turn. But as Michel de Certeau said, "An event is not what we see or know of it, but what it becomes (and first of all, for us)."

Étienne Anheim

Georges Duby, *Le dimanche de Bouvines, 27 juillet 1214* (Paris: Gallimard ["Trente journées qui ont fait la France"], 1973). Republished by Gallimard ("Folio"), 1985. Translated into English by Catherine Tihanyi as *The Legend of Bouvines: War, Religion, and Culture in the Middle Ages* (Berkeley: University of California Press, 1990).

1973

THE INTERPRETATION OF CULTURES: GEERTZ TURNS CULTURES INTO TEXTS TO BE INTERPRETED

In one of the chapters in *The Interpretation of Cultures*, Clifford Geertz (1926–2006) refers to Ruth Benedict's *Patterns of Culture*, published in 1934, as "the most popular anthropology book ever published" in the United States. Forty years later, it is a safe bet that Geertz's book now holds that title. It is part of the same "hermeneutic" tradition, yet in inverting the syntax of the title—plural for cultures, single for the interpreting act—it profoundly renewed American anthropology.

The Interpretation of Cultures is not a monographic treatise but a collection of fifteen texts (the oldest dating from 1957). However, like Claude Lévi-Strauss's *Anthropologie structurale* (*Structural Anthropology*), the book has a solid structure and great retrospective cohesion (the impact of the two books in their respective intellectual worlds was indeed similar). Geertz only retained those articles that helped redefine "the concept of culture," the goal he sets in his preface; he organized his texts into five parts, going from the most anthropological (considering the human species in its greatest generality) to the most ethnographical (the book closes on his famous analysis of Balinese cockfights), with the heart of the book being composed of discussion of classic ethnological concepts (social change, ritual, ideology, nationalism, religion, etc.) rooted in concrete examples. Above all, Geertz added an unpublished introductory chapter, "Thick Description: Toward an Interpretive Theory of Culture," summarizing his position and setting out a series of ideas and phrases that were soon quoted way beyond the precincts of anthropology: the opposition between thin and thick description, the first merely recording actions, the second seeking to convey their meaning in context; a "semiotic" concept of culture as a "network of meanings," man being compared to "an animal suspended in webs of significance he himself has spun"; a definition of anthropology "not [as] an experimental science in search of a law but an interpretive one in search of a meaning"; a comparison between ethnographic work and "trying to read a manuscript—foreign, faded, full of ellipses, incoherencies, suspicious emendations [. . .] written not in conventionalized graphs of sound but in transient examples of shaped behavior"; a characterization of ethnology as fiction, an "imaginative act" comparable to writing an novel.

The theoretical core of the book is twofold. First, anthropology is an interpretive science. Geertz takes up the opposition—developed by Wilhelm Dilthey and brought up to date by Paul Ricœur—between the natural sciences (explaining or searching for laws) and the human sciences (or sciences "of the mind," interpreting or building meaning). But for Geertz, this is less a matter of affiliation to a philosophical school than it is showing how fertile such a conception is, to which he adds concrete content based on his ethnographic experience, particularly in Java, Bali, and Morocco. The dominant metaphor is that of reading, with culture being envisaged as "an ensemble of texts, themselves ensembles, which the anthropologist strains to read over the shoulders of those to whom they properly belong." The work ends with a comparison (already found in the work of Edward Sapir and Ruth Benedict) between interpreting a culture and conducting a close reading of a poem, based on shuttling back and forth between the whole (culture) and the parts (such and such an action). In this undertaking, requiring both rigor and imagination, the key operation is the production of *context*, making it possible to dissipate the opacity or apparent absurdity of indigenous conduct or discourse by reconstructing a familiarity rendering them intelligible. Next—and consequent upon this "hermeneutic" approach—Geertz does not define the scholarly viewpoint as cut off from that of the actors (as is the case in the French sociological tradition). Instead, he sees it as an extension of indigenous interpretations, as a second- or third-order construct, further removed from direct experience but not different in kind.

129   *Geertz Turns Cultures into Texts to Be Interpreted*

Equally, at the other end of the chain, Geertz does not recognize a first order, some objective phenomenal reality of culture, but instead only interpretations, even at the "first order" (when events are perceived and experienced by a native).

The Interpretation of Cultures established Geertz as the most brilliant and most read anthropologist of his generation, in a context where, since the 1950s, "hard" forms of objectivist anthropology had dominated (the neo-evolutionism of Leslie White, "cultural materialism," and nascent cognitive anthropology). The book also established a language and tone, frequently pleasing and obstinately refusing jargon, based on suggestive ethnographic examples, even in its most theoretical passages.

The success of the book was equaled in scale by the attacks it attracted. It became a target for "textualist" rereadings (many contributors to 1986's *Writing Culture* were former students of Geertz) as well as for postcolonial theory, the objection being that this interpretive approach stemmed from a characteristic vision of the liberal and bourgeois world, which was blind to the power relations and forms of domination hidden behind falsely neutral concepts. In a way, the book embodies an age of innocence—a naive yet happy time—in the American social sciences when, united under the banner of interpretation, historians, literary critics, and anthropologists spoke the same language and the "fusion of horizons" and "productive dialogue" between scholars and natives were, if not accessible, at least conceivable and desirable ideals.

Vincent Debaene

Clifford Geertz, *The Interpretation of Cultures: Selected Essays* (New York: Basic Books, 1973). Republished by Fontana Press, 1993.

1974

THE MODERN WORLD-SYSTEM: WALLERSTEIN AND THE PLANETARY EXPANSION OF MODERN CAPITALISM

Immanuel Wallerstein (born 1930) is one of the most influential sociologists of the twentieth century. His research at Columbia University into African independence movements led him to question "methodological nationalism," which meant that the study of social protest against colonialism and intercontinental imperialism was conducted solely within the framework of states.

The first volume of *The Modern World-System*, translated into thirteen languages, drew inspiration from the work of Fernand Braudel on the *longue durée*. It inaugurated analysis of the development of Western capitalism on the planetary scale, pursued in three additional volumes: *Mercantilism and the Consolidation of the European World-Economy 1600–1750*, *The Second Great Expansion of the Capitalist World-Economy 1730–1840*, and *Centrist Liberalism Triumphant 1789–1914*.

His main thesis assimilates capitalism to the geographic expansion of an interstate system rooted in an intercontinental division of labor, structuring unequal commercial exchange between regions specializing in exporting raw materials, foodstuffs, and servile labor (the periphery) and regions producing manufactured and high-technology products (the core) with semi-peripheral rural zones lying between the two. Although this structuring effect was borrowed from the Latin American "dependency" school, Wallerstein went further in identifying a shared ideology and merchandise chains linked to innovative sectors. He also detected economic cycles, based on converging factors plus centuries-long trends, with alternating phases of expansion and contraction in trade, demographic and urban growth and shrinkage, and the emergence of hierarchies or rivalry between political formations. At the intersections and turning points in the cycles, there were phases of "hegemonic transition" in which there were massive transfers of technology and capital toward low-cost production regions, often cloaked by the ascending mobility of new political hegemons.

According to Wallerstein, the "capitalist world-economy" was born in sixteenth-century Europe on the ruins of feudalism, thanks to the discovery of the New World and the transformation of distant commerce in luxury goods into necessities. It then spread and incorporated other regions into its operation, previously organized into "empire-worlds" or "world mini-systems." The weakening of the Mongol and Byzantine empires, the decline of the Catholic Church, the crisis in seignorial revenues, and the establishment of a global market in cereals, wood, and precious metals drove the circulation of large flows of money in Europe and the development of centralized states. These were sufficiently powerful to control trade routes and thus guarantee their entrepreneurs a rational choice of labor regimes, thereby ensuring the profitability of distant commerce (slavery and serfdom on the peripheries, sharecropping in the semi-periphery; leasing and salaried employment in the core). The power of the states ultimately derived from the concentration on their territory of the production process, requiring capital and technology to sell goods on monopolistic markets, while weaker states housed production processes relying primarily on labor and arable land to export goods sold on competitive markets. This differential gave rise to the transfer of services between regions through trade.

The importance of this first volume lies in the foundations it establishes for a new current in the social sciences: world-system analysis. This approach rejects both the liberal theory of modernization and orthodox Marxism. Against the former, Wallerstein disputes that each state may move through the stages of growth and development by liberal public policy. And he reproaches the latter with having too narrow a vision of capitalism, restricted to the concept of industrial nation-states. By proposing the world-economy as the unit of analysis, Wallerstein brings out what these two approaches are unable to apprehend and render intelligible. In the first case, the fact is that world trade remains a zero-sum game in which, in tandem with growth, zones of very marked inequality and poverty move about the world and are reconfigured at a planetary scale. In the second case, the fact is that salaried employment and slavery are complementary to the accumulation of capital, each in regions where life expectancy, standard of living, political regimes, and forms of merchant production differ entirely from each other. The remuneration of workers in cities thus depended on the provision of low-cost food and clothing fiber by the peripheries, where slaves were exploited on plantations.

Wallerstein's book sparked much debate, triggering research, for instance, on the relative importance of international trade and colonization in Europe's rapid industrial development. Some criticized its holistic determinism, arguing that it neglected the capacity for initiative by social agents involved in the (dis)functioning of the system. Many historians have additionally reexamined the nature of labor regimes and the reality of their complementary division in different regions. Lastly, his analytical framework has been applied to other continents and earlier periods: The constitution of an Afro-Eurasian world-system has been identified, particularly by Philippe Beaujard in *Les mondes de l'océan Indien* (*The Worlds of the Indian Ocean*), from the urban revolution of the Bronze Age in western Asia through to the synchronization of centuries-long cycles affecting China and the Mediterranean since the beginning of our era and running over more than fifteen centuries.

If, as Wallerstein argues, our century is that of stagnation and the decomposition of the capitalist world-system, owing to its having reached ecological limits and to the absence of new external arenas that are essential to its expansion, then that means that the contemporary crisis is similar to that which marked the disintegration of feudalism, and that the current period of transition is likely to bring about a new world-system that, for the coming centuries, will require new epistemologies in the social sciences if we are to apprehend it in all its complexity.

Eric Mielants

Immanuel Wallerstein, *The Modern World-System*, vol. 1, *Capitalist Agriculture and the Origins of the European World-Economy in the Sixteenth Century* (New York: Academic Press, 1974).

1975

MAIDENS, MEALS, AND MONEY: MEILLASSOUX AND THE ALIMENTARY STRUCTURES OF KINSHIP

When Claude Meillassoux (1925–2005) published *Femmes, greniers et capitaux* (*Maidens, Meals, and Money*) nearly ten years after his *Anthropologie économique des Gouro de Côte d'Ivoire* (Economic anthropology of the Guro of the Ivory Coast, 1964), it would be an understatement to say that the second book was eagerly awaited. It built with rigorous logic on two articles from 1960 and 1963: "Essai d'interprétation du phénomène économique dans les sociétés traditionnelles d'auto-subsistance" (Essay to interpret the economic phenomenon in traditional self-subsistence societies) and "Élaboration d'un modèle socio-économique en ethnologie" (Elaborating a socioeconomic model in ethnology). After putting forward a theoretical framework for the study of "subsistence societies" and comparing this with reality using in-depth ethnography, he revisited his theoretical propositions to hone and supplement them, creating a demanding dialogue between fieldwork and theory. The 1960s were marked by the consequences of de-Stalinization, the end of the last French colonial war, and African independence movements. In this context, the intellectual excitement surrounding the events of 1968 fed into the creation of new critical approaches. The independence of former colonies, by changing relations with the countries that once ruled them, required new analytical tools, such as those developed by the economist Samir Amin with his theory of unequal exchange in *L'échange inégal et la loi de la valeur* (Unequal exchange and the law of value, 1973). "Classic" anthropology was thus denounced for its compromises with colonialism, while Marxist anthropology considerably increased its audience, influence, and international credibility. Meillassoux's book played a central part in this phenomenon. It is made up of two distinct yet indispensable parts, just as his political commitment and scholarly approach were linked yet separate. The first part is devoted to devising a theoretical model of the domestic agricultural community, while the second analyzes the ways in which it is linked to capitalism. The theoretical model put forward is notable for several innovations, such as the analytical distinction between production and reproduction. Productive units are built up based on the economic and social necessities of production, as detailed by Meillassoux. The size of the groups thus formed being insufficient for reproduction, groups enter into relation with each other to constitute a large enough whole to ensure their genetic and social reproduction. This analytical distinction is a heuristic sidestep that helps us to appreciate why and how it is necessary for "reproduction relations to become production relations." The model also addresses the historical conditions presiding over the invention of the agricultural community and domestic kinship relations. This was the first time a *historical* theory of kinship had been put forward, stripped of all universality and any naturalizing sequel, casting new light on the relations between generations and gender: groups of descent, genealogies, along with distinctions between older and younger and uterine and agnatic lineages were an invention correlated to the Neolithic revolution and the domestication of plants.

The domestic group reproduced following the cyclical time of advancing and restituting seeds and harvests, founding the anteriority of one generation on the other; its reproduction thus took place over the lengthy time of generational renewal. Ensuring renewal was ideologically given by recruitment through instituting the kinship relation of filiation, to which matrimonial strategies were subjected. While the notion of generation is essential for analyzing production relations, that of gender is central to thinking about social and demographic reproduction. For according to Meillassoux, the only way to ensure the renewal of generations is the exchange of women between domestic units, due to their reproductive capacity, as occurs in gynecomobile societies. Conversely, in gynecostatic societies, in which domestic units exchange husbands rather than wives, the correction of democratic imbalances is, he argues, brought about by abducting women, which "resumes and contains all the components in the undertaking to render women inferior, and preludes all the others."

The second part of *Femmes, greniers et capitaux* discusses, as Michel Panoff has observed, the encounter between "a capitalism looking for cheap labor and a system organized for centuries around drawing from its own substance everything needed to maintain and reproduce life." Meillassoux here rejects the theory of unequal exchange. He puts forward an analysis of the conditions for the exploitation of labor within the framework of imperialism, leading him to criticize Marx's theory of surplus value, which for its part applies to integral capitalism.

In France, debates in the journal *L'Homme* provided a platform reflecting the hostility the work provoked among structuralists and certain Marxists. Other scholars, with a more innovative form of Marxism, saluted Meillassoux's work without sparing it criticism: Pierre-Philippe Rey, for instance, questioned its materialist determinism and failure to take into account the class struggle between older and younger in the emergence of domestic modes of production within lineage societies.

The book was translated into six languages. Outside France, it renewed debates about applying the concept of mode of production to subsistence societies. It went on to decisively influence the anthropology of gender and economic anthropology but also development agronomy. Despite the advanced state of involution of domestic agricultural communities, it still provides a powerful heuristic for understanding them. No doubt, renewed interest will soon arise, resonating strongly with a line of Césaire's poetry: "resistance resuscitates around some phantoms more real than they appear, unfamiliar builders."

Jean-Luc Paul

Claude Meillassoux, *Femmes, greniers et capitaux* (Paris: Maspero ["Textes à l'appui"], 1975). Reprinted by L'Harmattan, 1992. Translated into English by Felicity Edholm as *Maidens, Meals, and Money: Capitalism and the Domestic Community* (Cambridge: Cambridge University Press, 1981).

1976

THE CHEESE AND THE WORMS: GINZBURG LAUNCHES MICROHISTORY

The events took place in 1583 in a village in the hills of Friuli, under Venetian domination at the time. The protagonist is a miller in his fifties, Domenico Scandella, whom everyone called Menocchio. Summoned to appear before the court of the Inquisition and interrogated about his beliefs, he blurted out a theory on the origin of the universe: "All was chaos, that is, earth, air, water, and fire were mixed together; and out of that bulk a mass formed—just as cheese is made out of milk—and worms appeared in it, and these were the angels. The most holy majesty decreed that these should be God and the angels, and among that number of angels, there was also God. . . ."

This set Carlo Ginzburg (born 1939) wondering how Menocchio could think that God had not created the universe. The Council of Trent had come to a close twenty years earlier, and the evangelization conducted by the Catholic Church had reached all the parishes in the Italian Peninsula. Nobody, be they illiterate or cultivated, could doubt the account in Genesis. Was Menocchio simpleminded? No. He was stubborn, talkative, and eccentric, but he was not mad. Had he been in contact with one of those clandestine Anabaptist groups still active in the region? No. The interrogation showed that Menocchio did not contest infant baptism. Had he learned this curious theory mixing cheese and transcendence in a text circulating despite the censorship? This was not the case either. Menocchio was an autodidact who had stumbled his way through barely a dozen books that he had borrowed or bought himself. Most of these books gave a highly orthodox treatment of religious subjects; a few had been placed on the index (such as the *Decameron*). But in none of them could Ginzburg detect a cosmogeny comparable to that of the miller. At this stage of the inquiry, he was as disconcerted as the judges had been four centuries earlier, confronted with a heresy they were unable to identify.

But Ginzburg formulated a new hypothesis: Not only had echoes of reformed theses disputing the ecclesiastical hierarchy reached Menocchio, who had read some nonorthodox books, but he had interpreted them in the light of an oral tradition "deeply rooted in the European countryside, that explains the tenacious persistence of a peasant religion intolerant of dogma and ritual, and tied to the cycles of nature, and fundamentally pre-Christian." Precisely because it was oral, such a tradition tended "not to leave any trace, or to leave only distorted traces of itself." And it was only by comparing these tenuous traces that one could work back up to the "popular roots of much of high European culture, both mediaeval and post-mediaeval."

Ginzburg had been driven toward this hypothesis by earlier research he had conducted into fertility cults in Friuli, which he had likewise approached through the trials of the Inquisition in *The Night Battles: Witchcraft and Agrarian Cults in the Sixteenth and Seventeenth Centuries* (1966). A few years later, his exploration of how witchcraft related to oral culture had led him to write a book on rituals of death across Eurasia: *Ecstasies: Deciphering the Witches' Sabbath* (1989). But it was *The Cheese and the Worms* that became an instant classic.

For, in 1976, Ginzburg was infringing not one but several taboos in historical scholarship. Like many other historians of these years, he drew on anthropology and preferred the history of ordinary people to that of elites. But from the outset he stood out for rejecting two approaches that were then in the avant-garde of research: quantitative methods (used to apprehend demographic behavior but also cultural and mass phenomena) and the influence of Foucault, which encouraged historians to analyze state power on the basis of administrative regulations and discursive forms, rather than the experience of actors. Through Menocchio, Ginzburg was expressing both his confidence in the possibility of reaching oral culture through written sources and the ethical tension pushing him toward reconstructing this experience.

Above all, Menocchio became synonymous with "microhistory." His life course, though not unique, was anomalous, and this border case, because it was truly extraordinary, was of irreplaceable heuristic value: It provided a way of unearthing evidence otherwise lost from view. Shortly after, in *Clues, Myths, and the Historical Method* (1986), Ginzburg named his method the "index paradigm" (in reference to the historian of science Thomas Kuhn), presenting it as an alternative to the paradigms that were then dominant in history and social sciences.

The Cheese and the Worms was translated into twenty-six languages and has attracted much praise and criticism. The changing responses it has engendered are testimony to its longevity. In the 1980s, when the linguistic turn was triumphant, Dominick LaCapra proposed a rhetorical and hermeneutical reading of Ginzburg's book in *History and Criticism* (1985), noting the equivalent of a psychoanalytic "transfer" between Ginzburg and his protagonist. Both of them, according to LaCapra, used writings to find confirmation of their prior convictions. Nowadays, when the relation between Europe and Islam is a central preoccupation, it is a different trace, which Ginzburg touched on only lightly, that has given rise to new inquiries (such as Pier Mattia Tommasino's *The Venetian Qur'an: A Renaissance Companion to Islam*, 2013): the possibility that Menocchio found the answers to some of his worries in the first translation of the Qur'an into the vernacular, which was in fact a vulgarized and polemical synopsis of Christian knowledge about Islam, and a collection of stories about biblical prophets and figures who would have been readily identifiable to a sixteenth-century reader. What new provocations will *The Cheese and the Worms* inspire in future?

Francesca Trivellato

Carlo Ginzburg, *Il formaggio e i vermi: Il cosmo di un mugnaio del '500* (Turin: Einaudi, 1976.) Translated into English by John and Anne Tedeschi as *The Cheese and the Worms: The Cosmos of a Sixteenth-Century Miller* (Baltimore: Johns Hopkins University Press, 1980).

1976

BREAD AND CIRCUSES: VEYNE AND THE LOGIC OF GOOD DEEDS

What is "euergetism"? The recurrence of the term (employed thirty years earlier by Henri-Irénée Marrou) in the work of an author who called for history to be "rid of its isms" did not fail to trigger snide remarks. But this must not obscure the fact that this now widespread neologism, forged from the Greek word *euergesia*, meaning "good deeds," does not refer to some historical method, theory, or school but to the object studied.

In his state doctorate *Le pain et le cirque* (*Bread and Circuses*), published by Seuil in 1976, when he had just been admitted to the Collège de France, Paul Veyne (born 1930) inquires into "gifts by an individual to the community," what he also calls "patronage," in the Greco-Roman world over a period of six centuries (from the third century BCE to the third century CE). "Let us imagine that most town halls, schools, and even hydroelectric dams were due to the munificence of regional capitalism, which, further, paid for workers' aperitifs or cinema tickets." This "controlled anachronism," typical of Veyne's writing, launches this imposing 800-page study of liberality in the Ancient world, viewed over the *longue durée*. These liberalities are examined in all their material, symbolic, and ideological ramifications because, for six centuries, they were pivotal to all aspects of the civic and imperial organization of Hellenistic and Roman society: gifts by notables to their cities ("Greek euergetism"), by Roman senators to their armies and clienteles ("the republican oligarchy in Rome"), and by the emperor to the megapolis of Rome ("the emperor and his capital"). This three-part analysis is preceded by theoretical and methodological considerations ("the agents and their behavior"). Lastly, most of the 174 pages of notes, in addition to the requisite erudition, provide what virtually amount to mini-articles or parallel investigations.

In 1971, five years before the book came out, Raymond Aron, writing in *Annales*, had greeted *Comment on écrit l'histoire* (*Writing History*), also by Paul Veyne, in terms that apply equally well to *Le pain et le cirque*: "An unpredictable book, an improbable draw in the lottery of intellectual works." In 1977, in his lectures at the Collège de France on *Sécurité, territoire, population* (*Security, Territory, Population*), Foucault referred to the importance of this earlier book, including for understanding power mechanisms in the modern period. Far removed from any principle of causality (predominantly represented in those days by Marxism), Paul Veyne emphasizes the irrational aspect that he perceives in "the agents" (benefactors and beneficiaries) and in "their behavior"—in an approach resembling that pursued in the United States by Peter Brown (*The Making of Late Antiquity*, 1978).

Although Paul Veyne's espousing of new theoretical lines was universally applauded, as was the scale of the erudition on which he drew, *Le pain et le cirque* came in for vigorous criticism in an article published in *Annales* in 1978 by Jean Andreau, Alain Schnapp, and Pauline Schmitt-Pantel, three historians of Greece and Roman. They virulently denounced its method and content, arguing that certain of Veyne's "invariants" were more a matter of psychology than social history, that the modern conceptualization failed to conduct lexical analysis on the documentation, that the book effaced politics in favor of a "theatrical conception" of history, that it displayed insufficient awareness of (or else deliberately downplayed) ancient law, that it conflated the idea of order with that of class, and so and so forth. Lastly and perhaps most importantly, "in *Le pain et le cirque*, it is a matter of being done with Marxism, which has lost all heuristic value."

The list of criticisms did not stop there. A few years later, in *Les cités grecques et leurs bienfaiteurs* (Greek cities and their benefactors, 1985), Philippe Gauthier upbraided Veyne for reading the epigraphic documentation with insufficient attention to clearly identify who these *euergetai* actually were. Were they, for example, citizens of the city, or from elsewhere? He also charges him with proceeding by generalization, failing to take specific

141   *Veyne and the Logic of Good Deeds*

geographical contexts (Africa, Asia Minor, the Black Sea) into account, and artificially dividing the classical from the Hellenistic world.

It was fifteen years before the book was translated into English, in a drastic abridgment by Oswald Murray (*Bread and Circuses: Historical Sociology and Political Pluralism*, 1990). In his foreword, Murray asserts that the theoretical discussions required in France in 1976 were no longer indispensable, and certain readers were thereupon relieved to see reduced the "density of the Gallic conceptualization" (such as Robert Garland, writing in the *Journal of Hellenic Studies* in 1991). However, in a particularly dense book review (*Journal of Romanic Studies*, 1991), the English historian Peter Garnsey regretted, on the contrary, seeing a "state doctorate" transformed into an "Oxford monograph." Basing his review on the French version, Garnsey sought to do justice to the subtlety, strength, and richness of a book whose content—as set out in the main body of the book as well as in the copious erudite footnotes—far exceeded a study of the mechanisms of euergetism. The title of this review, "The Generosity of Veyne," is an unambiguous reference to the topic studied, yet forty years after the book was first published, it could equally well apply to the scale of the prolific material *Le pain et le cirque* still offers, benevolently and good-naturedly, to the reader.

Yann Rivière

Paul Veyne, *Le pain et le cirque: Sociologie historique d'un pluralisme politique* (Paris: Éd. du Seuil ["L'Univers historique"], 1976). Republished by Points ("Histoire"), 1995. Translated into English by Brian Pearce as *Bread and Circuses: Historial Sociology and Political Pluralism* (London: Penguin Books, 1990).

1977

DEADLY WORDS: FAVRET-SAADA CASTS A SPELL ON POSITIVISM

The value of objectivity gives rise to sharper tensions in anthropology than in other disciplines. It is the vector distinguishing ethnographic discourse from that of the representatives of colonial power while also authorizing ethnographers to snatch away knowledge about humankind from literature and philosophy and make it the object of a new scientific discipline. But that does not preclude virtually all its practitioners from recognizing that there remains an irreducible substrate that does not match the constraints induced by the required objectivity of a monograph. Strategies are developed to work around this, in forewords, field journals, and first-person accounts that can accommodate the subjective and literary dimensions that are excluded from official knowledge.

The ethnography of *Les mots, la mort, les sorts* (*Deadly Words*) is wholly founded on the denunciation of this division. Jeanne Favret-Saada (born 1934) was assuredly not the only person in the late 1970s to call into question the positivist ideal that had taken hold with structuralism, but her decision to suspend objective knowledge and rely on subjectivation placed her on the sidelines of the anthropological community. In a context marked by the gathering strength of deconstruction and the beginnings of the postmodern current, she decided to work counter to the imperative to demystify. The watchword of Foucault, Derrida, and Lyotard might well have been to ditch thought systems and practices hitherto deemed self-evident; but for the ethnography of spells, what was needed, on the contrary, was to allow oneself to be drawn into its discourses and practices, which, as a modern rational subject, one was meant to have ditched as a matter of course.

The defenses erected by scientific discourse asserting that witchcraft could not exist in our modern societies, or at least could only exert a hold over the weak of mind, needed dismantling to allow for an investigation in the Normandy bocage, where the locals were hardly keen to play the role of credulous bumpkins. There was no point looking for good "informants" in a society where anyone saying they were bewitched was thereupon open to ridicule. People only spoke of witchcraft to make an accusation, or to ask for help against an aggressor. Any ethnographer wishing to break through the wall of silence would need to cast off the neutrality prescribed by the discipline and expose themselves to the violence of these deadly words.

Yet refusing to reduce the ethnography of spells to its critical preamble should not lead to neglecting the turning point it represents in the history of anthropology. The main problem encountered in building anthropological knowledge has long been that of the increased generality created by deindexing spatiotemporal coordinates. Drawing on Benveniste, Favret-Saada shows how there is a more fundamental type of deindexation before any comparison that one might term *personal deindexation*. To satisfy the requirements of science, the ethnographer must occult the personal anchoring of their discourse behind their description of a culture, ritual, or belief. This amounts to a full-scale denial of ethnographic interlocution, reducing the status of the indigenous to an object.

This is what gives rise to the problem of belief that, from Edward Tylor through to the emergence of the cognitive sciences, continually occupied anthropologists: In order to account for the behavior and discourse of individuals removed from concrete situations of action or utterance, one needed to invent something along the lines of an erroneous theory of causality, something like a "primitive mentality." As Favret-Saada points out, this causes indigenous people to be completely "irrealized" and to come across as puppets moved by collective interests or false beliefs.

This refusal to objectivize leads to a new way of doing ethnography, probably the point where the book had the greatest influence. This approach may be defined using the concept of the *impossible position*. The reversal brought about in *Les mots, la mort, les sorts* consists in assuming, in the first person, the position of the bewitched—that is, of the person only ever

144   *Deadly Words*

described as the absolute opposite of the rational scientific subject. It is precisely to the extent that she was affected by the discourse of witchcraft, using the services of a *désorceleuse* (someone who breaks spells), that Jeanne Favret-Saada's work moves beyond the stage of a collection of anecdotes to which all folklorist discourse is ultimately reduced.

One of the key consequences of this new form of investigation is the way it promotes the narrating of events. This narrative turns out to be crucial. First, because the position from which ethnography is written is so improbable, it needs to go over how it got there. Much of the work consists in explaining how this position was first missed, then reached, over a far from smooth course of events. But this narrative also transpires as the only way of talking about the ethnographer's interlocutors as real people—that is, named individual agents who are situated and caught up in a life course. It forbids the ethnographer from immediately dissolving their discourse within a social group, status position, or belief, for it is first and foremost the narrative of *interlocution situations*.

To Favret-Saada's mind, despite these many virtues, narrative has never constituted the crux of anthropology: *Les mots, la mort, les sorts* was devised as the starting point for a second book meant to use the "system of places" characterizing witchcraft in the bocage. The fact that three decades elapsed between the first book and the second, *Désorceler*, was not without incident on the course taken by anthropology. As the ethnography of spells has shown us, silences often weigh no less heavily than words, and there is no doubt that the postmodern radicalization of calls for subjectivity was fueled by this thirty-year reticence.

Gildas Salmon

Jeanne Favret-Saada, *Les mots, la mort, les sorts: La sorcellerie dans le bocage* (Paris: Gallimard ["Bibliothèque des sciences humaines"], 1977). Republished by Gallimard ("Folio"), 1985. Translated into English by Catherine Cullen as *Deadly Words: Witchcraft in the Bocage* (Cambridge: Cambridge University Press, 1980).

1977

THE DOMESTICATION OF THE SAVAGE MIND: GOODY EXPLORES THE INTELLECTUAL TECHNOLOGIES CONNECTED TO WRITING

The Domestication of the Savage Mind, by the anthropologist Jack Goody (1919–2015), was published by Cambridge University Press in 1977. It was an immediate success, as shown by its being reprinted the following year and then published in a French translation by Jean Bazin and Alban Bensa in 1979 under a slightly different title, *La raison graphique, la domestication de la pensée sauvage*. The book's impact was exceptional: It influenced many disciplines (including anthropology, linguistics, sociology, history, philosophy, education sciences, and communication studies), sparked many controversies (including the powerful current from which new literacy studies issued), and inspired various professions (teachers, typographers, and graphic designers).

The book's strength lies in its linking up three lines of argument: a thesis positing the existence of "graphic reasoning," the bringing to light and deconstruction of an ideology of a "great divide," and an epistemological critique of anthropology bearing on the fact that ethnological study has not examined its own graphic condition, as Bazin and Bensa note.

Goody's main thesis is that writing played a central role in the scientific development of Occidental societies, based on abstraction and generalization. More specifically, he argues that the graphic forms used since the appearance of writing in Sumer script modified the cognitive practices facilitating abstract language processing, particularly the operations of classification and categorization. Lists and dual-entry tables are, for Goody, the most striking examples of this graphic culture of writing societies. Writing further provided the literate with a way of "stocking" information, transmitting it, and constructing critical traditions, thus paving the way for analysis of language, critical history, literature, and the study of law.

Goody denounces racialist theories opposing primitive to evolved mentalities, scientific to primitive minds, or superior to inferior societies, which thereby envisage a virtually natural "great divide" into "them" and "us," without taking the consequences of writing into account. For Goody, it is also a matter of refusing more edulcorated versions of the "great divide," opposing savage and domesticated minds or hot and cold societies (particularly in Lévi-Strauss). In emphasizing the importance of writing as a factor for scientific rationality, the book reinforces an entire current of materialist thought that accords decisive importance to the conditions in which science is produced. The great divide does not exist; it is rather the relations between modes of thought and the usages of writing that trace the provisional contours of the differences between the literate and the nonliterate. Subjecting the ways that ethnologists work to reflexive scrutiny, Goody puts forward a closely argued critique of the consequences of using writing in building knowledge about oral or largely illiterate societies. Thus, the fact of analyzing a myth based on a written transcript fixes one version among others, erasing the inherent variability of recitation and the particular utterance in situations. Similarly, drawing up a table of the classification systems attributed to a nonliterate society produces distortions because it introduces an inappropriate binary logic. Many scholarly operations extract situated practices from their contexts, favoring unwarranted rationalizations and debatable systematism. It is not only the Durkheimian legacy which thus comes in for criticism, but structuralism too, with its pretension to decipher mythic accounts better than the actors themselves and to produce knowledge independent of the social relations at play in nonliterate societies.

The Domestication of the Savage Mind was written at a time when the theme of writing was on the rise. In France, as of the 1950s, a series of leading publications, some of them revolutionary, had placed this theme front and center: Roland Barthes's *Le degré zéro de l'écriture* (*Writing Degree Zero*, 1953); Marcel Cohen's *La grande invention de l'écriture* (*The Great Invention of Writing*, 1958); Gilles-Gaston Granger's *Pensée formelle et sciences de l'homme* (*Formal Thought and the Sciences of Man*, 1960), which already asserted that "scientific discourse is primarily graphic"; Jacques Derrida's *De la grammatologie* (*Of Grammatology*, 1967); Jacques Bertin's *La sémiologie graphique* (*Semiology of Graphics*, 1967); and *L'espace et la lettre* (Spaces and letters, 1977) edited by Anne-Marie Christin. These books removed writing from the relegation to which it had been condemned by Ferdinand de Saussure, drawing particular attention to its visual, graphic, and spatial resources. They no doubt laid the groundwork for the immediate success of *The Domestication of the Savage Mind*. Goody also drew on many works that had renewed the approach to writing, such as those by the linguists Ignace J. Gelb, and Josef Vachek of the Prague school, and especially those of the Russian psychologist Lev S. Vygotsky, who had put forward the hypothesis of a form of graphic reasoning back in 1934.

The book marked a turning point for Goody, an anthropologist previously known for his work on *Comparative Studies in Kinship* (1969) and whose interest in writing had only appeared in muted form. Goody went on to expand on his ideas on literacy, particularly in *Writing and the Organization of Society* (1986) and *The Interface between the Written and the Oral* (1987). *The Domestication of the Savage Mind* opened a new chapter in work on writing. In fact, it was an entire interdisciplinary research field, the anthropology of writing, that Goody ended up creating.

Béatrice Fraenkel

Jack Goody, *The Domestication of the Savage Mind* (Cambridge: Cambridge University Press, 1977).

1978

INTERPRETING THE FRENCH REVOLUTION: FURET CONSIGNS THE REVOLUTION TO THE PAST

Certain books, like certain events, mark a change in period. The essay published in 1978 by François Furet (1927–1997) is such a work: there is a before *Penser la Révolution française* and an after.

Despite this, the book is not an easy read, both because of the density of its analyses and the sudden shifts in tone, swerving from the learned to the polemical. The essays on the "possible histories of the revolution" contain a vitriolic attack on the then-dominant Jacobin historical scholarship.

What most struck people about this set of texts was their starting point. "The French Revolution is over," Furet stated: that is, over *qua* event, ever since the consolidation of the Republic in the late nineteenth century, and over *qua* prefiguration of another revolution, that of the proletariat rather than the bourgeoisie, in 1917, since real socialism had shown its true face, the gulag. Aleksandr Solzhenitsyn's book, published in 1974, not only ruled out talk of the French Revolution in the terms the "Marxist" school had used for half a century, it further imposed a critical reinterpretation of the French "precedent." The idea of revolution had been stripped of its innocence. It was henceforth impossible to absolve the Terror on the grounds of circumstances, since Solzhenitsyn showed that Terror lay at the heart of the Bolshevik project, for which, it was argued, the French Revolution had provided the mold.

The historians of the Jacobin school had sacrificed historical knowledge on the altar of celebrating the idea of revolution. The time had now come to turn the page. "We need to break the vicious circle of commemorative scholarship," Furet wrote. "Scholarship about the Revolution is, to my mind, burdened down by intellectual laziness and the regurgitation of respectful platitudes. It is surely time for [. . .] it to revert to intellectual curiosity and the untrammeled activity of knowledge about past." The judgment, though harsh, was not wrong. It had been a long time since the erudition of Georges Lefebvre had prevented the social interpretation of the Revolution—the reign of the "bourgeoisie" and of capitalism following on from that of the aristocracy and of "feudality"—from congealing into a "vulgate." Other, less subtle historians had succeeded him; Furet castigated them; they never forgave him.

It would be unfair to attribute the fall of the Jacobin house to the single-handed efforts of François Furet. By 1978, English-speaking historians, necessarily less sensitive to the delights of purely French quarrels and shielded by their solid empiricism from the allure of the philosophy of history, had broken down the doors of the "Marxist" citadel. George Taylor and Alfred Cobban had been the first to comb through the archives and turn up not the slightest specimen of the "bourgeois" said to have chased out and replaced the nobility. The Revolution was not born of the bourgeoisie; rather, the bourgeoisie was born of the Revolution.

Back in 1965, Furet had published *La Révolution française*. This book, cowritten with Denis Richet, had been his first attack to cause a stir, and we cannot understand his 1978 book without it. Although it still referred to the concept of the "bourgeois revolution," it dismantled the idea that the Revolution's tumultuous course was attributable to pure "circumstances," along with the idea that the political sphere depended strictly on social interests. Yet *Penser la Révolution française* was not a mere offshoot of the 1965 work. It accorded politics, the true religion of the men of 1789, its true place. With the idea of the autonomy of politics from the social realm, the meaning of the open and even unpredictable nature of history returned to the fore, together with questions about democracy and modern individualism for which the revolutionary decade provided a host of examples. Alexis de Tocqueville and Augustin Cochin were not chosen at random to illustrate the "possible histories" of the French Revolution. Tocqueville was chosen for outlining a history privileging the long-term results of the Revolution, to gauge the extent to which the apparent rupture masked continuity; Cochin,

150   *Interpreting the French Revolution*

for sketching a phenomenology of the rupture and the events. Both insisted on the forms and weight of a French political culture that had been central to issues debated in the nineteenth century, from Benjamin Constant and François Guizot to Jules Michelet and Edgar Quinet, but had been pushed into the background by interpretations of the Revolution in terms of social interests.

The line of questioning raised in *Penser la Révolution française* inspired Furet's works until his death. Everything that followed, from *La Révolution: De Turgot à Jules Ferry* (*The Revolution: From Turgot to Jules Ferry*, 1988) to *Le Passé d'une illusion* (*The Passing of an Illusion*, 1995), acted as a development or explanation of the groundwork laid in the 1978 work. Many authors' oeuvres arise from a series of encounters with different topics. Furet's was of a rarer kind, being constructed—not to say planned—around a question, namely that of the "revolutionary passion" that had gripped his generation so strongly.

Not everyone admired *Penser la Révolution française*. Quite the contrary. The battle was fierce yet brief. The verdict fell with the bicentenary in 1989. With its low-key celebrations and speeches shorn of conviction, it was far removed from the centenary of 1889. To avoid ruffling feathers, Carnot and Danton, the heroes celebrated in 1889, gave way to more consensual and less colorful figures, Condorcet and the Abbé Grégoire. It was democracy that was commemorated, not its origin. Ten years after *Penser la Révolution française*, the revolution was well and truly over.

Patrice Gueniffey

François Furet, *Penser la Révolution française* (Paris: Gallimard ["Bibliothèque des histoires"], 1978). Republished by Gallimard ("Folio"), 1985. Translated into English by Elborg Forster as *Interpreting the French Revolution* (Cambridge: Cambridge University Press, 1981).

1978

ORIENTALISM: SAID VIEWS THE ORIENT IN THE MIRROR OF THE WEST

When Routledge and Kegan Paul published *Orientalism*, an essay by a young professor at the prestigious Columbia University in New York, they probably had little idea how successful it would be. The previous works of Edward Said (1935–2003)—a post-structuralist analysis of the concept of beginnings in modern literature, following a doctorate on how Joseph Conrad had built his biography—had certainly been widely discussed. But this debate had remained internal to the world of literary studies. In 1977, Said had become a member of the Palestinian National Council and had already published political texts. But their readership barely reached beyond the circle of those who supported the Palestinian cause.

With its open-ended yet scathing title, *Orientalism* set its sights on larger aims. It was soon translated into many languages and the subject of many interpretations. In the wake of Foucault, Said charts a "global institution" that he calls "orientalism," forming an order of discourse constitutive of both the Orient and the Occident, sapping the former and energizing the latter. This raises a sensitive issue. Lying at the heart of the countries and people who are the subject of his analysis, from Mesopotamia to the Nile valley, is Palestine, Said's land of birth. And in the late 1970s, Palestine was a paradigmatic cause for intellectuals around the world committed to combating colonialism, imperialism, and racism. The State of Israel had occupied the West Bank since June 1967, and in 1978 the Israeli army had taken control of southern Lebanon, which was embroiled in civil war. Said sought to provide his readers with a way of emancipating themselves through awareness of power structures that were so integrated as to have become invisible. Above and beyond the economic and political alienation already denounced by Marxists and democrats, he revealed the presence of a deep cultural alienation not stemming from the former but obeying its own logic. He thus responded to the desires of a readership looking for new means of emancipation on American campuses, in Europe, and in what was still called the third world.

Admittedly, Said formulates criticisms already made by others before him. For example, in 1963, the sociologist Anouar Abdel Malek had already questioned the propensity of Western scholars to restrict themselves to a textual, decontextualized, and essentializing approach to the Orient: By privileging elements from the past, they produced an image of an immobile and backward world, thereby condoning its domination by the European powers where they lived. But these criticisms gained new resonance when penned by an American academic, with an incisive style, in a book combining theoretical sophistication and polemical punch. The fact that most American specialists of the Middle East were subservient to a policy of American power and support for Israel, which Said sets out to denounce, acquires a different direction once placed within the framework of Orientalist discourse through the centuries. This framework allows him to transform what could have been a polemical flash in the pan into a work that soon became a benchmark. The ambition of his project and the prestige of the authors discussed (such as Giambattista Vico, Nietzsche, and Antonio Gramsci) give his attacks unequaled force, making the work one of the founding books of postcolonial studies. After having defined the domain of Orientalism, Said analyzes how it was structured in the nineteenth century, before turning his eye to its contemporary forms. He is original in considering all the components making up Orientalist discourse: scholarly production but also artistic and ordinary works. Indeed, he went on to write a book on how Islam was treated in the media.

The fact that Said bases his analysis on a loosely defined corpus, assuming the decision not to consider how a work related to its referent (its degree of truth), attracted many criticisms, particularly from specialists of Islam and of the Arab world. Those hoping to find a history of Orientalism were bound

153   *Said Views the Orient in the Mirror of the West*

to be disappointed. Said discusses a limited space (the Near and Middle East), giving correspondingly little room to German philology, and his writing often lacks precision. He only works with printed texts and often fails to place them clearly in context. Yet the success of *Orientalism* no doubt facilitated the development of a critical history of Orientalism in both social and political terms. In France, readers were less sensitive to the political scope of the work than those in the United States, perhaps partly due to a flat translation, or rather adaptation. Scholars such as Jean-Pierre Tieck, Maxime Rodinson, and Michel Seurat, writing in *Revue des études palestiniennes*, though stating their sympathy for the principle, expressed frank misgivings about the content. In failing to provide any true alternative to the Orientalism he critiqued, did not Said run the risk of authorizing solely "internal" points of view, thus ultimately reinforcing new essentialisms? Was he not reviving an ancient suspicion against the *mustachrikûn*, the Arabic term for translating "orientalist," holding them to be spies in the service of foreign powers seeking to impose their domination? The silence of literary critics and the reservations of the few historians to review the French translation of *Culture and Imperialism* (1993), a collection of texts expanding on ideas formulated in *Orientalism*, clearly reveals a certain embarrassment at the hybrid nature of a work combining militant and scholarly registers.

Nowadays, we can still appreciate how *Orientalism* passes from one level of analysis to another, always on the move to avoid being caught in the structures underpinning our representations. Or, to use the title of Said's fine autobiography, his last book, published in 1999, it is a way of thinking that was forever *Out of Place*.

Alain Messaoudi

Edward W. Said, *Orientalism* (London: Routledge & Kegan Paul, 1978).

1979

FUTURES PAST: KOSELLECK SETS OUT HIS THEORY OF HISTORICAL TIME

On being published in Germany, *Vergangene Zukunft: Zur Semantik geschichtlicher Zeiten* (*Futures Past*) established Reinhart Koselleck (1923–2006) as a theoretician of history—though the meaning of these terms needs clarification. Any reader expecting to find a systematic exposé—such as in Johann Gustav Droysen's *Historik*, a point of reference from an earlier age in Germany—is in for a surprise. *Futures Past* offers no such thing, being a series of articles grouped into three parts, of which the first two give pride of place to the issue of temporalities while the third looks more closely at historical semantics and the history of concepts. In fact, this organization is more for the sake of convenience, for these various aspects repeatedly overlap. Articles were, as a rule, Koselleck's preferred format (excluding his theses), and this is particularly clear with *Futures Past*, given that he wrote the book gradually alongside the great project that occupied him for twenty years (1972–1992) as the main editor of the eight-volume *Geschichtliche Grundbegriffe* (*Basic Concepts in History: A Historical Dictionary of Political and Social Language in Germany*). This encyclopedia of landmark concepts, viewed historically, combining political, social, legal, economic, intellectual, and philosophical history, is no mere lexicon of the history of ideas. It was within the framework of this joint project that he honed the conceptual history (*Begriffsgeschichte*) with which his name is associated, even though, to his mind, this was only ever an instrument, preparatory to doing history, not a discipline or even a subdiscipline, as it has since become for certain historians.

Le futur passé was published in French eleven years later. The translation was by Jochen Hoock (a former pupil of Koselleck's) and his wife. French readers had previously been able to read Koselleck's chapter in a book called *L'âge des révolutions*, which he had written with Louis Bergeron and François Furet, and an (incomplete) translation of his thesis, published in 1979 as *Le règne de la critique*. In these works, he came across as a historian of the eighteenth and nineteenth centuries, examining the period he described as *Sattelzeit* (a watershed), that of the Enlightenment, revolutions, philosophies of history, and the rise of the bourgeoisie. In addition, there was an original collection in French, *L'expérience de l'histoire* (1997).

The unity of *Vergangene Zukunft* (for it truly does form a book) derives from the central issue, a theory of historical time, and from Koselleck's way of addressing it systematically based on precise empirical study. The book thus presents a series of case studies seeking to apprehend the emergence of a (specifically) historical time—alongside a natural, astronomic, geological, or divine time—whose central theme is the concept of experience (*Erfahrung*). Since the second half of the eighteenth century, Koselleck writes that "history no longer occurs in, but through, time. Time becomes a dynamic and historical force in its own right." This time, both actor and agent are borne along by progress and perceived as accelerating. This was how contemporaries experienced the French Revolution, for instance. This new time brought with it a new concept of history, henceforth viewed as a "collective singular": no longer histories but history in the singular, history "in itself," "without any object being subordinated to it nor priorly imposed object." In the wake of this, Koselleck examines many other concepts, such as "revolution," "chance," "prognosis," and "modern times" (*Neuzeit*).

This historical time needs to be immediately put in the plural, for there is not a single time but multiple times. The investigation consists in detecting how within each present, the categories of the past and of the future were related to one another, and how, between the sixteenth and the late eighteenth century, the content of these categories was profoundly altered. Indeed, there was a shift from a future still caught up with eschatological expectations to another future that, as of the seventeenth century, granted room to prognosis—that is, rational calculation, postulating that the future would not exceed the past. But here we remain on known ground: that on which the diplomacy of classical monarchies was played out, for example.

It is afterward that a new future became established, paving the way for a new future based on progress that, as Condorcet declared, was "indefinite" by principle. It is thus a whole series of "futures past" that Koselleck pinpoints, associated with experiences of time undergoing continuous change. Equally, when he studies in a now-famous section the "dissolution of the *topos* of the *historia magistra vitae*," he apprehends how the past ended up losing its former function as a reservoir of examples, instead giving way to a history attentive to the unique, to that which was not repeated, to the event. The transition between the two historical regimes may be resumed by the formulation attributed to Frederik II: "the only lesson of history is that there is no lesson."

In drawing up his theory of historical time, Koselleck draws on two categories that ran through all his subsequent reflection on history, for, thanks to their degree of generality, they are the preconditions for all history: experience and expectation. Weaving past and future together, they may be used to "thematize" historical time. More exactly, Koselleck views the "field of experience" and the "horizon of expectation" as the two poles between which historical time is generated. It is precisely with modern times, this time that is advancing ever more quickly, that the distance between experience and expectation is continually stretched, potentially to breaking point. Great crises, from modern times through to the present day, may thus be analyzed from this angle.

François Hartog

Reinhart Koselleck, *Vergangene Zukunft: Zur Semantik geschichtlicher Zeiten* (Frankfurt: Suhrkamp, 1979). Translated into English by Keith Tribe as *Futures Past: On the Semantics of Historical Time* (Cambridge, MA: MIT Press, 1985).

1979

DISTINCTION: BOURDIEU AND THE SOCIAL PRODUCTION OF TASTE

What links mountaineering, visiting museums, a preference for Goya and Kandinsky, listening to the *Art of the Fugue*, and a taste for exotic cuisine? These practices characterize the "lifestyle" of academics, which differs from that of other segments of the dominant classes, such as captains of industry and commerce, who have more "economic capital" but less "cultural capital."

This is what results from a vast study of the cultural practices of the French conducted by the sociologist Pierre Bourdieu (1930–2002)—a professor at the Centre de sociologie de l'éducation et de la culture at the École des hautes études en sciences sociales (EHESS)—which was published in 1979 by the Éditions de Minuit as *La distinction: Critique sociale du jugement* (*Distinction: A Social Critique of the Judgement of Taste*). This imposing work, which sets out an innovative analysis of the social structure by bringing to light the social conditions for the production of taste, had a major impact on the social sciences of its day.

Against an intellectual backdrop of two conflicting dominant paradigms, structuralism and Marxism, Bourdieu adopted the relational approach they shared, combining this with a topographic approach attentive to the positions held in a hierarchical social space, to analyze social classes in a new way. Against the Marxist theory, which takes culture as a mere superstructure reflecting economic power imbalances, he demonstrated the relative autonomy of fields of cultural production, engendering, with the ideal of educational meritocracy, a distinct species of capital: "cultural capital." The social structure thus transpires as a chiasmatic structure, depending on the volume and composition of the capital. Unlike approaches examining social stratification, which adopt fixed revenue-based hierarchization criteria, this is a dynamic space undergoing constant transformation—a space of symbolic struggle to define cultural legitimacy.

To apprehend relations between classes and segments of classes, Bourdieu introduces the method of structural analysis that identifies systems of differential gaps of cultural significance. Thus, the dominant classes, who are differentiated from the dominated classes by their overall volume of capital of all sorts, further distinguish themselves by marking, through their tastes and lifestyles, how far they are from need. However, there is also opposition among the various dominant segments based on their cultural practices and preferences as a function of the composition of their capital: Those with the greatest cultural capital (the intellectual and artistic professions) are in a dominated position within the field of power in relation to the segments holding economic and political power, while the liberal professions lie between these two poles. They are differentiated through their lifestyles and privileged objects of consumption (Goya as opposed to Renoir), as well as through their categories of judgment and ways in which they appropriate artworks, with the former opposing material appropriation (acquisition), which is not within their means, to symbolic appreciation through "pure" and "disinterested" contemplation in museums, corresponding to their ascetic dispositions. The Kantian theory of disinterested aesthetic pleasure thus only concerns one of the ways—admittedly the more distinguished and distinctive way—of appropriating works, issuing from the autonomy claimed for fields of cultural production. Similar principles of differentiation may be found within the dominated classes between, for example, the intellectual petite bourgeoisie (primary schoolteachers, librarians, etc.), who exhibit their "cultural willingness," and the commercial petite bourgeoisie, turned toward material goods. The concept of "habitus" designates this system of ethical, aesthetic, and political dispositions acquired through education by interiorizing social structures, which in turn structure the perception, judgment, and practices of social groups.

La distinction received great coverage in the French media when it was published, then, after initial translations into German, Italian, and English, in the foreign press. The critical dimension of the book, particularly the analysis of taste as an instrument of domination, was greeted as an attempt to demystify "snobbery." Certain reviewers emphasized the dual critique of populism and aesthetic formalism. In addition to its theoretical contributions, the work provided a research program—in Imre Lakatos's meaning of the term—for many working in the social sciences. Its reception in the United States helped drive the development of the sociology of culture. Within the space of a few years, it became Bourdieu's most cited book, and the concept of cultural capital the most borrowed from his theory. Quantitative studies drawing on multiple correspondence analysis were conducted in Norway, Portugal, and the United Kingdom. In 2009, an international conference called *Trente ans après La distinction* (Thirty years after *La distinction*) was attended by researchers from sixteen countries (with the proceedings being published by La Découverte in 2013).

International comparisons have raised fruitful questions, calling for further work on this research program: Has the differentiation between economic capital and cultural capital come into effect everywhere? What are the indicators of cultural capital in different societies? Do "gender" and "race" have any incidence as such? What is the case with "eclectic" practices (such as rock and classical music, for example)? Is there such a thing as transnational cultural capital? Under what conditions is cultural capital transmitted and reproduced in the age of globalization?

Gisèle Sapiro

Pierre Bourdieu, *La distinction: Critique sociale du jugement* (Paris: Éditions de Minuit ["Le Sens commun"], 1979). Republished by Éditions de Minuit, 1992. Translated into English by Richard Nice as *Distinction: A Social Critique of the Judgement of Taste* (London: Routledge & Kegan Paul, 1984).

1980

THE PRACTICE OF EVERYDAY LIFE: DE CERTEAU AND THE CREATIVITY OF ORDINARY PRACTICE

Within the prolific and diverse oeuvre of Michel de Certeau (1925–1986), *L'invention du quotidien* (*The Practice of Everyday Life*) holds a special place. It was immediately brought out as a paperback, and of all his books, it is the one that enjoyed the most immediate success. It reached a wide public, first in France and soon elsewhere.

L'invention du quotidien started out as a report on research conducted with Luce Giard and Pierre Mayol from 1974 to 1977. This work had been financed by the Délégation générale à la recherche scientifique et technique, a public agency supporting research under the very loose label of "cultural forecasting," in a project giving substantial leeway to those conducting it. The Ministry of Culture had just published the first statistical investigation into "the cultural practices of the French." However, the three researchers headed off in a completely different direction, focusing less on global statistical distributions than on culture users' "ways of operating or doing things." The book was published in two volumes: The first, *Arts de faire*, written solely by de Certeau, sets out thoughts on the art of practice; the second presents the results of Giard and Mayol's surveys of dwelling and culinary practices. With the passage of time, one may wonder what made this difficult and ambitious work successful when most research reports wind up in ministerial archives. One obvious reason is the intellectual demands of the program, but the political and cultural circumstances also need to be considered.

As of the 1950s, the mass production and consumption of culture had given rise to questions, debates, and many different stances. Did this provide an opportunity for further emancipation, or was it merely an additional form of alienation? The appearance of paperbacks had given rise to bitter debate: Were they real books? Were their readers real readers? More generally, the position attributed to so-called popular culture was highly ideologized. At one extreme lay moral and aesthetic overvaluation of supposedly popular products (most of which were outdated—it was "the beauty of death"); at the other extreme were denunciations of manipulation said to subjugate the masses to the interests of the mighty. This debate, which was political in nature, also traversed the social sciences. Sociologists, philosophers, and historians conducted investigations whose most useful outcome was to call into question the very idea of popular culture. Nevertheless, in the 1970s, theories of cultural domination had the upper hand. The most sophisticated versions had been put forward by Michel Foucault (the progressive disciplinarization of society) and by Pierre Bourdieu (distinction and the theory of the *habitus*). For both these authors, behavior and choices were driven by unthinking logics.

It was with such positions that *Arts de faire*—a book dedicated "to the ordinary man. To a common hero, a ubiquitous character, walking in countless thousands"—took issue. Combining a number of approaches in many different areas with intuitive field observations, de Certeau develops countless variations on the theme of cultural actors' autonomy, arguing that their consumption needs to be understood as creative appropriation—that is, as productions. Against the anonymous strategies discussed in global approaches, he opposes the minute, dispersed tactics cobbled together by individuals and groups who evade collective constraints and norms or else have learned how to accommodate them. Ways of using a town, of walking, speaking, reading, and cooking, allow him to identify autonomous fluid logics: "pushed to their limits, these procedures and ploys of consumers form the network of an anti-discipline which is the subject of this book."

It is still surprising that this ambitious, often difficult work met with such success. This may be attributed to a combination of factors. The 1970s saw the erosion of great models claiming to account for the social world and of the very idea of society as a whole, at a time when societies were entering a crisis they were not able to describe, much less understand. As a result, social actors were once again under analysis, together with their agency. The pragmatic turn, without ignoring the constraints weighing on actors, focused on the holds afforded by the gaps and jumps in a social world now perceived as more irregular. These themes were emerging concurrently in the first formulations of Italian microhistory and of German *Alltagsgeschichte*. They may also be linked back to earlier attempts to account for common usages, such as the sociology of the Chicago school, the works of Erving Goffman, Henri Lefebvre's critiques of everyday life (1958), and especially the dazzling interpretation of the English working class's cultural practices put forward by Richard Hoggart in *The Uses of Literacy* (1957). But the late 1970s crystallized the themes that Michel de Certeau's analysis then bound together. His ideas fed into the spectacular development of cultural studies (and "studies" in general) in the English-speaking world, seeped into the imaginary of alternative movements, as well as fueling the attention paid more generally to the form, style, and issues of cultural practices by historians, sociologists, anthropologists, and philosophers, for whom everyday life ceased being something silent and self-evident and instead became an object for investigation into the meaning of ordinary practice.

Jacques Revel

Michel de Certeau, *L'invention du quotidien*, vol. 1, *Arts de faire* (Paris: Union générale d'éditions ["10–18"], 1980). Republished by Gallimard ("Folio"), 1990. Translated into English by Steven F. Rendall as *The Practice of Everyday Life* (Berkeley: University of California Press, 1984).

1981

PORTRAIT OF THE KING: MARIN AND THE POWER OF REPRESENTATION

Rereading Louis Marin's *Le portrait du roi* (*Portrait of the King*) more than thirty-five years after it was first published is a revealing experience: Some of its hypotheses are central to present-day thought on how images relate to power, while others have remained partially misunderstood despite their heuristic potency. One such misunderstanding arises from his choice of terminology. Marin (1931–1992) uses the term "portrait," and even more frequently "representation," where one would today expect to see "image" and "agency." The term "portrait" may seem surprising once one realizes the book is not about painting but about a set of texts ranging from Pelisson's plans for a history of the king (1670) to the history of metal during the reign of Louis, from Gomboust's plans for Paris (1652) to two texts by Félibien, one a guide to Versailles and the other a description of a party held by the king on returning from conquering Franche-Comté in 1674. What Marin calls the "portrait of the king" is composed of all these discursive, ritual, and visual forms by which the king is represented as a figure while his physical body is absent. At the heart of this "multimedia" construction, Marin places an idea that, while simple, has endless consequences: The king is only king in representation. In other words, royal power does not preexist the discursive, performative, and ritual forms representing it. Marin's semiotic is substitutive: Representation substitutes a present sign for the absent king. At the same time, it is also energetic: The operation presenting the king is not limited to replacing the absent monarch, for it also confers him with a presence that is not only powerful and fascinating, hence likely to induce terror and love in his subjects, but also just and having the value of law. In a passage written a year before the publication of *Portrait du roi* and reprinted in the texts collected in *Politiques de la représentation* in 2005, Marin sums up what he means in stating that the power of the king is his representation.

> So, what is power? Power is being capable of performing an action on someone or something; not acting or doing, but having the power, having the strength to do or to act. Power is, in its most general sense, being capable of force, having a reserve of force that is not spent but is capable of being spent. One may even wonder what a force that does not manifest itself might be. Power thus means first having power, but it is also and especially valuing this power as an obligatory constraint, generating duty as law. In this meaning, power is instituting power as law, with the former itself conceived as the possibility and capacity for force. And this is where representation will play its role, because it will be both a means of power and its underpinning. In other words, my working hypothesis is that representative mechanisms transform force into power, first by holding force in reserve, which amounts to power, and second by valuing this power as a legitimate obligatory state, by justifying power.[1]

Combining analyses of many sorts of images and texts, *Le portrait du roi* shows how representation holds force in reserve in signs and how it signifies force in discourse on law. Marin provided the social sciences with a set of decisive heuristic tools. First, his conception of the sign/representation as energy throws light on how forms relate to forces; this relationship, which is crucial for analyzing the "work of images" and their effects, eludes approaches investigating how forms relate to meanings. Second, in galvanizing reflection on the performative dimension of the sign/representation, Marin reestablishes links between the image and anthropology, and with theology even.

The idea of representation as wielded by Marin involves a dual operation: Representation admittedly had a mimetic or transitive purpose, representing something—the king. At the same time, it had a reflexive and

---

[1] Louis Marin, "Le pouvoir et ses representations" (1980), in *Politiques de la représentation*, ed. Alain Cantillon (Paris: Collège International de Philosophie, Kimé, 2005), 73–74.

pragmatic dimension. It presents him and imposes his presence with even greater force since this ostensible dimension is naturalized. If we remove the idea of representation, the pragmatic and reflexive dimension of "presenting oneself," and instead consider only its transitive and mimetic dimension, we soon lose our way in the "critique of representation" as this developed, for example, in the modernist perspective issuing from the affirmation of abstract art or in works examining nonmimetic semiotics specific to non-Western cultures or lying outside the so-called classical period. The interest in the way Marin links the idea of representation to that of power has no doubt suffered from this "critique of representation." Not only is Marin's thought foreign to such critique, but it may also be used to better elaborate it, going far beyond visual studies with which it shares a concern for situating images within the power relations in which they are caught. Marin never just denounces the "true face" lying beneath the fine appearances of art. He penetrates to the bottom of each of the subjects studied through a very particular form of analytical description conveyed in a precise, rich, and agile language enacting the play of the text.

Giovanni Careri

Louis Marin, *Le portrait du roi* (Paris: Éditions de Minuit ["Le Sens commun"], 1981). Translated into English by Martha M. Houle as *Portrait of the King* (London: Macmillan, 1988).

1981

L'EXERCICE DE LA PARENTÉ: HÉRITIER UNIFIES THE FIELD OF KINSHIP

L'exercice de la parenté (The exercise of kinship) had a curious fate. As soon as it was published, it was recognized as a major landmark in kinship studies: Its theoretical ambition, the importance of the results presented, its limpid and concise style—all predestined it, in the eyes of contemporary readers, to becoming a classic. However, five years elapsed before the publication of any in-depth reviews emphasizing its contributions or discussing its analytical premises. If this major book did not initially have the impact it deserved, it was because, within the evolving field of kinship studies, it was both ahead of its time, answering a question hitherto left pending, and behind its time, in espousing the structuralist paradigm which was losing ground.

On the face of it, the book looks like a supplement to the structuralist theory of kinship, expanding on analysis first put forward by *Structures élémentaires de la parenté* (*The Elementary Structures of Kinship*). Françoise Héritier (born 1933) sets out to analyze a type of system that Lévi-Strauss had called "semi-complex" and "complex" but had deferred studying for want of the statistical analytical tools needed to understand how these systems functioned. They are characterized by the fact that marriage, far from following a prescriptive model (as is the case in so-called elementary systems), is governed solely by prohibitions, apparently leading to arbitrary individual choices. *L'exercice de la parenté* provides a powerfully argued solution to the puzzle these systems raised, drawing on a novel method of computerized data analysis of a large set of actual marriages. Using the example of the Samo of Burkina Faso, Héritier draws out two hitherto unnoticed features.

First, she shows that prohibitions cannot be explained solely in terms of unilineal filiation since they exceed the lineage framework and are dropped after several generations (running counter to the logic of permanent lineage); additionally, they do not apply uniformly to all lines within a lineage. Second, and above all, she shows that the effect of these prohibitions differs widely depending on whether the individuals impacted by two successive marriages in the same line are of the same sex (father and son, brothers, etc.) or the opposite sex (brother/sister, mother/son, etc.). This difference is crucial, for it makes it possible, without violating established prohibitions, to exchange sisters and repeat previous alliances, formulas associated with the functioning of elementary systems of restricted or expanded exchange. Statistical processing of Samo marriages confirms what this line of arguing suggests. Far from being exposed to the randomness of history and individual strategies, they are well and truly structured by a mechanism pointing them toward precise zones in the matrimonial field: The choice of spouse pushes up as closely as possible against the limits set out by prohibitions. In other words, the prohibitions specific to semi-complex systems implicitly sketch "rules" for marriage that are just as (if not more) restrictive than those governing so-called prescriptive alliance systems. Is the same true of "complex" systems (found particularly in European societies), where prohibitions relate to genealogical positions rather than units divided up by filiation and where the field of permissible spouses would appear to be even more open? Large quantitative datasets of marriage, though rare at the period, allowed Héritier to detect replications, duplications, and sequences of alliance in these systems, sketching out zones of preferential endogamy over time. She deduced the existence of subjacent structures identical to those operating in semi-complex systems, likewise resulting in marriages being channeled fairly precisely while being linked to non-lineage ways of dividing up the social field.

In bringing to light the continuities between the alliance formulas of elementary systems and those that lie hidden at the heart of semi-complex and complex systems, Héritier unified the field of kinship. Yet however decisive this contribution was, her theoretical ambition was even greater. She wanted to consolidate the foundations of this field by redefining its "fundamental laws." That is the purpose of her first chapter, where she advances two strong theses. The first is that whenever it is a matter of positing a relation of difference or identity, a "parallel" relationship (such as that between brothers) will always be preferred over a "crossed" relationship (between a brother and sister). The second relates to the "differential valence of the sexes," giving rise to systematic asymmetry in kinship terminologies between the masculine and feminine points of view, with the former always dominating the latter.

The virtually transcendental nature granted to these principles has sparked debate: According to Hériter, they belong to the "realm of the feasible," while other criticisms have focused on the categorization of forms of kinship, preferring to see in the examples studied particular regimes of alliance structures rather than distinct "systems." Héritier has also been accused of positing too simple a relationship between terminologies and marriage formulas. Lastly, more radical criticisms from constructivist-type theorizations centered on notions of relatedness have targeted her conceptualization of the biological substrate of kinship, deemed ethnocentric. Nevertheless, her book remains a dazzling demonstration of the fertility of the structuralist approach and a key contribution to understanding marriage forms based on prohibitions.

Anne-Christine Taylor

Françoise Héritier, *L'exercice de la parenté* (Paris: Gallimard-Le Seuil-Éditions de l'EHESS ["Hautes études"], 1981).

1982

SLAVERY AND SOCIAL DEATH: PATTERSON DEFINES SLAVERY AS SOCIAL DEATH

What is slavery? Inaccurately called the "peculiar institution" in the United States, it has existed in various forms on all continents at all periods. Is it possible, and heuristically useful, to propose a universal transhistorical definition? No doubt it is possible, and it provides a way of analyzing the intrinsic functioning of the phenomenon while differentiating slavery from other relations of domination such as serfdom. Defining slavery and thus understanding what it does to slaves is not purely an academic problem: despite now being legally forbidden everywhere, slavery persists throughout today's world, making it a major political issue as well.

When Orlando Patterson (born 1940) started working on *Slavery and Social Death* in 1973, he had been a professor at Harvard's department of sociology for just two years and was only the second Black professor to obtain a permanent position within the Graduate School of Arts and Sciences. He was a Jamaican sociologist who had studied at the University College of the West Indies and then the London School of Economics. His doctorate, *The Sociology of Slavery*, was published in 1967. With the exception of Cyril L. R. James's *The Black Jacobins*, it was the first study to focus on Caribbean slavery from the slaves' point of view. Influenced by Stanley Elkins, Patterson insisted on the destructive and anomic effects of the Jamaican slavery system. He argued that after the abolition of slavery, this original chaos gave birth not to a single Creole culture but to two distinct cultures, one European and one Afro-Jamaican. Wishing to better understand the primordial institution that still shaped Jamaican society, which was then going through the challenges of independence, he launched himself into a comparative historical sociology of slavery throughout the world.

Working well before the "global turn," Patterson sought to throw off the Western-centric bias in slave studies, and so he considered all systems of slavery equally. From the sample of 196 cultures drawn up by the anthropologist George Murdock, he selected sixty-six societies having practiced slavery, from Babylon around 1750 BCE through to the Lolo people in the Taliang Shan mountains in southwestern China in the first half of the twentieth century. The historical and ethnographic literature allowed him to complete this quantitative and qualitative data. Hence his dataset included a large set of societies employing various forms of enslavement, whose masters responded to plural motivations ranging from social prestige to economic profit, with different demographic proportions of slaves and varying degrees of openness, depending on the relative ease of obtaining manumission and the status of the freed and their descendants.

On the basis of this comparison, Patterson derived an original definition of slavery emphasizing its social effects: "Slavery is the permanent, violent domination of natally alienated and generally dishonored persons." Natal alienation stems from slaves being snatched from all social ties in which they were placed before enslavement, with masters recognizing them as having no independent social existence. Rootless and isolated, slaves are reduced to a condition of social death. Such a conception leaves no room for law (property) or economy (labor), unlike the classical definitions of historians or those in the Convention to Suppress the Slave Trade and Slavery signed under the auspices of the League of Nations in 1926.

This definition of slavery as social death is associated with a dynamic perspective linking slavery and manumission. Here, Patterson no longer views the phenomenon as a personal relationship but as an institutional process. Nearly all systems of slavery allow for the possibility of manumission, with the promise of freedom constituting an instrument of social control: To perpetuate itself, slavery needs its negation. Just as being enslaved is thought of as a substitute for violent death, compensated by servile status, manumission is assimilated to a gift calling forth a counter-gift and does not put an end to the relationship of dependency between master and former slave. Still, masters are no less dependent on their slaves than slaves are on their masters. In fact, slavery may easily transform into a parasitical relationship. It is thus not surprising that the outcome is freedom. This idea, which emerges at the end of *Slavery and Social Death*, was explored by Patterson in his other great book, *Freedom in the Making of Western Culture*, published in 1991.

Nearly thirty years after it first came out, *Slavery and Social Death* is the first reference to which all researchers interested in slavery still turn. It is a transdisciplinary book, used by sociologists and anthropologists as much as by historians. No other comparative work of similar global scale has been produced since. Additionally, the concept of "social death" has been taken up by specialists working in many different fields. Nevertheless, the work has been much debated. Each of the three components of Patterson's definition—power, natal alienation, and dishonor—has been criticized. Above all, he is accused of focusing on the master-slave relationship and considering it solely from the angle of the ideology of masters. It is true that while Patterson does emphasize slave resistance to their desocialization and degradation, he does not place the conflict inherent to the master-slave relationship at the heart of his analysis, despite the paradigm of slave agency having dominated scholarship since the 1960s. Some researchers have rejected its definition, others have sought to revise it, but all still position themselves in relation to Patterson. His work has never ceased to inspire debate on what constitutes one of the most extreme forms of domination.

Cécile Vidal

Orlando Patterson, *Slavery and Social Death: A Comparative Study* (Cambridge, MA: Harvard University Press, 1982).

1982

ART WORLDS: BECKER TURNS ART INTO A JOB LIKE ANY OTHER

In freely adapting the idea of an art world, first put forward by the philosopher Arthur Danto, and turning it into a sociological tool that went on to become paradigmatic, Howard Becker (born 1928) brought art into the circle of legitimate sociological objects. Yet one of the most significant effects of the upheaval that the book *Art Worlds* triggered was repositioning the sociology of art within the sociology of work, of which it was henceforth but a particularized form. Recognizing the object seemed to strip it of its exceptional character. One of the objections frequently made against Becker has been that his sociology did not address art as such but rather the jobs and forms of cooperation by which aesthetic objects were produced and distributed. Becker has never dodged this issue: in his preface, he states that he has treated art as "the work people do," adding that he was "more concerned with patterns of cooperation among the people who make the works than in the works themselves or with those conventionally defined as their creators."

It is this shift that lends the work its sociological quality. Becker is not impressed by the religion of art, which issues the feeling of the sacred without divinity as developed by the moderns. He had played piano in bars around Chicago and was well placed to know that audiences were rarely stirred by legitimist impulses. His early years in Chicago and musical apprenticeship on the job left him with what he calls a "congenital antielitism," giving rise to his deflationary vision "treating art as not so very different from other kinds of work, and treating people defined as artists as not so very different from other kinds of workers, especially the other workers who participate in the making of art works."

The book's great strength is that it is entirely centered around a simple and effective idea: that of a "world." From Danto's definition, Becker retained the contextual, institutional, and artifactual dimension of art. But to this he added what the interactionist sociology he had learned in Chicago in the 1950s owed to the ideas of Everett Hughes and Herbert Blumer. Social life took place in the dynamic specific to interactions between individuals; agents are guided by the meanings borne by the objects peopling their world; their passage through social space is based on information provided by interactions with other agents and on the complex play fueled by interpreting situations. In the domain of art, as in all other sectors of social life, actors feel the need to cooperate as a function of a limited number of conventional procedures framing the interaction. While the plasticity of these links makes it possible to rearrange and partially rewrite conventions, one should not conclude that they are thereby ephemeral or reduce to the here and now interaction in art worlds—which display, on the contrary, surprising durability.

Becker's model largely resists the conventional charge brought against it by structuralism, which reduces interactionism to brief face-to-face encounters, occulting the considerable part played by conventional mechanisms. Becker never forgets that the arts have a long history. He defines the art world as "the network of people whose cooperative activity, organized via their joint knowledge of conventional means of doing things, produces the kind of art works that art world is noted for." The chapter on "Arts and Crafts" provides a way of grasping Becker's approach, which is both elaborate and homespun. The distinction between arts and crafts derives primarily from a way of naming productive activities. A given object may be considered as the product of an artist or a craftsman depending on how it is viewed, which results from a certain state of conventional arrangements and social relations: The theory of art worlds is from this point of view an extension of the labeling theory that Becker had propounded in his first major book, *Outsiders* (1963). In this chapter, Becker sets out a veritable theory of aesthetic change, accounting

174   *Art Worlds*

for the processes by which different statuses are assigned successively to the production of forms.

The idea of a "world" met with great success, while also giving rise to some misunderstandings, with certain users seeing it as relaxing the structural constraints ordinarily imputed to Pierre Bourdieu's field theory and as a form of methodological anarchy. But the idea of "convention" as used by Becker is in fact very rigorous. The emphasis on cooperative interplay has often led people to think that Becker neglected the agonistic direction of artistic competition. Over thirty years after the work was published, it is still used to support art analysis, and it still feeds controversy. In France, Pierre-Michel Menger, who wrote a noted foreword to the French translation, removed the issue of art as work from its interactionist envelope to explore new avenues. And, just like the concepts of field, stage, and network, that of a world continues to shape a wide variety of empirical analyses.

Jean-Louis Fabiani

Howard S. Becker, *Art Worlds* (Berkeley: University of California Press, 1982).

1982

THE FOUL AND THE FRAGRANT: CORBIN ENDOWS OUR SENSES WITH A HISTORY

When Alain Corbin (born 1936) published *Le miasme et la jonquille* (The miasma and the daffodil) in 1982, he was forty-six years old and a professor at the Université de Tours specializing in nineteenth-century French history. A doctorate on the Limousin region of France had been followed by a book on prostitutes, published in 1978 and received as a historical approach to the types of deviance that Michel Foucault had made into a fashionable research topic. But it was already more than just that.

He now published another book on what, on the face of it, seemed a most surprising subject: the history of smell. Historians had not thought of that before. The idea came to Corbin on noting how much was said about the smell of "women for hire" and the existence of the first bathrooms in luxury brothels. But he remained prudent. He did not claim to have produced a comprehensive work on the matter, even less to announce a turning point in historical scholarship. Perhaps this was a matter of common sense, but nowadays, decades after the proclamation of so many turning points, it comes across as an act of rare modesty.

Corbin assures his readers that he has simply gathered material for a history as yet unwritten, merely suggesting that the sense of smell had a history. In fact, he did far more than this. *Le miasme et la jonquille* analyzes the great undertaking to deodorize bodies between the mid-eighteenth and the late nineteenth century, together with the parallel invention of the perfumery industry. Musk, amber, and civet gave way to subtle floral scents. Perhaps the movement only affected a certain social elite, but that is significant in itself: The working classes, who had remained attached to strong smells and their belief in the therapeutic virtues of bodily effluvia and excrement, were increasingly identified by their foul smells. Those visiting the poor noted with ever-greater insistence that the poor were those who smelled bad—they truly were the "great unwashed."

Corbin emphasizes the hold of neo-Hippocratism over society of the period. However, the theory of humors was on the wane, and doctors said illness was caused by miasma, which was generated by the lack of movement of air and water, detectable by bad smells. Efforts were made to eliminate these environmental causes of illness: Sewer networks were one direct consequence. From the soldier's tent to the ship's cabin, from prison cells to hospital rooms, confined spaces with their suspect odors came in for close attention. People moved out from the first floor of buildings to settle on the second floor. To those who complained of illness, doctors responded with a new injunction: a change of air. (Corbin took this as the starting point for his next book, on the origins and development of sea bathing.) It was not until the Pasteurian revolution at the end of the nineteenth century that one could state, in the words of Dr. Paul Brouardel, that "everything which stinks does not kill, and everything which kills does not stink"—leading to a reappraisal of various swathes of human activity.

In the days of "new history," Corbin's investigation was very well received, attracting eulogiums in newspapers and journals and being translated into many languages. One unexpected consequence of the German translation was Patrick Süskind's best seller, *Das Parfum*, published in 1985 and partly inspired by his reading *Le miasme et la jonquille*. In 1988, when Corbin had just been elected to a chair at Université Paris 1, Jacques Le Goff referred to the book on smells as one of the recent pointers, together with Jean Delumeau's *La peur en Occident* and Pierre Vidal-Naquet's *Le chasseur noir*, of "the development of histories of representations." The terminology was not yet stabilized: soon one spoke of the history of representations.

In his own way, Corbin was in fact continuing the long inquiry Lucien Febvre had suggested into the "affective life" of times gone by. Febvre spoke of "sensibility"; this project had been taken up by historians of "mentalities." Corbin transformed it by defining an original method for investigating how

177 *Corbin Endows Our Senses with a History*

scientific and medical creeds, ideological beliefs, moral and religious norms, aesthetic and literary codes, and the uses of the senses shaped the life of people in society. Studying systems of representations and the figures expressing them lies at the heart of this "history of sensibilities," written in the flowing style Corbin employed in all his books, expanding his research program to embrace the history of sight, touch, and hearing. The 1982 book, the starting point of "sensorial anthropology," was thus something truly new. Recent comprehensive works on the history of bodies, virility, and the emotions are among its offshoots.

In inviting its readers to study the "social imaginary," *Le miasme et la jonquille* suggested the existence of countless systems of representation at work in our societies, an intuition that led Corbin to become an inexhaustible source of new subjects, both for him and his pupils. Each time, the rule remains the one established by his study of smell. Writing in 1982, Corbin stated that discourse on the object, the sociology of behaviors and their interpretation by scholars, individual expectations, and strategies implemented by authorities formed "a fragmented field of study within which the real and imaginary are mixed to the point that it would be simplistic to wish to divide them at all costs and at any moment." That too was new: Corbin was asking historians to carry on tracking down social reality in documents of the period, but with the proviso that they think of this reality as a jumble of practices and representations and certainly not as a set of forces opposing fiction—a lesson we may still usefully learn from today.

Sylvain Venayre

Alain Corbin, *Le miasme et la jonquille: L'odorat et l'imaginaire social, XVIIIe–XIXe siècles* (Paris: Aubier ["Collection historique"], 1982). Republished by Flammarion ("Champs"), 2016. Translated into English by Miriam L. Kochan, Dr. Roy Porter, and Christopher Prendergast as *The Foul and the Fragrant: Odor and the French Social Imagination* (Cambridge, MA: Harvard University Press, 1986).

1982

THE MAKING OF GREAT MEN: GODELIER AND THE MULTIPLE FORMS OF DOMINATION

The Baruya people of New Guinea, with a population of about 2,000, live in villages and hamlets at altitudes between 1500 and 2000 meters, where they grow crops, rear pigs, and produce salt from plants. They made their first appearance in the anthropological literature after the first field trip by their first ethnologist, Maurice Godelier (born 1934).

La production des Grands Hommes (*The Making of Great Men*) is no doubt one of the most accomplished monographs of its period that shaped subsequent anthropology of Oceania. It is still of interest today because it addresses fundamental questions. Let us look at two of the most general issues it tackles: first, the relations of social distinction and domination, which within a given human group, allow actors to conceive of and perform various forms of belonging, roles, and social statuses; and second, the principles governing power relations, which despite (and even because of) their diversity, legitimize social reproduction.

One of the main points of interest of Godelier's way of tackling these issues is that he inverts the dominant lines of analysis. His work does not approach society as an object as such, as a given fact, or simply as a locus to be studied. It is understood as the consequence of consented power relationships based on forms of representation that justify them. Far from being lasting and timeless, Baruya society is discussed as the product of a long history of migrations, conflicts, and conquests, underpinned by a body of shared beliefs that are reproduced in ritual activity, connecting various forms of social distinctions and domination.

These beliefs take three forms: The first is domination in relation to the hierarchy of clans that followed the arrival of the Baruya clan, which, on being evicted from its territory, imposed itself locally through conquest and alliance, eventually giving its name to the entire society. Second are the norms inherent to the domination of men over women, and third, the forms of domination among males with a hierarchy distinguishing Great Men (great shamans, warriors, and great hunters) from the other men. Baruya society is based on the relationship between these three forms of domination and their reproduction.

Male domination is pivotal. Although women have their own rituals, myths, and social spaces, they are not allowed to make or own tools, weapons, musical instruments, or sacred objects. They are excluded from landownership and from the great initiatory cycles whose purpose is to reproduce social cohesion; they bear the attributes of impurity and of danger, which the male world is supposed to control. But once again, Godelier inverts the causality. Going against feminist anthropology, he establishes an interplay between male domination and female subordination: The wielding of physical and symbolic violence includes the consent of those who are dominated. This consent ensures the reproduction of domination over time, with male and female initiation rites anchoring the conveyed ideology in the minds and bodies of the society. While it only takes two weeks to transform a pubescent girl into a potential mother, boys have to live for twelve years in the house of initiates, a time during which they endure four long ritual cycles before they are allowed to marry and procreate. While female initiations explain the importance of regularly swallowing their husband's sperm, male initiatory secrets focus on the obligation for young novices to perform fellatio on their older co-initiates, who have not yet come into any contact with a vagina. This regular ingestion is presumed to make them grow stronger during their reclusion and more powerful than women. Consent to male domination is rooted in sharing the same cosmology, attributing a limited capacity for action to women and major agency to the sun, which is at the origin of living beings, as well as to the sun's legitimate representatives—men. The power of the sun's energy is meant to be embodied in sperm, from which maternal milk is said to derive. This ritual homosexuality limited to the house of initiates gives men the imaginary power to give birth to boys a second time, outside their mother's womb, who are thus stripped of their procreative capacity.

While the first set of distinctions and dominations connects the various clans and repositions social structures in its historical dynamics, this second set is transversal, linking the question of dominance and subordination within relations between the sexes. As for the third, it relates to the conditions in which political power emerges and is wielded. In a 1963 article that has become a classic ("Poor Man, Rich Man, Big Man, Chief"), Marshall Sahlins distinguished between two ideal-typical types of power in Oceania: Polynesian chiefs and Melanesian Big Men. While the former inherited power through their genealogical position, the latter acquired fame and power by accumulating and redistributing goods, by contracting debts, and by setting up networks of interdependence. Godelier discovered a third ideal-type of political power in Oceania: that of Great Men, who differ markedly from Big Men in that their fame and power derive from their individual skills and exploits, independent of wealth and its distribution.

The Baruya monograph provides an ethnographically and theoretically rich analysis from which fundamental anthropological questions that are still at stake may be addressed.

Laurent Dousset

Maurice Godelier, *La production des Grands Hommes: Pouvoir et domination masculine chez les Baruya de Nouvelle-Guinée* (Paris: Fayard ["L'espace du politique"], 1982). Republished by Flammarion ("Champs"), 2003. Translated into English by Rupert Swyer as *The Making of Great Men: Male Domination and Power among the New Guinea Baruya* (Cambridge: Cambridge University Press, 1986).

1983

ELEMENTARY ASPECTS OF PEASANT INSURGENCY IN COLONIAL INDIA: GUHA REHABILITATES THE POLITICAL CONSCIOUSNESS OF SUBALTERNS

Elementary Aspects of Peasant Insurgency in Colonial India is the major work by Ranajit Guha (born 1923), the founding father of the Indian subaltern school of historiography. When this book came out in 1983, Guha had just launched the series of volumes of collected papers entitled *Subaltern Studies* that gave its name to this current of historical scholarship. But he had previously been working on it for ten years, and it was during this period of gestation, accompanied by debates with a team of young researchers working alongside him, that the initial theoretical and methodological framework of *Subaltern Studies* took shape. Guha, a politically committed Bengali historian, had joined the Communist Party of India (CPI) as a student during the Second World War and served six years as a full-time party worker from 1947. He returned to university studies and history teaching in Calcutta in 1953, resigned from the CPI in 1956, and eventually settled in Britain in 1960. He was familiar with the work of the British radical historians' group, a brilliant collective of critical Marxist scholars significantly influenced by Gramsci's thought (such as Edward P. Thompson, Eric Hobsbawm, and others), and with their mode of history-writing known as "history from below." In the Indian context, he rejected (as did the local pro-Chinese dissident communists) the CPI's support for the ruling national bourgeoisie, accused of having betrayed the social promises made during the struggle for independence. When on a study visit to India in 1970 and 1971, he met students who had recently been involved in the Naxalite (Maoist) insurgency launched in northern Bengal in 1967. He identified with this populist idealism of an ultra-left-wing organization fighting for the emancipation of the disinherited rural masses and switched focus to the history of Indian peasant uprisings.

The purpose of *Elementary Aspects* is to rehabilitate the political consciousness of the peasantry, going against Marx's famous metaphor comparing it to a "sack of potatoes" expressing its inaptitude, as a multitude plunged into false consciousness, for any form of organized autonomous collective resistance. In a smart move, Guha banishes any essentializing attempt to represent the subjectivity of the peasants, instead focusing on their concrete rebellious practices. In establishing a repertoire of recurrent forms of insurgent mobilization and action (the "elementary forms of resistance" announced in the book's title), he seeks to reveal what he calls the "logic of peasant rebel consciousness." His investigation opens in 1783 with the first rebellion mentioned in the colonial archives and closes in 1900, so as to apprehend this rebel consciousness in its original "purity," before nationalist politics penetrated the countryside. He details peasant insurgency practices in six thematic chapters entitled "Negation" (the popular conception of resistance), "Ambiguity" (the fuzzy boundary between crime and insurgency), "Modality" (the forms of collective action and organization), "Solidarity" (unity and discord within the rebellion), "Transmission" (rebellion as communication), and "Territoriality" (the spatial horizon of the rebellions).

The book, strongly argued and written in a lucid and elegant style, was praised for its rigor and for the wealth of empirical work accomplished. But its methodological options and idealization of the people were much discussed. Because the only way to gain access to the events was through the distorting lens of the archives of state repression, Guha had to read his official sources "against the grain" to decipher the experience of the insurgents, but this decoding could never make up for the many silences of these records. The sociological analysis of the movements is deficient, for the generic label "peasant rebellions" encompasses revolts of weakly stratified tribal groups in mountainous forest zones as well as uprisings occurring among ancient and richly differentiated peasantries of the great plains. Similarly, the general term "peasant" makes no distinction between landowning farmers, tenants, and agricultural laborers, whose objective interests and capacities for resistance could differ. Finally, the priority given to the forms of rebel behavior works to the detriment of exploring their causes and of a linear narrative of the course of events. Yet, Guha's approach here prefigured what Michel Dobry, a specialist of the sociology of political crises, has called "the etiological illusion," which tends to reduce the actual causes of a crisis to its potential determinants, thus implying a mechanistic explanation of human behavior. Guha's decontextualizing of the uprisings arose from his radical rejection of economism and of the infantilizing fable of "spontaneous" peasant revolts. By stripping the rebellions of their historical singularity in order to extract common characteristics and grouping these thematically, he was on the contrary seeking to demonstrate the existence, in a sort of structural atemporality, of a coherent and autonomous political culture of subalternity, enabling us to hear what he later called "the small voice of history."

How did this brilliant book, although built on such disputed premises, become an emblematic text? It deserves full credit for importing into mainstream historical discourse the category (borrowed from Gramsci) of the subaltern, which connotes a notion of power, thus shifting the focus of "history from below" from economic and social critique to the political critique of domination. The acclimatization of the term within the social sciences as a whole was then carried forward by the planetary vogue of subaltern studies as of the 1990s. But it is above all the project of rehabilitating the politics of the people that made *Elementary Aspects* a symbolic reference. *Subaltern Studies*, which expanded on it, initiated the first line of social science research with a global outreach to have issued from the formerly colonized world, engendering emulation in many countries of the South. As the subaltern school rose to academic prominence, it undeniably took a postmodernist turn, which made it deviate from its initial trajectory. But Guha's *Elementary Aspects* stands out among social science research as the most accomplished outcome of the initial questionings of this intellectual venture.

Jacques Pouchepadass

Ranajit Guha, *Elementary Aspects of Peasant Insurgency in Colonial India* (Delhi: Oxford University Press, 1983).

1983

ESSAYS ON INDIVIDUALISM: DUMONT PLACES WESTERN EXCEPTION IN PERSPECTIVE

Essais sur l'individualisme (*Essays on Individualism*) by Louis Dumont (1911–1998) is a collection of seven seemingly very disparate texts. The table of contents, in distinguishing between studies about modern ideology and those on the "comparative principle," gives no indication of what lends the volume its unity. Yet, while the book may disconcert readers with its diverse references and topics, it follows an overall purpose.

The idea is that social anthropology—in other words, the comparative study of human societies—may contribute to our way thinking about two "major political problems" facing modern societies.

What are the two problems? The first stems from the fact that our world is becoming ever more intercultural. "Non-modern cultures are going to weigh more and more heavily in the making of the world's common civilization." By cultural interaction, Dumont was designating the phenomenon not yet called globalization, whose effect (the emergence of anti-individualist claims within individualism, such as the assertion of "minority rights," for instance) transpires both in the dominant (individualist) culture and in dominated (holistic) cultures. The second problem is the "diseases of democracy." Totalitarianism, though seemingly opposed to democracy, is not the resurgence of some premodern ideology, but a contradictory form assumed by democracy "once it loses sight of its limitations, strives to perfect realization, and, checked by the facts, ends up divided against itself." These aporia are clearly as topical as ever.

What might an anthropological perspective on these problems be? Dumont states that all his research is indebted to the thought of Marcel

Mauss, from whom he takes two lessons. First, anthropology needs to be a sociology, and hence it must relate the phenomena studied to a particular englobing society (rather than to human nature or the mind). Second, anthropology, precisely because it is social, works on the "comparative principle." Saying anthropology is comparative does not mean it needs to proceed by detecting comparable features in different societies, which would entail losing reference to concrete societies. It needs to conduct a more radical kind of comparison, calling into question the researcher in person. Dumont cites Mauss's precept: "Sociological explanation is completed once one has seen *what* people believe and think, and *who* the people believing and thinking that are." To be faithful to Mauss, Dumont argues that "*who* the people believing and thinking that are" needs to be completed by adding "in comparison to us who believe this."

If the anthropologist comes up with a pertinent comparison—here, between us Westerners and India—this makes it possible to adopt a global perspective on our ideas and so bring out their *configuration*. This word needs to be taken in the structuralist or Gestaltist meaning of the term: the ideas and values to be studied are not semantic atoms that we may isolate from one another, but they derive their content from their position in a whole, which needs to be apprehended as such.

Dumont reckons that he has thereby responded to the objection that an anthropologist must study practices, material facts, rather than representations. Before being able to address material facts escaping our modern ideology, we first need to critique its categories for describing and conceiving of them. And the difficulty of the two major problems mentioned earlier stems from the fact that our categories—economics, politics, religion, and so on—are inadequate, precisely because they partake in the individualist configuration defining our ideology, whereas the problems facing us signal the persistence or gathering strength of values and experiences belonging to the opposed configuration: that of a holistic ideology placing cardinal value on community.

Dumont's goal is thus to replace our commonsense ideas with concepts that are more satisfying from an anthropological point of view because they are more sociological, and more sociological because they are reached via

186   *Essays on Individualism*

comparison. Hence the studies in the first part provide comparative definitions of the individual, in the normative sense, and of the category of politics, of the nation, of socialism, and of totalitarianism.

An anthropology of modernity shows that individualist culture is an *exception* within universal history. One way of understanding this exception is to expose how it came about, which Dumont does in his first two chapters. In many histories of ideas, the Middle Ages do not really exist, failing to find their place between the ancients and the moderns. But in the retrospective portrait sketched by Dumont, not only is there a middle period between classical antiquity and modernity, but this period plays a decisive role. The question has often been raised whether the individual existed in the Middle Ages. Dumont answers by describing in his first chapter how the individual-out-of-the-world (the early Christians) metamorphosed into an individual-in-the-world (the persons of modern natural law). Another classic debate relates to what defines modern political thought. Dumont answers by going over the transition in which the modern state, the bearer of ultimate political values in their order, inherited the sovereign function held by the Church in the Middle Ages.

Vincent Descombes

Louis Dumont, *Essais sur l'individualisme: Une perspective anthropologique sur l'idéologie moderne* (Paris: Éditions du Seuil ["Esprit"], 1983). Republished by Éditions du Seuil, 1993. Translated into English as *Essays on Individualism: Modern Ideology in Anthropological Perspective* (Chicago: University of Chicago Press, 1986).

1983

IMAGINED COMMUNITIES: ANDERSON UNVEILS NATIONS' FICTIONAL UNDERPINNINGS

It would be hard to come up with a more arresting title than *Imagined Communities: Reflections on the Origin and Spread of Nationalism*. If it contributed substantially to the book's success, it was because the title announced a short, accessible essay, specified the content, and gathered the thesis into a lastingly successful idea, an "imagined community." It is immediately clear that contemporary nations are cultural creations, hence contingent by nature.

The book by Benedict Anderson (1936–2015), rather than sparking a passing vogue for "identity creation," fundamentally altered the field of nationalism studies. *Imagined Communities* argues against all those who seek the origin of nations in an ethnic group, custom, language, or the slow sedimentation of history and identity. The particularism to which nations lay claim becomes an imaginary construct, a fiction, a great narrative that has ended up being embodied in social practices; though each nation claims to be exceptional and historically grounded, this conceals a common process linked to the history of the merchant capitalist world. Yet the book's reception worldwide stemmed less from this original theory than from Anderson's elegant and concise defense of a clear stance in the great debate about nations, which was of fundamental importance in the social sciences of the 1980s and 1990s and marked by major texts by Ernest Gellner, Anthony Smith, Partha Chatterjee, and Eric Hobsbawm, among others.

Anderson's argument draws on British Marxism, of which he was one of the most brilliant proponents, as well as on the Annales school together with Walter Benjamin and the Frankfurt school. It takes nationalism as one of the avatars of print capitalism, inquiring at length into the early modern period, with the Gutenberg invention, the development of a publishing and book market, and the appearance of newspapers. This engendered two watersheds: first, the beginning of the era of reproducibility and mass diffusion of cultural products, thanks to technical inventions and the expansion of capitalism; second, the foundation by certain elites (whose description falls outside the book's remit) of communities of interpretation untrammeled by the former denominational monopolies on laying down truth. The vernacular languages asserted themselves over sacred languages, through "national" literature, for instance. They signaled and conveyed a territorialization of the imaginary and its withdrawal behind borders and within a people. The nation thus appears as an unprecedented set of images, symbols, and words opposing "traditional" cosmologies, producing a new way of understanding time, space, and memory: this intelligibility was primarily imaginary and textual, becoming established as a self-realizing prophecy, spanning the centuries, thanks to techniques and expanding publics.

The success of *Imagined Communities* is surprising, given Anderson's original intention. He said he had written it to understand the possibility of war between countries in the socialist bloc; luckily, the events that soon consigned this ambition to the past also saw the book triumph. The fall of the Berlin Wall, collapse of the Soviet Union, and correlating increase in sovereignties and conflicts in Europe and Asia seemed to indicate the victory of the nationality mindset, yoking the national question to issues of ethnicity, as during the wars in the former Yugoslavia.

The theme might appear old-fashioned in these days of histories of specific worlds and the vogue for matters of circulation. What remains of the concept of nation in these globalized times, now that historians have shifted their interest to global, imperial, and Atlantic perspectives? The diffusionism governing the book's main thesis also looks outdated: recent scholarship no longer privileges the hypothesis of the capillarity of the imaginary running from the "top" toward the "bottom," spreading "elite culture" to the nationalized masses through techniques and the market.

But any such criticism would miss the source of the book's originality. With the social sciences currently wary of the concept of identity, *Imagined*

Communities provides a salutary conceptual toolkit to avoid the snares of essentialism. But the principal originality lies in Anderson's approach, for he tackles a canonical subject in political science and history from a "decentered" specialism. It was precisely because he was a specialist of Southeast Asia that he could advance a thesis that, though seeming so paradoxical, was fundamentally right. The intimate nature of nationalism may best be understood far from the great canonical models relating to Europe, for it is to Latin America that we must turn to understand its origins. Anderson argues that seventeenth-century reforms gave rise to a closed group of metropolitan administrators whose esprit de corps was built up over the course of their peregrinations around the empire. This identity opposed them to local elites, from whom they confiscated imperial government. And on being thus excluded from power, white Creoles developed an early form of national thought, diffused in the nascent press. Although this interpretation has since been disproved by a different interpretation of independences, these societies were nevertheless marked by the many human contributions, statuses, and colors that were originally pure fabrications that could not be underpinned by any ethnic or historical unit. Anderson's originality lies precisely in this bold move to leave Europe behind and *provincialize* it, the better to apprehend it. The move remains as fertile as ever, given the extent to which history and the social sciences are still wedded to the idea of conceptual matrices and models supposed, rightly or wrongly, to have originated in Europe or the West.

Clément Thibaud

Benedict Anderson, *Imagined Communities: Reflections on the Origin and Spread of Nationalism* (London: Verso, 1983).

1984

THE PASTEURIZATION OF FRANCE: LATOUR MAKES ROOM FOR THE NONHUMAN

With its power struggles, invisible enemies, ordeals, betrayals, battles, victories, duels, harangues, alliances, and control of the land, *Les microbes: Guerre et paix* (*The Pasteurization of France*) is an epic saga. By the time Bruno Latour (born 1947), a young anthropologist, published his first book in French in 1984, he had already written (with Steve Woolgar) an important ethnographic study, *Laboratory Life* (1979), combining life sciences, fieldwork, sociology of science, and anthropology. Like Pasteur (whose "sideways movement" from one discipline to another he describes), Latour transposes what he learned from Africanists, and then in microbiology laboratories in California, to a historical and philosophical domain.

The work is an open attack on all reductions: the great macro-historical accounts explaining episodes in the history of science in terms of revolutions, epistemological ruptures, and great men, and hence the choice of one figure, Pasteur, and one emblematic event, the discovery of microbes ("the least questionable episode in the history of science") to build an a fortiori argument. Pasteur seems to be the perfect example of a "scientific manner of convincing untouched by compromise, tinkering, and dispute." Latour does not dismantle the great figure, but approaches him differently, showing his displacements, pointing out his allies, thereby telling a history wholly different to that of the solitary scholar. Pasteur's immediate success was less due to his singular genius than to his position as spokesman and amplifier for a movement that already existed, a combination of sanitation, urban planning, moralization, and advocacy of living conditions, known at the time as hygienism. This is one of the earliest formulations in Actor Network Theory (ANT): "An idea, even one of genius, even an idea that is to save millions of people, never moves of its own accord. It requires a force to fetch it, seize upon it for its own purposes, move it; and often transform it." Movement lies at the heart of Latour's analysis: the "sideways movement" that led Pasteur from crystallography to microbiology, allowing him to apply what he had learned in other disciplines to new ones, thus becoming a pioneer in all; the move in which Pasteur's acolytes took the question of infectious disease into the laboratory, even though the problem did not look like it fell within their remit; the moving of this laboratory to Pouilly-le-Fort, in the Seine-et-Marne countryside, where the anthrax epidemic was raging and the crucial experiment was conducted that gave real-scale proof that Pasteur's hypotheses were right; then the return to Rue d'Ulm, this time to disseminate vaccines and spread new pasteurization practices. No doubt Pasteur was a genius, Latour argues—just not for the reasons we think.

The title of an article Latour published a year earlier, "Donnez-moi un laboratoire et je soulèverai le monde" ("Give me a laboratory and I will raise the world") clearly resumes his way of thinking of the laboratory as a place for inverting forces, where humanity can master the nonhuman because it may be isolated, cultivated, and measured there. With a laboratory it is possible to sample a component of reality, to move it to a new yet favorable environment, where nothing else obscures the view. The laboratory on Rue d'Ulm is "what makes agents visible," while the farm at Pouilly-le-Fort is the dazzling public display of this unprecedented mastery of the "invisible enemy," now finally unmasked. Pouilly-le-Fort, lying between the laboratory and the peasants' field, is the tipping point where the Archimedes principle may be performed. His apparatus needed to be similar enough to the Paris laboratory to make it possible to control microbes by vaccination, yet different enough to prevent any accusations that Pasteur was working with "laboratory microbes"—illustrating how small gestures in the laboratory may have immense impacts outside it.

What is a microbe? It is an actant within a narrative. Microbes force us to "recompose society differently," to leave solely human relations behind and make room for these invisible entities acting as forces, systematically

192 *The Pasteurization of France*

deviating trajectories we believed straightforward. Pasteurians and their hygienist allies had to place social links on a new footing to include microbes, just as anthropologists of science were forced to rethink their discipline to open it up to the nonhuman. Actors, agents, actants, characters—there is no clearer illustration of how the idea of agency is primarily a semiotic concept, implying symmetry between natural and social actors. In 1984, nascent science studies focused mainly on humans, not on ecology and natural beings. It was Latour and his *Microbes* that brought science studies into contact with ecology, leading to the developments with which we are familiar in philosophical and anthropological thought over the past thirty-odd years.

Combining an empirical argument with a philosophical text, the book had a considerable impact, and in conjunction with his 1987 *Science in Action*, it initiated a major shift in studying and understanding scientific practice. *Les microbes* and *Irréductions* defend a metaphysics that does not accept a distinction between nature and society, inviting us to leave behind any transcendent conception of science as the only field where the irrefutable certainty of facts allows us to escape the bothersome tinkering of politics. These works thus launched a research program that Latour has continued to develop over thirty years in books of key importance in contemporary thought, from *Nous n'avons jamais été modernes* (*We Have Never Been Modern*) to *Face à Gaïa* (*Facing Gaia*).

Frédérique Aït-Touati

Bruno Latour, *Les microbes: Guerre et paix*, followed by *Irréductions* (Paris: Métailié ["Pandore"], 1984). Republished by La Découverte, 2011, under the title *Pasteur: Guerre et paix des microbes*. Translated into English by Alan Sheridan and John Law as *The Pasteurization of France* (Cambridge, MA: Harvard University Press, 1988).

1985

TIME AND NARRATIVE: RICŒUR REFIGURES TIME

We live in time, and time is inherent to being; however, speculation on time is an "inconclusive rumination." Confronting this aporia, Paul Ricœur (1913–2005) suggests exploring the path provided by narrative: "Temporality cannot be spoken of in the direct discourse of phenomenology, but rather requires the mediation of the indirect discourse of narration." This is the idea underlying the three volumes of *Temps et récit* (*Time and Narrative*), written during Ricœur's "American period," when he divided his time between Paris and Chicago. This shuttling back and forth across the Atlantic led him to develop a lengthy conversation between phenomenology, analytic philosophy, narratology, and historiography.

The core of his argument is "triple mimesis," mediating between time and narrative, an active process imitating or representing action. Mimesis I relates to the preunderstanding we have of lived temporality; mimesis II to the actual plotting proposed by the configuration of the work and its specific interplay of tradition with innovation; and mimesis III to the readers' refiguration not only of the work but also of their own world and ways of feeling and acting. The entire exploration of literary narrative, conducted in discussion with Northrop Frye, seeks to show that the advent of the novel as a "form without form" and the "end of the art of telling" in no way means the end of plotting: the birth of new narrative forms proves that the narrative function, while it may undergo profound changes, does not disappear.

Fictional accounts reconfigure our temporal experience, which is always confused, formless, and mute, as it were. They do not resolve the paradoxes of time but put them to work and make them productive. Far from being vicious, the time-narrative circle is "in good health," for each half reinforces the other. Thus, the three "fables about time" selected by Ricœur (*In Search of Lost Time, The Magic Mountain*, and *Mrs. Dalloway*) fictively enrich human experience of time through "imaginative variations." All three point out the discordance of times, the gap between chronological time and lived time, inserting the dimension of conflict into time. Not only is the time of day only externally the same for all, while differing within the intimate realm, public time too is eroded by incompatible visions: it does not bring together; it sets apart.

Historical narratives too are a response to the aporias of temporal experience. But that presupposes expanding our concepts of event and narrative. Ricœur shows that despite Braudel's proclamations, he did not manage to do away with individuals, events, and narrative. Far from being evacuated, action remains central, and the very idea of *longue durée* history is inseparable from the dramatic event—that is, the plotting of event. Ricœur thus strips events of their impetuous character (it is not necessarily "brief and nervous, like an explosion") and instead assigns them the status of symptoms or testimonies.

Temps et récit proposes a long and complex path, grounded in an "indirect connection of derivation." Ricœur recognizes that history is a narrative practice and analyzes the overlaps between history and fiction. Both evolve through reciprocal borrowings: Historical intentionality "becomes effective by incorporating into its intended object the resources of fictionalization stemming from the narrative form of imagination," while the intentionality of fiction "produces its effects of detecting and transforming acting and suffering only by symmetrically assuming the resources of historicization presented it by attempts to reconstruct the actual past." However, unlike Hayden White, Ricœur is careful to maintain the distinction between the two types of narrative discourse. "Only history can claim a reference inscribed in empirical reality [. . .]. Even if the past no longer exists and if, in Augustine's expression, it could be reached only in the present of the past, that is, through the traces of the past become documents for the historian, still it did happen." This has two consequences.

First, the problem of truth remains fundamental in history: The past is defined as the reference point to which historical knowledge seeks to correspond appropriately. "With the documents and by way of documentary proof, the historian is subject to what once happened. He has a debt to the past, a debt of recognition of the dead, which makes of him an insolvent debtor." Second, precisely because history pursues objectivity, it may raise the question of the limits of objectivity as a specific problem. For this reason, any naive vision of the concept of reality applied to the pastness of the past is disqualified. Hence there is asymmetry and complementarity between the referential models and respective purposes of history and fiction.

Narrative, the guardian of time: The formula enjoyed great success. It also gave rise to some misunderstandings, despite Ricœur carefully setting out its limits. For him, there is no total narrative, no "plot of all plots" (meaning we must renounce Hegelian temptations). Furthermore, the idea of making up for the aporia of time via poesis does not imply that there is nothing beyond narrative. Ricœur sees narrative as a decisive mediator between chronological time and subjective lived experience, yet he recognizes that there are aspects of time that narrative per se cannot apprehend or assume, and that what happens does not already have the form of narrative.

Sabina Loriga

Paul Ricœur, *Temps et récit*, tome 1, *L'intrigue et le récit historique*, tome 2, *La configuration dans le récit de fiction*, tome 3, *Le temps raconté* (Paris: Éditions du Seuil ["L'Ordre philosophique"], 1985). Republished by Points ("Essais"), 1991. Translated into English by Kathleen McLaughlin, David Pellauer, and Kathleen Blamey as *Time and Narrative*, 3 vols. (Chicago: University of Chicago Press, 1984, 1985, 1988).

1986

RISK SOCIETY: BECK ANNOUNCES SCIENCE'S SELF-DISENCHANTMENT

When Ulrich Beck (1944–2015) published *Risikogesellschaft* (*Risk Society*), he was already a recognized intellectual in Germany. Selling 60,000 copies in five years, the book reached an audience far beyond academia and profoundly influenced German political ecology. No doubt the book's success was partly due to its tone: rather than setting out the results of rigorous empirical research, it is an essay in which Beck readily adopts a polemical stance, and his prime objective is to pinpoint the specificities of contemporary societies.

He thus puts forward a general theory of modern societies. The book primarily examines contemporary individualism, analyzing how it reconfigures social inequalities, together with gender relations, the family, and work, not to mention science and technology. The key idea is that of "reflexivity." Thus, while contemporary individualism leads to each of us being progressively emancipated from the institutions characterizing industrial society (social class, the nuclear family, etc.), this emancipation results from our capacity—and indissociably the injunction—to construct and redirect our own biographical trajectory. By virtue of social organization, the latter is increasingly less determined by tradition or class and, formally, depends more and more on our own decisions. That is why individualism may be said to be reflexive: We are led to question what we are, especially what we wish to become, to call into question what was previously described and accepted as self-evident. Carrying on from this book, translated into English in 1992 yet into French only in 2001, Beck worked with other theoreticians of reflexive modernity such as Anthony Giddens and Scott Lash.

Still, it is mainly what Beck has to say about science and risk that won it notoriety. The idea of reflexivity plays a key role here once again, with Beck distinguishing two phases in the process of scientific rationalization that progressively reshaped our societies. First, science applied its methodical doubt to nature and to men, thus helping to "disenchant" the world: This was the era of "simple modernity." Then, over the course of the twentieth century, science started to apply this approach to itself, examining its hypotheses, calling into doubt its tools, methods, and results along with their social and environmental consequences. Science thus disenchanted itself, torpedoing any faith in progress at the same time. Beck notes that the human and social sciences have played a crucial role in this demystification of science, particularly the epistemology and sociology of science and knowledge.

With the development of the reflexive modern era, contemporary sciences now produce partial, provisional, contested knowledge. They have become "balkanized," and we are witnessing a process in which science, quasi-science, and pseudo-science are being placed on the same level, and in which the latter may turn "science's" own arguments back against it. Beck describes science as a sort of supermarket, in which we may each choose between multiple competing forms of knowledge in the light of our beliefs and interests. Science is therefore in a state of structural crisis, especially as it is confronted with new risks that it helped cause but about which it is incapable of producing stable consensual knowledge for tackling them. These new risks are the primarily the by-products of wealth-producing activities, involving a sizable dollop of science. They are also invisible, escaping detection by our senses, unlike the wealth produced, thus facilitating their silent proliferation. Lastly, they often pose risks of such unprecedented scale as to be "democratic," since no one may ultimately escape them. Beck here refers to the many microscopic pollutants we inhale and ingest on a daily basis without anybody really knowing what the consequences on our health might be. But it was ultimately current affairs that best illustrated his analyses, decisively contributing to their success. *Risikogesellschaft* came out in 1986, the same year as the Chernobyl nuclear catastrophe, while the BSE crisis (also called mad cow disease) occurred just a few years after the book was translated into English. And what are radioactive dust or prions other than invisible risks we cannot apprehend from which no one may escape, produced by economic activities assisted by science?

From this point of view, the book's success is paradoxically best illustrated by the obsolescence of some of its theses. Nowadays, many "new risks" are no longer proliferating silently; rather, they are triggering widespread concern, and outcry even. Not all those who worry have read Beck, but all have experienced some of the crises and catastrophes that he announced. Additionally, the idea of reflexive modernity, though giving rise to stimulating criticism, continues to be of use. Perhaps the most fertile of Beck's analyses relates to the disenchantment of science through developments in the sociology of science and its analysis of controversy. It is revealing that Brian Wynne was one of the authors of the foreword to the English edition while the French edition's foreword was written by Bruno Latour, both eminent figures in science studies. At a time when many commentators are speaking of "post-truth" or a "post-factual" society, it may no doubt be useful to reread the bracing analyses of the status of truth in contemporary societies by an author who considered the prefix "post" to be the defining word of our era.

Patrick Peretti-Watel

Ulrich Beck, *Risikogesellschaft: Auf dem Weg in eine andere Moderne* (Frankfurt: Suhrkamp, 1986). Translated into English by Mark Ritter as *Risk Society: Towards a New Modernity* (London: Sage, 1992).

1987

THE CULTURAL USES OF PRINT IN EARLY MODERN FRANCE: CHARTIER AND THE CULTURAL HISTORY OF THE SOCIAL REALM

Usages, skills, and acumen; tactics, repurposings, and deviations; differential appropriations rather than univocal effects; multiple divides rather than hierarchies: The history of the "cultural course taken by France from the sixteenth to the nineteenth century" as proposed by Roger Chartier (born 1945) in this collection of articles depicts a complex, multiple, shifting social realm in early modern France. It injects a lexicon centered on actors' dispositions and practices into social history, building up a vision attentive to social dynamics and how individuals of the past constructed the meaning of their existence. Against a fixed description of a world divided into the people and the elites, against a chronology that takes the seventeenth century as a radical break (with an absolutist state and the Catholic Reformation), against the opposition between traditional oral culture and a modernity based on the written word, the book plots a course that complexifies and recomposes the sociocultural landscape of early modern France. This reconfiguration is based on a radical critique of the concept of "popular culture": Michel de Certeau, in "La beauté du mort," written with Dominique Julia and Jacques Revel in 1970, had pointed out how the very idea and interest in popular culture was grounded "in that which suppresses it," in reifying it in its forms and contents, in shearing it of any subversive dimension. Chartier takes this refutation a step further, displaying the complexity of ancien régime *cultures*. He points out the extent to which writing penetrated worlds where literacy held little or no sway, questions the watertight division between oral societies and worlds of writing, and shows how any disciplinary or constraining mechanisms contained in written objects (on what constitutes a good death, on civility, etc.) secretes "tactics which subvert it" and how any divulgation of a cultural model gives rise to new practices of distinction.

This is not a matter of coming up with an account to replace one that preceded it. Chartier presents a series of studies on *questions* (town dwellers' practices concerning the printed word, peasants' reading) and on *corpuses* ("arts of dying," civility manuals, the "Bibliothèque bleue"), all acting as windows onto singular yet linked cultural worlds. Reading is at the heart of the book, but not just as an object of research: By endowing reading with all the density of a signifying social action, Chartier overturns how historians relate to their printed sources. Historians of early modern French culture, such as Robert Mandrou, had often identified textual *contents* with social groups—people and elites. *Lectures et lecteurs dans la France d'Ancien Régime* first emphasizes the "usages of literate texts by readers who were not literate," and vice versa. The social characteristics of culture are thus to be identified in terms of usages and practices. The three studies on the "Bibliothèque bleue" (cheap works produced in Troyes from the sixteenth to the nineteenth century) point out how they constantly reused texts from the learned tradition together with literary novelties: The printers and publishers in Troyes adapted, cut up, and recomposed these writings in a common publishing format that circulated in town and countryside alike. While it is impossible to identify a "popular culture" with specific texts and forms, Chartier describes how these publishers, in setting out these works for printing, incorporated the representations they had of their readers' skills: the short paragraphs of the "livres bleus" with their simplified plots, often punctuated by images, implicitly postulate discontinuous, halting, and elementary reading.

This brings about a major methodological shift. For by paying attention to the *materiality of the written word* and to *setting out works for printing*, the written word, printed material, and books become, *as objects*, the sources for a sociocultural history focusing on practices. It is no longer a matter of just noting the unequal distribution of printed works in inventories drawn up when people died, which can only tell us about the limited social worlds of the wealthiest and nothing at all about practices. Instead, the printed work becomes the archive of its usages, via ways of setting out texts for printing, their materiality, their formal aspects, page layouts, typographical choices, all of which postulate types of reading and possible usages for writings. This is one of the main thrusts in Chartier's work, in dialogue with a sociology of texts that had been renewed by the "material bibliography" of Donald McKenzie and with examination into the expectations of readers stemming from a critical reading of "reception aesthetics." But it does not stop there. For *Lectures et lecteurs dans la France d'Ancien Régime* also paved the way to a renewal in the political history of early modern France. In 1990, in *Les origines culturelles de la Révolution française* (*The Cultural Origins of the French Revolution*), Chartier returned to reading practices and the circulation of printed material, emphasizing their role in the process of desacralization characterizing the final decades of the eighteenth century. The impact of books stemmed both from their subversive content and from a way of reading that no longer respected meaning-prescribing authorities. This reveals just how far Chartier had traveled from the history of ideas dominating understanding of the Enlightenment.

In encouraging social and political historians as well as text specialists to examine how printed material was used, and to envisage them in their materiality, Chartier taught us to not decide in advance what we think we know about the cultural behavior of men and women of the past. For the history of reading practices is alert to what eludes it, to the actual singular, ephemeral appropriations that leave no traces. And this disquiet is one of the lasting lessons of his book.

Judith Lyon-Caen

Roger Chartier, *Lectures et lecteurs dans la France d'Ancien Régime* (Paris: Éditions du Seuil ["L'Univers historique"], 1987). Translated into English, with two additional chapters, by Linda G. Cochrane as *The Cultural Uses of Print in Early Modern France* (Princeton, NJ: Princeton University Press, 1987).

1987

FAMILY FORTUNES: DAVIDOFF AND HALL ANALYZE THE CO-CONSTRUCTION OF GENDER AND CLASS

By 1987, a new "gender history" was fast emerging from the various social and cultural histories produced by feminist historians in the 1960s and early 1970s. No longer content merely to add women to a historical narrative from which they had been excluded, scholars such as Caroline Bynum, Jacqueline Jones, and Christiane Klapisch (to name but a few) sought instead to write histories of women *and* men, of masculinity *and* femininity, and thus explore the multiple ways in which these two categories are always mutually constructed. As we shall see, *Family Fortunes* played an important role in this larger effort to cast gender as a *relational* concept. This move would allow scholars to locate ideas about gender difference and gendered structures of inequality at the heart of more global histories of society, culture, and politics. But the book was also written in dialogue with those historians and sociologists who were studying processes of class formation in modern Britain. The prologue by Catherine Hall (born 1946) and Leonore Davidoff (1932–2014) thus announces that theirs is a study of the "institutions and practices of the English middle-class from the late eighteenth to the mid nineteenth centuries [which] concern both men and women." In language that echoes Edward P. Thompson's pathbreaking book on the formation of the British working class, the authors further state their conviction that "gender and class always operate together, and that consciousness of class always takes a gendered form."

This ambitious program was received by some with a mixture of suspicion and disdain. Often these reviews were marked by their authors' fear of the threat that so-called militant research posed to the alleged neutrality of a long historical tradition that, in fact, focused solely on the activities of men. Norman McCord thus asserted that *Family Fortunes* could hardly be considered a work of scholarship, thanks to its authors' "tenacious devotion" to "preconceived dogmas," while Harold Perkin declared that "Hall and Davidoff were blinded" by a feminist agenda that rendered them "incapable" of understanding the feelings of "dutifully dedicated and willfully contented wives and mothers."[1]

But in 1987, the time had passed when research into women and gender could be pushed to one side by the dismissive readings of the most conservative guardians of the profession and its masculine hierarchies. Hence, *Family Fortunes* also sparked great interest—critical interest, to be sure, but serious and engaged nonetheless—from feminist, Marxist, and Marxist feminist historians, for whom the book opened many new perspectives. Forty years later, its importance is confirmed by the fact that its then-novel thesis—that gender is central to class formation—now strikes us as obvious. Yet once we resituate the book in the context of the late 1980s, we can clearly see the extent to which *Family Fortunes* transformed social history by demonstrating how the formation of social classes is always fashioned by gender relations. Hall and Davidoff's theses were strikingly new at the time: Miriam Slater applauded their abandonment of a strict division between the public and private in favor of an approach that stresses their interconnection, while John Gillis stated that *Family Fortunes* had "transformed" our way of thinking about the period, offering historians and sociologists alike a "model" for studying the family in other contexts or moments of history.

This enthusiastic reception has at least four roots: One is the authors' insistence that identities are necessarily gendered and that the organization of sexual difference is central to social organization. Second is their novel

---

[1] See Norman McCord, review of *Family Fortunes: Men and Women of the English Middle Class, 1780–1850*, by Leonore Davidoff and Catherine Hall, *English Historical Review* 103, no. 409 (October 1988): 996; and Harold Perkin's review in *Economic History Review* 41, no. 2 (May 1988):309.

understanding of gender categories as unstable, caught up in processes of construction, contestation, and reconfiguration that continually play out within social practices and institutions. Drawing on Gramsci, Hall and Davidoff argue that these processes give rise to diverse, even conflicting, perceptions of gender roles and that this plurality of meaning creates spaces for negotiation and change. Yet there is always an apparently unified "common sense" to gender distinctions that arches over and above these diverse interpretations, concealing their existence behind a seemingly unified structure and significance. Third, the authors repeatedly demonstrate that the boundaries between public and private are in fact porous and mobile and that the family, as an institution binding the market to the domestic sphere, acts as a mediator between the public and private spheres. Finally, the idea of studying men too as gendered beings, and the conviction that masculinity was itself a social construct, meant that *Family Fortunes* heralded later work in masculinity studies.

The book thus played a crucial role in elaborating a new history of gender. It did this by drawing on a vast range of family and literary sources: marriage records, wills, letters, diaries, archives of family businesses and local associations, censuses, together with songs, poetry, and novels written by doctors, priests, and local authors. With its ambitious and precise use of the techniques of social history, *Family Fortunes* provides an alternative to Joan Scott's "Gender: A Useful Category of Historical Analysis" (1986), published just a few months previously, which advocates a post-structuralist approach based on the principle that gendered categories are constructed through discourse and representations rather than at the level of practices. During the ensuing "theory wars"—fierce conflicts over the most useful methods for furthering thought about women and gender—*Family Fortunes* would inspire an entire generation of historians attentive to the force of social practices and structures.

The book was finally translated into French in 2014, illustrating a certain lack of permeability in nineteenth-century French history to works in English. But the French edition came out in a climate of resistance to neoliberalism and the crisis of capitalism. *Family Fortunes* thus found a new public, one that was attracted by renewed interest in the idea of class and the increasingly widespread sentiment that, whatever their field of expertise, historians can ill afford to sideline the gendered dimensions of their research.

Laura Lee Downs

Leonore Davidoff and Catherine Hall, *Family Fortunes: Men and Women of the English Middle Class, 1780–1850* (Chicago: Chicago University Press, 1987).

1988

THE GENDER OF THE GIFT: STRATHERN TURNS GENDER INTO A CAPACITY FOR ACTION

In 1988, anthropologists of Melanesia discovered a book with a most perplexing title, content, and style. *The Gender of the Gift* was a radical departure from what had hitherto been written about this part of the world, transforming gender from a property of people into a capacity for acting and relating.

Since the mid-1970s, Papua New Guinea had been the subject of many ethnographic works by women who, driven by the feminist wave, suspected male bias in the works of certain of their male counterparts. Marilyn Strathern (born 1941) was a good ten years ahead of them in devoting her research to women's activities and their scope for action among a population of the New Guinea Highlands, the Melpa (or Hagen). She had discovered that persons were defined as men or women on the basis not so much of fixed attributes than of modes of action: namely, production (of trade goods) for women and transaction for men, in a society where the main collective affair was ceremonial and competitive exchange between groups.

In the early 1980s, Strathern's thoughts on gender in Melanesia were stimulated by criticism from other women working on Melanesia and feminists who accused her of falling into the trap of male bias or of deeming that anthropology and feminism sat awkwardly with each other. Her willingness to consider feminism with the distance and lack of concession that is part of any rigorous analysis was probably perceived as a lack of loyalty by female colleagues involved in debates seeking to make their mark in the public sphere.

As indicated by the subtitle, *Problems with Women and Problems with Society in Melanesia*, the book associates thinking on the discipline and its analytical categories with an interpretation of the world of Melanesian ideas and practices based on two of its pillars: gender and gift. The result of this vast undertaking was to fundamentally alter the way English-speaking anthropology analyzed the forms of social life and ideas in this region of the South Pacific. French anthropology, however, was not immediately affected.

The book is based on the idea that for Melanesians, the concepts of society and culture are not entirely relevant, making it necessary to find an alternative that is neither holistic nor individualistic in order to make sense of the way these peoples think and act together. Using a critique of both "pre-feminist" and feminist approaches, *The GOG*—as the book is commonly called—seeks to bring to light a set of ideas and practices in which many collective activities consist in unmaking relations, in disassembling them, thereby revealing their hidden significations and causing that which was invisible to rise to the surface. These symbolic processes of representation are implemented during sequences of events, most often ritualized, an analysis of which makes it possible to apprehend the Melanesian way of being related to each other ("sociality").

People and objects are at the heart of these processes. The notion of "dividual person," taken from McKim Marriott, emphasizes the diverse influences bearing on and constituting persons. The person, Marilyn Strathern notes, is a microcosm of relations who begins life as the product of others' actions. Children are thus said to be "complete" or "cross-sex" because they issue from the mixing of paternal and maternal substances. Because of this completeness, they are incapable of reproduction. A child subsequently becomes an "incomplete," "same-sex," or "single-sex" person after a symbolic detachment or extraction of a part of themselves (through a rite involving bloodletting, for example). It is only then that they are capable of reproduction and, more generally, of being an agent. According to Strathern's model, a person's life is thus conceived as alternating variable internal states that bring relational states to light. For, though not defined by Strathern, the key word is "relation," a concept that Melanesian society erects as a value, that is, "with which it works."

208   *The Gender of the Gift*

The Gender of the Gift is brimming with ideas, giving the impression that it mirrors the Melanesian ethnographic material the author is seeking to make sense of: It is never understood once and for all, and one has to revisit it to discover hidden levels, those which were inaccessible on first reading. Alfred Gell did the readers a great service by producing diagrams and drawings in a paper humorously called "Strathernograms" (1999), depicting Strathern's hypotheses on the "partible person," on the relations in which a domestic pig is embedded, or on the "mediated" or "unmediated" nature of the relations between human beings, depending on whether or not an object circulates between them.

It is also Gell who mischievously described the set of ideas built by Marilyn Strathern in *The GOG* as the "system M," with M standing for Melanesia or Marilyn as one preferred. He probably thus wished to signal an ambiguity: Was the "system M" the mode of thinking of each of the populations whose ethnographic descriptions are analyzed by Marilyn Strathern, or was it a common denominator smoothing over variability and never genuinely represented anywhere? Be that as it may, *The Gender of the Gift* has provided plentiful food for thought for anthropologists of Melanesia and further afield, and it has made a permanent mark on gender research.

Pascale Bonnemère

Marilyn Strathern, *The Gender of the Gift: Problems with Women and Problems with Society in Melanesia* (Berkeley: University of California Press, 1988).

1989

PRIMATE VISIONS: HARAWAY FINDS IN PRIMATOLOGY TOOLS FOR RADICAL PROTEST

While France was celebrating with great publishing and republican pomp the bicentenary of the French Revolution, Donna Haraway (born 1944) published her first major work, *Primate Visions*, a 500-page illustrated octavo. This comprehensive survey provides both a history of knowledge about primates and a political history of the invention of the West. Repurposing Foucault, who had repurposed Clausewitz, Donna Haraway states that "primatology is politics by other means." Knowledge about primates is interpreted as a complex scientific construct "of self and other, culture and nature, human and animal, of what is defined as purpose and resource, actor and acted upon."

Knowledge in primatology here transpires as so many deeds to produce the West and man. The Enlightenment "man" (not mankind) of knowledge, the universal male of instrumental reason, man as political subject, the white man of the industrial period, man the colonizer, man the grabber of nature. Haraway's enterprise is a genealogy unbound. For her object is precisely to question the boundaries modernity erects between science and non-science, culture and nature, man and woman, human and animal, Westerner and colonized.

Primates, the objects of inquiry, are situated at the symptomatic place where these great devices are inscribed. They are the mirror of how "we" (white rational modern man, hence excluding the possibility of a female author) have gone about writing "our" great scientific, political, and racial narratives of the production and transformation of the world, of the domination and exclusion of "others." As a historian and anthropologist of science, a feminist theoretician attuned to the powerful voices of Black feminism, Haraway questions the whiteness and masculinity of this "we" whose neutrality went unquestioned in bicentenary France—a France where inquiring into the universality of the republican model or the situated nature of the production of knowledge was violently slapped down and which was closed to all *foreign* incursions, to any of the reflexive critique embodied in the various "studies."

Primate Visions transports us to many places and many attempts to study primates, man's origin, the history of evolution, or to understand man on the basis of the animal; the rhesus monkey that gives its name to the system for classifying human blood has long been used as material for experiments in science laboratories. The reader thus moves through a patiently reconstructed world, from the museum to the laboratory, to the zoo, up into space (with the first apes sent there), then "to paradise" when the first female primate ethologists (such as Jane Goodall) were placed in the spotlight, like vestal virgins at nature's bedside in the garden of Eden.

The book casts its net wide: the gorillas presented in the diorama at the New York Museum of Natural History (hunted, naturalized, and staged "naturally" as an American nuclear family); the baby macaque tortured by Harry Harlow in his behavioral psychology laboratory (and whose suffering fueled psychosocial doxa about how to assist single-parent, mainly Black families in 1950s America); the wise Ham (the first cyborg chimpanzee whose acronym, bestowed by science, came from the "Holloman Aerospace Medical Center") who was sent into space to explore the allotopic future of a Western civilization saturated in technology; the countless gardens provided by tropical milieus for exploring and hierarchizing (human and animal) species, the natural living environment for primates, and the resource-world defined by the West as "third world." The stories might change but all are an inextricable tangle of science and society.

The work is empirical and theoretical, unparalleled and non-reproducible, but it lit a fuse under the perception of the Enlightenment as a hardworking positivist workshop for the social sciences; it also lit a fuse under the "hard" sciences and their exegetes. Against decades of rhetoric asserting the purity of science, whose internal logic was exulted in all ignorance of what was deemed to be "external" (social structures, cultural and social environments, relationships of domination and power), Haraway proposed a radical, excoriating, and learned reading of the sciences forming primatology and of how primatology was shaped and conditioned by these worlds. Coming after her earlier work, *A Cyborg Manifesto* (1984), which resonated worldwide, *Primate Visions* established Haraway as one of the major voices in social studies of science, cultural studies, and feminist critique of the sciences (in the wake of Evelyn Fox Keller, Sandra Harding, and Carolyn Merchant). The biologist Anne Fausto-Sterling, a pioneer in the field, hailed it as a major work defining "new standards" for writing the history of science that she felt "difficult to surpass."

Primate Visions is one of the high points in an oeuvre being constantly rewritten, in critical dialogue with Bruno Latour, Isabelle Stengers, and Vinciane Despret. Haraway's oeuvre, drawing on the work of disciples, activists, and artists who at times use her works in new ways, is driven by the relation to the animal world, which became one of her main objects of inquiry: examining the human condition as a biosocial condition but also the "nature" of *our* "species relations" and the type of policies we may adopt toward environments within which we co-evolve, transforming both them and us.

Primate Visions is a vast undertaking, poaching and filching across epistemic and political boundaries. It is also an amazing workshop for writing history and narrating possibilities for the present. In 1989, in the dying days of Marxism, Donna Haraway sketched out new maps of power and knowledge. Fausto-Sterling, who acknowledges that she lost her "innocence" on reading this book, asks whether "historians will henceforth work open-eyed, or else continue to live in ignorance?"

Delphine Gardey

Donna J. Haraway, *Primate Visions: Gender, Race, and Nature in the World of Modern Science* (New York: Routledge, 1989).

1990

GENDER TROUBLE: BUTLER SOWS TROUBLE IN GENDER

Where we have been accustomed to thinking of the difference between the (two) "sexes" as a biological universal, the social sciences introduced the idea of "gender" to think about cultural variability. From one society to the next, the role of women and of men differ or are even inverted. With Margaret Mead, it became clear that if there are cultures where the sexual division of labor does not correspond to the models we deemed "natural," it is because biology has nothing to do with the definition of social roles. Equally, the existence of societies where there are more than two "genders," where one is not necessarily classified as a "woman" or a "man," reinforces the idea that gender is a social category that is indifferent to the lessons of biology. In psychology too, research by Robert Stoller and sex reassignment operations on newborns by John Money not only showed that one could equally well produce a social man as a social woman from a given biological substrate but also that "gender" was imposed on individuals by formatting their very anatomy even. Thus "gender" was definitively emancipated from "sex."

When Judith Butler (born 1956) published *Gender Trouble* in 1990, with the subtitle *Feminism and the Subversion of Identity*, she reshuffled the cards in the sex/gender dichotomy. The concept of "sex" left the biological terrain and entered the feminist sphere, being just as much a cultural construct as gender. Far from "sex" forming the architectonic ground onto which "gender" differences were then grafted, "perhaps it was always already gender, with the consequence that the distinction between sex and gender turns out to be no distinction at all." She thus posits the primacy of gender, which becomes "this construction of 'sex' as the radically unconstructed," with the latter only emerging subsequently.

Borrowing the concept of performance from the philosopher of language John L. Austin, Butler argues that individuals become "gendered" through what they do. But certain parodic performances "really sow trouble," where others end up being domesticated and circulating "as instruments of cultural domination." This "gender performance" paves the way to queer thought and practices. *Gender Trouble* thus theorizes the subversion and deconstruction of norms by the subject. But is this not an illusion?

While *Gender Trouble* stands out for being positioned within the field of psychoanalysis, particularly through its discussion of Joan Riviere's concept of "masquerade," Butler additionally conducts a biting critique of the gendered norms of cultural intelligibility: those which "institute and maintain relations of coherence and continuity among sex, gender, sexual practice, and desire." Assigning an individual to a "sex" brings with it a gender identity linked to an obligation to desire a member of the opposite gender and sex—what Butler calls the "heterosexual matrix." This heterosexual imperative makes certain identifications possible while excluding or disavowing others. Thus far, from asserting the individual's freedom concerning their gender, Butler thinks of it as a restrictive system: gender is what institutes the fact that *there are two sexes*.

Gender is thus defined as the sustained "stylization of the body," making the body a product of repetition. More generally, the body, and particularly its "sex," becomes a particularly dense site of power. In the wake of Michel Foucault, Butler thinks through the "disciplinary production of gender" as a set of regulatory, discursive, and physical practices producing a "significant corporeality," a "viable" identity. Our sexual identities, gender, and sexuality are not "chosen" but produced by different processes of incorporation and interiorization, which are mainly hidden from view.

Gender Trouble attracted much criticism, some based on misreading. Against Butler's idea of the body as fashioned by political forces, in whose interest it is that the body continue be constituted by "sex markers," it has been argued that materiality is not the effect of power. The idea of the body has thus been included on the charge sheet brought against the post-structuralist current and Derridean deconstruction: In Butler's world, it is said, all is "text," all is "construction" and "language games." This reception was even more accentuated in France, where Cynthia Kraus's translation was only published in 2005, fifteen years after the original, at a time when the notion of "social construct" had become a topic of fierce debate.

Butler responded to these criticisms with *Bodies That Matter: On the Discursive Limits of "Sex"* (1993). But once again, from the title onward, the word "sex" only ever appears in scare quotes. For Butler, thinking the matter of bodies necessarily leads to other domains, so that *materiality* is approached solely through the political processes of *materialization*. The category of sex is normative: It constitutes a "regulatory practice which produces the body it governs," or a "regulatory ideal" in Foucault's meaning of the term. Butler attributes the subject with "originary complicity with power," which means that becoming a subject is necessarily a subjectivation. It is always by citing power that the *I* may accede to existence and take a lasting hold there. This way of thinking about subjection or becoming a subject, absorbing power the better to subvert it, is debatable, particularly from a psychoanalytic point of view that invites us to remove the subject from the subjection/subjectivation dichotomy.

Gender Trouble is a brilliant demonstration of the impossibility of acceding to nondiscursive sex, showing that all discourse about sex conveys power relations. But enclosing the subject in a world without any externality seems a questionable way of conceiving the emergence of resistance and of plotting the path toward transforming the world.

Thierry Hoquet

Judith Butler, *Gender Trouble: Feminism and the Subversion of Identity* (New York: Routledge, 1990).

1990

LE CARREFOUR JAVANAIS: LOMBARD RESHUFFLES THE CARDS OF GLOBAL HISTORY

Le carrefour javanais: Essai d'histoire globale (The Javanese crossroads: Toward a global history) stands out for the extent of its documentary material, for its spatial and temporal scale, and for its arguments. While this masterwork by Denys Lombard (1938–1998) focuses on the period from the late fifteenth to the first half of the twentieth century, Lombard does not shy away from mentioning the latest developments in prehistoric research or tackling very contemporary issues. Additionally, the Java in question is in no way limited to the coasts of the eponymous island, since it acts as a confluence basin where "influences" converge from distant origins, all of which, be they Indian, Chinese, Islamic, or European, take root and sprout hybrid growths on an archaic local "substrate."

To paraphrase Michelet, the worlds of Asia, the Middle East, and especially Europe are not too much to explain Java. But from the outset, the book subverts the intuitive hierarchy between significant "influences." The first volume sets the tone in providing an inventory not only of the legacies but also the "limits" of "Westernization," for perhaps the encounter with Europe—with the Portuguese as of the 1510s, then the Dutch and British in the following decades—was not the determining event: In any case, Java long remained confined to the limited arenas of coastal forts and factories. Some of the basic features of Javanese thought owe next to nothing to Europe, such as the categories of time and space, carried over from India at the time of the great Hindu-Buddhist empires, or the idea of a reflexive "self," a refuge in mystical rapport with God, stemming from the "Islamic stimulus" washing over the archipelago in the age of the sultanates. While the European vein is often the most visible, it is not necessarily the most precious, sparkling misleadingly like mica.

The other two volumes of the book examine deeper seams, the "Asian networks" and the "legacy of concentric kingdoms," respectively, where the latter expression refers to the Javanese political orders, the *negara* carved out of the forest and whose ritual sovereignty was distributed iteratively in accordance with the Buddhist model of the *mandala*. Lombard is certainly one of the first authors to make us appreciate how much the "Southeast Asian Mediterranean" owes to its regional environment. The reference to Braudel—which contributed to the book's initial fortune—is no mere hat-doffing: if the Indonesian world forms a "Mediterranean," it is primarily because it is a series of "little seas" linking up fractions of territories with deep economic and political ties.

Despite their powerful steamers, neither the British, who settled on the Malay Peninsula and in northern Borneo, nor the Dutch, who expanded their hold over virtually all the archipelago in a series of jumps, managed to exert full mastery over these maritime spaces. In the eighteenth and nineteenth centuries, "aquatic societies" of reef and foreshore gatherers entirely concentrating on long-distance trade and seafaring kingdoms, like that of the Bugis, continued to operate along the borderlands and in the interstices of European domination. The peoples of the Straits provided pearls, tortoiseshell, and sea cucumbers (*trepang*) for the Chinese market, forming the subaltern segment in long-distance trade networks, the first link in these "Asian networks" with which Europeans, being unable to control them, had to broker arrangements.

If there was a "Westernization" with powerful repercussions, it was brought about by "Islamization." The Islamization of the Indonesian world progressed in fits and starts, and while its exact chronology remains open to debate, a conservative estimate places its beginnings in the mid-fourteenth century. According to Lombard, this marked the arrival of a specific modernity. For several months each year, the sultanates lying along the course of ships following the trade winds were home to monsoon passengers, Yemeni, Gujarati, and Chinese merchants loading cargoes of spices, rare resins, and sea produce, then patiently waiting for the winds to turn. These political units were thus, by necessity, contract societies based on commercial transactions surrounded by myriad guarantees, as under the Malacca laws (circa 1450–1470). Lombard makes the pioneering suggestion that this model of contractual relation, which recognizes *equality in* law if not *legal equality* between the signatories, was not limited to the domain of merchant transactions. Thus, the *Taj us-Salatin*, composed in 1603, modeled on Arabic and Persian "princes' mirrors," proposes a specifically contractualist version of relations between the *raja* and his people (*rakyat*), bound by a set of reciprocal obligations, respecting which prevents toppling into tyranny and dissent (*fitnah*). Lombard's analyses, presenting Islam as the source of literary, political, and philosophical modernity, not as a lead blanket weighing down on individual consciences and public freedoms, are as topical as ever.

So, is this dazzling fresco of the Indonesian world an "essay in global history"? Yes, provided the pattern is not British- or American-style global history, which anachronistically peoples its vast social deserts with capitalized entities, but rather the "total history" dear to the Annales school. Shunning any teleology, the analysis passes from one order of causality to another, embracing the "short time" of literary events and the "cyclical time" of economic conjunctures and of transformations to literary concepts and canons. *Le carrefour javanais* is a choral chronicle of a contact zone, carefully catching in full each horizon of historicity in play. It may thus be deemed a precursor to "connected history."

Romain Bertrand

Denys Lombard, *Le carrefour javanais: Essai d'histoire globale*, tome 1, *Les limites de l'occidentalisation*, tome 2, *Les réseaux asiatiques*, tome 3, *L'héritage des royaumes concentriques* (Paris: Éditions de l'EHESS, 1990).

1991

THE MIDDLE GROUND: RICHARD WHITE AND INTERCULTURAL ACCOMMODATIONS

The fourth book by Richard White (born 1947) came out when he was a professor at the University of Washington (Seattle). In 1991, this prolific author published an overview of the American West (*"It's Your Misfortune and None of My Own": A New History of the American West*) as well as *The Middle Ground*, a more ambitious work that invented a new way of apprehending the history of contact between Europeans and Amerindians. This dense book of over 500 pages is a masterstroke. The concept of the middle ground, an intermediary place of understanding where cultures mingle and create agreements, soon became a key reference in historical scholarship. It rendered obsolete the earlier yet persistent framework of analysis: that of the frontier, the line separating colonized zones from "virgin" lands, which according to Frederick Jackson Turner (1893) had acted as the melting pot for the singular characteristics of American democracy.

On its publication, *The Middle Ground* won plaudits from North American historians, along with many prizes. It established White as one of the leading American historians and thereby helped normalize Amerindian history. Yet White was not the first to slate Turner's thesis, which was judged too ethnocentric and teleological. His two 1991 books in fact flowed from three currents in historical scholarship that were very active at the time: new Indian history, which emerged on American campuses in the late 1960s, seeking to make Amerindians the actors of their history and to give them a "voice"; environmental history, examining the history of Indians from the angle of ecological change; and new western history, which adopted a more inclusive approach to the history of the American West and sought to break with the habitual narrative of the white man's triumph in the "wilderness." Lying at the confluence of these three currents and rejecting "simplistic" accounts of conquest, assimilation, and resistance, White sought to provide American history with "more complex and less linear" stories.

The germ of the book came from a transformation that may be described as "Braudelian." It was initially meant to be built around an illustrious figure, Tecumseh, a Shawnee chief and traditional hero of Indian "resistance" in the early nineteenth century. But as the writing advanced, this figure lost his central place in favor of an exploration of a territory, the Great Lakes region, named the Pays d'en Haut by French settlers in the seventeenth century. Like Philip II in Braudel's *La Méditerranée* (*The Mediterranean*), Tecumseh was finally only studied at the end of the book, as embodying the death throes of the process of intercultural accommodation comprising the middle ground. White's account thus follows a circular path: the middle ground sprang up in the Pays d'en Haut in the mid-seventeenth century, in a region of political importance to the Indians, before disappearing around 1815 when the region vanished.

The Middle Ground is neither a historical portrait of an Amerindian chief nor the history of a "tribe" (along the lines of Bruce G. Trigger's *The Children of Aataentsic: A History of the Huron People to 1660*, published in 1976). Nor does it provide analysis of colonial policies toward Indians, and it pays but scant attention to the cultural transformations affecting native societies. White did not seek to write a history solely from the Indians' viewpoint: Given the lack of adequate sources, such a study struck him as difficult to conduct. By sketching an astonishing series of historical vignettes, drawing on abundant and underexploited colonial sources, some in French, he sets about studying a dynamic process by which the American Indians and the white settlers, placed in a situation of interdependence, forged mixed practices through mutual adjustments. These new practices, White argues, were cobbled together on the basis of the (sometimes biased) understanding each actor had of the other's culture. White thus subtly subjects the idea of the frontier to metamorphosis, for relations between Indians and whites were the locus where "something new" emerged.

Since 1991, *The Middle Ground* has continually influenced how the history of the relation between Europeans and "others" is written. This success, extending far beyond the field of North American history, is no doubt because White in no way skates over the misunderstandings of the encounter even while he emphasizes the possibility of intercultural accommodations. The book also came out at a time when structuralist and culturalist anthropology was on the wane. White was thus able to consolidate suggestions by two influential authors, quoted at the head of his first chapter and introduction. From Eric R. Wolf, he borrowed the idea that we need to historicize so-called primitive societies; that is, these societies, far from being just the victims of the European colonizers, contributed to the advent of the modern world, and it is impossible to study a society by considering it in isolation. And in unison with James Clifford, White denounces historical accounts dominated by an obsession with the purity and authenticity of cultures (or identities). He seeks to de-essentialize the American Indians, whom he sees neither as good ecological savages nor bogged down in tradition. What interests White is not cultural difference itself but the compromises that spring up between cultures and lead to the invention of new norms. He tells us that history is fluidity and always in movement. The contact between Europeans and Amerindians provides a textbook illustration.

Gilles Havard

Richard White, *The Middle Ground: Indians, Empires, and Republics in the Great Lakes Region, 1650–1815* (Cambridge: Cambridge University Press, 1991).

1992

IDENTITY AND CONTROL: HARRISON WHITE AND EMERGING SOCIAL FORMATIONS

In the 1950s, British anthropologists (particularly John Barnes and Elizabeth Bott) studied certain types of relations that emerge through interactions between people or groups and are characterized by crossing borders between the instituted groups. To make sense of the structure such relations form, they forged the idea of a "social network." This laid the groundwork for a research current that has continued to grow, now called "social network analysis." This draws its main ideas from anthropology, together with such varied sources as Georg Simmel's sociology, Jacob Moreno's social psychology, and mathematical graph theory.

Its expansion owed much to North American sociologists specializing in quantitative methods, with Harrison White (born 1930) being a leading proponent. He had initially studied theoretical physics before turning to sociology. After noted work on kinship, art markets, and professional careers viewed as chains of positions within a structure, he shifted his attention to social networks. He proposed new approaches (particularly using the idea of structural equivalence) and taught students who went on to become famous (including Mark Granovetter, Barry Wellman, and John Padgett, among many others) or with whom he renewed economic sociology. Further still, he initiated coherent theoretical thought grounded in network analyses, which had initially been more of a patchwork of different methods. *Identity and Control* is the result. The work was expectantly awaited as the great work that would establish network analysis within the landscape of social science theory.

It in fact went much further. Unlike many network analysts, White did not fall into the trap of making networks a fundamental structure from which the rest of the social world issued. Thus, he did not write a manifesto of "relational sociology" (something others subsequently tried their hand at) but sought rather to rigorously tease out the consequences of a conception of the social world in which "there is no tidy atom and no clear-cut world, only complex striations and long strings repeating as in a polymer goo." Social structures are here perceived as if they were forever emerging, forever transforming, with networks only constituting one form, among others.

The work has seven chapters setting out the main concepts, starting in the first chapter with that of identity, referring either to humans caught up in certain contexts or else to events. From the outset, this concept deconstructs, deflects any idea of person or "actor." The second chapter presents the forms of emerging order—"disciplines." The third examines networks, reduced to their interpretive dimension. Identities generate stories that "weave interpretation into and around relationships, as they then interweave over time into network forms." The fourth chapter then turns to institutions: caste systems (to which university disciplines are compared), clientelism, corporatism, and additionally, anything with a normative dimension. The fifth chapter folds networks and disciplines into the more general concept of style, seen as a source of partial coherence for interpretations which, inter alia, may give meaning to the idea of a person. The sixth chapter seeks to understand how action may emerge in this magma of interacting social forms. A final chapter looks at "rhetorics" (taken in a broadly normative meaning, associated with institutions) and attacks the idea of rationality, before returning to the two fundamental concepts of identity and control.

The text is complex, and often unsettling. It introduces a very large number of concepts in a language specific to White. There are many digressions and a plethora of empirical examples. Suggestions by some of White's colleagues to make the work more accessible and a proposal by French sociologists for a translation led to a collective rewriting (with each chapter now being cosigned), resulting in a second edition, published in English in 2008 and in French in 2011. The subtitle was new (*How Social Formations Emerge*), and the chapters were reordered, with the theme of control (which is not power but the search for footings in a social material seen as a chaos whence partial forms of order emerge) now placed earlier. The chapter on networks comes between those on identities and disciplines. Style now precedes institutions. The concept of regime, a certain balance to institutions, is developed in its own right, and the book closes with a summary formalizing the links between the concepts.

Some books in social sciences initially dazzle their readers but disappoint over the course of subsequent rereadings. But it is the exact opposite with *Identity and Control*: Readers discover new riches each time they revisit it. Andrew Abbott, in a commentary published in *Social Forces* in 1994, explained that the best idea was to first read the entire book to get an overall idea, without stumbling over more difficult passages, then reread the most important parts with this overall idea in mind, sometimes drawing on works by thinkers with a similar outlook to White. Readers who make the effort then discover what, for Abbott, is "one of the truly important books of the past forty years," capable of profoundly transforming how one perceives the social world.

Michel Grossetti

Harrison C. White, *Identity and Control: A Structural Theory of Social Action* (Princeton, NJ: Princeton University Press, 1992).

1993

THE POLITICS OF LARGE NUMBERS: DESROSIÈRES INVESTIGATES THE ONTOLOGY OF STATISTICAL KNOWLEDGE

With two revised editions in French and many translations around the world, *La politique des grands nombres* (*The Politics of Large Numbers*) by Alain Desrosières (1940–2013) is undoubtably the work that dominated the abundant scholarship into the history of statistics in France during the 1990s. The journals that published reviews included many leading publications in such varied fields as sociology, demography, economics, philosophy, history of science, political science, and, of course, statistics.

This visibility stems, first, from the content and scope of the book, which provides a lengthy historical long-term comparative vision of the relationship between statistics and the state, backed up by countless analyses of statistical concepts, methods, debates, and applications. Focusing on the nineteenth and twentieth centuries, the book leads onto a comparative political sociology of France, the United Kingdom, Germany, and the United States, in each case sketching out the different form and place that each accorded to statistics. In arguing that statistical science and administrative statistics only converged and led to a robust construct toward the beginning of the twentieth century, Desrosières conducts an archaeology of ideas (representativeness), tools (probability, means, correlations and regressions, econometrics), and ways of constructing objects (administrative inquiries, polls). The elaboration and practice of statistics appear as a revelatory product of the great changes affecting states during this period, with the concern for unification, the shift from the local to the national, and expansion into social regulation and protection.

The book's success also stems from the fact that, around 1990, the history of statistics was of crucial interest in the social sciences. In the light of Foucault's suggestion of studying *categories* of knowledge and action, it was a "strategic" field of application. Going beyond 1980s-style analysis of representations and constructs of the "social" realm, the book did not shy away from the problem of using numbers to construct objects, in the wake of Lorraine Daston, Ian Hacking, Ted Porter, and the "Bielefeld group." The history of statistics was also furthered by the success of science studies—with Bruno Latour in France—and the anthropology of knowledge, in which the impact of Jack Goody's *The Domestication of the Savage Mind* cannot be overemphasized. Likewise, the 1980s saw state institutions make a noted comeback in history and social sciences. By placing statistics under the dual lens of science and administration, Desrosières gave material form to this confluence between two bubbling currents.

One may further add Desrosière's original sociological stance. Before becoming an administrator at the French national office of statistics—Institut national de la statistique et des études économiques (INSEE)—Desrosières had attended lectures by Pierre Boudieu, from which he retained a critical stance that led him, in a courageous move for a state statistician, to historicize and deconstruct the ideas and methods used by INSEE. In the 1980s he drew fresh inspiration from lines of inquiry opened up by Luc Boltanski and Laurent Thévenot, with whom he had published a work on socio-professional categories five years earlier.

The success of *La politique des grands nombres* benefited from the hopes placed in the "sociology of conventions." Around 1990, it was expected this would provide a way of moving forward from Bourdieusian orthodoxy while also providing a new grounding for economics through an alliance with the social sciences. The central place given in the book to coding and equating is indicative of this thought. This was meant to resolve the dichotomies influencing how statistics was constructed—dichotomies between science and administration, between internalism (big figures and big ideas) and externalism (institutions and policies), between realism (objects in the social world are endowed with intrinsic existence) and relativism (these objects are constructed by statistics).

This theoretical choice was the most discussed aspect at the time. While many commentators praised the book for its ambition and many fields of observation, not only in statistics but also in social and political matters (poverty and unemployment), the issue was also raised of its theoretical framework—more specifically a tension that Desrosières dismissed in the revised edition. Did he truly historicize statistics or, as Libby Schweber wrote in *Revue française de sociologie* in 1996, did he rather seek to characterize its essence, its ontology, without managing to avoid the "ahistorical metaphysical language" of the theory of conventions, as Éric Brian observed in *Genèses* (1992)?

The debate is less obscure than it might seem. One year before *La politique des grands nombres*, a question had been raised concerning the long series established by Olivier Marchand and Claude Thélot in *Deux siècles de travail en France* (Two centuries of work in France, 1991): Is it permissible to aggregate figures produced in incommensurable contexts using incommensurable methods, and if so, how? A quarter of a century later, the question is still not settled and has been raised once again, particularly concerning Thomas Piketty's *Capital au XXI* *siècle* (*Capital in the Twenty-First Century*). Contemporary reception on the use of *La politique des grands nombres* in history, economics, and the social sciences is still divided along the two lines of interpretation put forward at the time of its publication: an analytical critique of how statistics operates, on the one hand, and a call for its greater historical contextualization, on the other. The former does not always avoid the pseudo-Foucauldian reduction of statistics to social control. Since then, the latter has shown that, at a stage well before the twentieth century, the rationality of "science" needs to be tied in closely with that of "administration."

Paul-André Rosental

Alain Desrosières, *La politique des grands nombres: Histoire de la raison statistique* (Paris: La Découverte ["Textes à l'appui"], 1993). Republished by La Découverte-poche, 2000. Translated into English by Camille Nash as *The Politics of Large Numbers: A History of Statistical Reasoning* (Cambridge, MA: Harvard University Press, 1998).

1994

THE AGE OF EXTREMES: HOBSBAWM RECOUNTS THE END OF NINETEENTH-CENTURY BOURGEOIS SOCIETY

The works of Eric J. Hobsbawm (1917–2012), one of the most reputed British historians of the twentieth century, were translated into French at an early stage. It is thus surprising that *The Age of Extremes* is best known in France for the quarrel sparked when several Parisian publishing houses refused to translate it, even though it had already come out in forty or so languages. In 1997, Pierre Nora, whose journal *Le Débat* was devoting a dossier to Hobsbawm, justified this refusal on the grounds of the "Zeitgeist," which was said to disfavor works of Marxist inspiration at a time when the tone seemed to be set by François Furet's 1995 book *Le passé d'une illusion: Essai sur l'idée communiste au XXe siècle* (*The Passing of an Illusion*). In short, there was apparently no chance of this book finding a public in France. The editors of *Le Monde diplomatique*, stung into action, commissioned a translation in 1999, ensuring it met with great success.

From the outset, the book was mired in controversy, no doubt to Hobsbawm's displeasure. There was no denying that he was a politically committed historian, but it must have been hurtful to him to see how certain people in France cast him as crypto-Stalinist author (he had been sidelined from any major academic position in the United Kingdom until 1971 because of his communist beliefs).

The Age of Extremes needs to be taken for what it is: A great overview intended to be used as a textbook, from the same stable as Hobsbawm's three previous books—*The Age of Revolution, Europe, 1789–1848*; *The Age of Capital, 1848–1875*; and *The Age of Empire, 1875–1914*. In fact, these publications were brought out at ten-year intervals (1962, 1975, and 1987). It must also be recognized that ever fewer professional historians are prepared to try their hand at great historical portraits, preferring to take refuge in erudition. It is also no doubt true that Hobsbawm was straying from his specialty, which was the nineteenth century. He combines history and his stories, adding personal memories of "things seen" from his youth wandering around Europe through to his long stays in California and Latin America. As a cosmopolitan internationalist, Hobsbawm is equally attentive to political and social causes as he is to differing cultural practices around the world. Under his pen, great historical trends and events take on particular substance, gaining in intensity, color, and emotion. The historian is here both "engaged spectator" and "participating observer," capable of objectifying the retrospective gaze cast backward over this century of noise and fury or these *Interesting Times*, as the self-ironically understated title of his autobiography put it.

The chronology Hobsbawm adopts holds no surprises. The period from 1914 to 1945 is that of "catastrophes": The "great edifice of nineteenth-century civilization" was swept away by two world wars, general bankruptcy, the first cracks in colonial empires, and the emergence of the Soviet and Nazi regimes (which Hobsbawm, like Moshe Lewin, refuses to interpret through the fallacious prism of "totalitarianism").

The ensuing "golden age," playing out against the backdrop of the Cold War, was dominated by the exceptional thirty-year boom that contemporaries imagined would never end, running until the 1973 oil crisis, which opened a final sequence bluntly described as a "landslide." The long economic crisis was accompanied by a dislocation of democratic countries' political structures and raised questions about the impact of technical revolutions and lifestyle changes, while the gulf of global inequalities expanded unabated. This "short twentieth century" closes on the fall of the Berlin Wall and the collapse of the USSR in 1989–1991.

In this essay, Hobsbawm uses the telescope rather than the microscope, far from the preoccupations of "history from below" characterizing his other works. The virtuosity with which he combines continental, regional, and local scales nevertheless allows him to tease out several key lines of analysis. His canvas is dominated by two major and overlapping collective actors, classes and nations, whose combats he places within an overall economic approach, following in the wake of Marx and Schumpeter. To him, the key question is that of the collapse of nineteenth-century bourgeois liberal society and the successive restructurings of capitalism.

Certain critics regretted that the singularity of events was sometimes glossed over: Hitler's rise to power in January 1933 is barely analyzed, while May 1968 receives cursory treatment. Hobsbawm was also accused of having little to say about Auschwitz or the gulags. Concerning the Holocaust, he answered: "I do not think such horrors can find adequate expression." Hence, curiously, in this century of extreme violence, the victims are reduced to abstract quantities. Another inconvenience of his synoptic approach is that his focus remains more or less centered on Europe, and the revolt by colonized peoples and their transformation into political subjects fail to transpire as a major aspect of the century. Lastly, his supposed indulgence toward the USSR was regretted. In fact, he never denied the crimes of Stalinism, but given that he does not analyze the cogs in the Soviet and gulag machine, he is reduced to presenting them as inevitable, given a context that left no alternative.

The book is nevertheless thrilling, borne aloft by Hobsbawm's great erudition and ability to marshal vast amounts of documentation to tease out global perspectives, all served by his agile style. As he observed, "Historians should not write only for their colleagues." In exposing himself to a different form of criticism, Hobsbawm sought to improve general understanding of the world.

Philippe Minard

Eric J. Hobsbawm, *The Age of Extremes: The Short Twentieth Century, 1914–1991* (London: Michael Joseph, 1994).

1995

FROM MANUAL WORKERS TO WAGE LABORERS: CASTEL AND THE EROSION OF THE WAGE SYSTEM

When Robert Castel (1933–2013) published his most important book, *Les métamorphoses de la question sociale* (*From Manual Workers to Wage Laborers: Transformation of the Social Question*) in 1995, at the age of sixty-one, he was nearing the end of a career for which he was best known for his works on the world of psychiatry, mainly conducted in the 1970s, and more generally, the treatment of mental illness in modern societies. This book, which he had been working on for ten years, thus marked a change in direction.

In fact, the hiatus between the two phases in his career is less radical than it might seem. In the 1980s, before he became a professor at the École des hautes études en sciences sociales (EHESS), Castel had headed a research laboratory examining policies targeting the poor, the relegated, and the disaffiliated (the Groupe de recherche et d'analyse sur le social et la sociabilité). Feeling that he had broadly dealt with the question of psychiatry, he shifted his research focus to job insecurity and flaws in the social protection system. He read with great interest the work of economists of regulation, from whom he borrowed the concept of the wage society—notably, Michel Aglietta and Anton Brender's *Les métamorphoses de la société salariale* (The metamorphoses of wage society, 1984). He had the brilliant idea of placing degradations in the labor market not within the short cycle of economic crisis but, on the contrary, the long cycle in transformations to wage relationships, once again drawing inspiration from Michel Foucault's genealogical approach as he had for his earlier works.

The book's success is of course due to Castel's talent for portraying a broad historical canvas stretching back to the Middle Ages, though the social and political context of the day was also a factor. A few months after the book was published, a powerful movement formed in France—the largest since 1968—to protest against proposed pension reforms. Two years earlier, Pierre Bourdieu and his team had published *La misère du monde* (*The Weight of the World*), to considerable success. In distinguishing poverty resulting from condition from poverty resulting from position, Bourdieu repositioned the question of social exclusion at the heart of society, rather than on its margins, and thus examined how social suffering is produced. With *Métamorphoses*, Castel drove the nail home by arguing that it is not solely on the margins of society that the social question needs to be examined, but also in the erosion of the wage system—that is, in the progressive questioning of the raft of protections and statuses that had allowed the postwar working classes to accede to mass consumption and leisure and to envisage the future with greater tranquility of mind. To demonstrate this, he goes over the long process by which this wage society had emerged since the industrial revolution, from the question of pauperism in the nineteenth century through to the social accomplishments of the twentieth century. The generalization of welfare and of the wage system, and access to social housing and public services, were key stages shaping the link between citizens and society through their participation in the world of work.

After having once been the condition of the poor, the wage system became the elementary form of social integration in a society profoundly organized and regulated around work by the welfare state. But, Castel warned, this could well become a dangerous situation, at least for ever larger swathes of the population. Society as a whole was once again threatened. Castel never stopped hammering out this warning, both in academia, where his book was instantly recognized as a classic, and in many circles of stakeholders, activists, and trade unionists in France and abroad.

Still, the book also has its limits, as Castel was well aware. At the end of his preface, he inserted a note on comparatism justifying his approach. The first half, from the Middle Ages through to the Renaissance, concerns Europe west of the Elba. The work then studies the situation in England through to the late eighteenth century, before zooming in on the French situation to address the transformations of the nineteenth and twentieth century. The problem is that the more we approach the conditions in which the wage society was formed and then eroded, constituting the heart of the work, the more the analysis focuses on the sole example of France. It is striking that there is not a single reference to Gøsta Esping-Andersen's *The Three Worlds of Welfare Capitalism*, published five years earlier, even though it had become a benchmark for international comparison of the wage society. Castel justified his approach by arguing that it was impossible to take different national contexts into account. Nowadays, owing to progress in comparative research, it is clear that *Les métamorphoses de la question sociale* is primarily about the "continental" or "corporatist" regime. The United States and countries close to the "liberal" regime have never built up a raft of statutory protections comparable to those found in France or Germany. The Nordic countries, close to the social democratic regime, have also adopted ways of preventing and regulating social risks, together with policies to reduce inequalities, which are still in striking contrast to other European countries.

Twenty years after the book was first published, it is still a benchmark. It is a treasure trove for historians, sociologists, and political scientists alike, and a magisterial example of what a *history of the present* may be.

Serge Paugam

Robert Castel, *Les métamorphoses de la question sociale: Une chronique du salariat* (Paris: Fayard ["L'Espace du politique"], 1995). Republished by Gallimard ("Folio"), 1999. Translated into English by Richard Boyd as *From Manual Workers to Wage Laborers: Transformation of the Social Question* (New Brunswick, NJ: Transaction Publishers, 2003)

1996

SAINT LOUIS: LE GOFF MEETS SAINT LOUIS

It might seem ironic that Jacques Le Goff (1924–2014), an advocate of "new history" and one of the major representatives of the Annales school, should write a historical biography, *Saint Louis*—about a king, moreover, and favored figure of historians of political events of the most traditional stamp. Was this yielding to fashion or taking an easy option? Or perhaps a ruse, portraying a national glory as cover for examining "Saint Louis's century," the "marvelous thirteenth century" of urban renewal, which saw the birth of universities and the building of cathedrals? Not at all. The content corresponds to what the title unfussily announces: It is Saint Louis himself, the individual Louis IX, from his birth in 1214 through to his death in 1270, with a "life supplement" running through to his canonization in 1297. The book deals with the individual person of the king and, to the extent that a historian may have access to them, his conscience, motivations, fits of anger, and conflictual relations with his mother. After an initial surprise, the reader readily recognizes that it is in fact a highly ambitious book, responding to a real challenge. Jacques Le Goff's conception of "historical biography" is more like an "anti-biography." Throughout, he raises the question of whether it is possible to write such a book, especially given the gaps and biases in the (relatively numerous) sources, many of which are biographies, or hagiographies even, written during the king's lifetime or shortly after his death.

Le Goff even feigns to doubt. "Did Saint Louis exist?" he asks, by which he means: Can the historian, reaching across the centuries, using sources that both reveal and mask the king, *really* approach Saint Louis in his period?

"History as a problem," of the kind dear to Marc Bloch and Lucien Febvre, loses none of its rights. Quite the contrary, since Le Goff deploys all his power of analysis, immense culture, and gifts as a narrator to rethink and legitimize a new "territory for the historian."

The first part of the book is about "Saint Louis's life." Though it follows chronological order, the time of a life is not neutral but flexible and qualitative. Hence the king's existence entered a decisive turn in 1254, on his return from crusade to the Holy Lands and captivity at the hand of the sultan. This ordeal made the king aware of his past faults and of the urgent need to repent. The great reforming ordinance of the kingdom in 1254, the peace with the English crown, then the renewed departure on crusade to Tunis in 1270, all flowed from this. The book's second part, on "the production of royal memory," is a demonstration in method. The central question—"Did Saint Louis exist?"—acquires all its pertinence. How are we to find the "true" Louis in the documents, especially those that already saw the saint behind the figure of the king? The sources are of distinct genres, whose specificities need to be taken into account. For clerics, Louis IX was a new Josiah, the biblical king. Even when Joinville, writing forty years after the death of his royal friend, portrays him speaking his mother tongue, French, and reports his personal memories, can the historian take him at his word? Or should we make do with collecting "isles of truth" on a sea of *topoi*? Le Goff's tour de force consists in turning the question around: For him, the truth is to be sought in these models of royalty, of saintliness even, given the extent to which the king, post-1254, sought to embody them for his contemporaries to the point of appearing to nascent "public opinion" as the new Christ-king, a fact recognized by the pope who canonized him twenty-seven years after his death, but without assimilating him to a martyr. The final part of the book, "Saint Louis, a unique and ideal king," analyzes all the components of this model made flesh. It shows how embodying the ideal figure of the holy king was a deliberate choice, entailing work on himself and on others to appropriate conceptions of royalty and saintliness, some of which were very ancient, others more recent. Revising the conclusions of Marc Bloch, Le Goff shows that Louis IX turned the "royal touch" into a regular rite of the Capetian monarchy. He also shows that he ensured the royal Christly worship of relics would continue by acquiring the crown of thorns for the Sainte Chapelle. The idea of "royal saintliness" underwent a notable shift with Saint Louis. It was no longer centered on the virtues claimed for a sovereign by the Church, but instead valued individual daily suffering, the quest for mortification, without necessarily leading on to the ultimate stage of kingly passion. Le Goff thus sets up a mirror with the other great thirteenth-century saint, Saint Francis, to whom he devoted a series of interlinked articles in 1999. Both Francis and Louis humbly embodied the *imago Christi* among men, including the lowliest, but each in his own fashion: One as a monk preaching in the world, while the other, refusing to yield to the attraction of the friars minor, fully assumed his role as a crowned layman. While the former experienced the grace of stigmata, the latter experienced the uncommon grace of dying in front of Tunis "at the same hour" as Christ.

Le Goff's final great book is also one of his most personal. Not only does he reveal the complexity of models of social action at a crucial period in the formation of Europe, but he also narrates the encounter—one that is not without warmth, empathy, and emotion, despite the passing centuries—between a leading historian and another exceptional man of flesh.

Jean-Claude Schmitt

Jacques Le Goff, *Saint Louis* (Paris: Gallimard ["Bibliothèque des histoires"], 1996). Republished by Gallimard ("Folio"), 2013. Translated into English by Gareth Evan Gollrad as *Saint Louis* (Notre Dame, IN: University of Notre Dame Press, 2009).

1997

THE DIVIDED CITY: LORAUX SHOWS FORGETTING IS CENTRAL TO POLITICS

La cité divisée (*The Divided City*) dazzles by its analysis, by the rigor of its approach, and by the abundance of its insights into the key idea of *stasis*, the division of the city. Nicole Loraux (1943–2003) noted that it was her prototypical work, combining major articles (including "To Forget in the City" and "To Repoliticize the City") and new texts ("And Athenian Democracy Forgot *Kratos*"), focusing on the issue of "forgetting" in the city's politics.

This approach was primarily part of an internal debate in historical scholarship on Ancient Greece. The question of historical anthropology and the potential tensions and convergences between historians and anthropologists was a major live issue. Loraux argued that in placing (especially) Athens within a regulated, unchanging civic time, punctuated by ritual and characterized by concord, "anthropologists" were enclosing the city in a representation that it produced of itself, and they were depoliticizing it. She called on them to place conflict at the center of this history, contrary to the bland image of a "cooled" city, and so understand how the city evacuated and repressed any image of its own division, drawing on real conflicts and their civic, literary, and memorial treatment.

The book is built around the restoration of democracy in Athens in 403 BCE, after a period of civil war and oligarchic violence under the "Thirty Tyrants." Loraux examines how the return of peace was accompanied by an injunction not to evoke past misfortunes. Why proclaim an amnesty? She starts by showing that the city "thinks," and thinks of itself as a fantasied indivisible whole. She contrasts Roman thought of the *civitas*, as a plurality of citizens, to the oneness of the Greek city, an indivisible primacy. She points out the methodological "price to pay," writing that "along the way, we might be led to claim that the city thinks, which amounts to treating the city as a subject." On this point, her approach tallies with her affinities with psychoanalysis, with her reading of Freud's *Moses and Monotheism*, and especially with her regular cooperation with psychanalysts and contributions to the *Nouvelle Revue de psychanalyse*, for example. The city thus has a soul.

But paradoxically, in refusing to be broken into parts, the city placed division at its heart—and thus at the heart of politics. Athenians' perpetual condemnation of stasis, an absolute condemnation of confrontation or of tension (a more static notion) between two parties, while admittedly a way of idealizing consensus and not thinking of real division, was also a way of thinking of it as a structural element that was already present. It was a forgetting of politics as such, and Loraux analyzes the way democrats themselves were led to erase any idea of *kratos*, for this term marks the victory of one camp over another, of one party over another party, even were this the democratic victory of the people.

This powerful examination of forgetting and of the return of politics was of pressing concern in the final quarter of the twentieth century. It was a major issue in scholarship, with memory and forgetting acquiring a central place in historical anthropology and the philosophy of history. But it was especially of political topicality, with the emergence of revisionist thought and the Papon trial in France sparking much debate and leading to the 1990 Gayssot Act, under which it is a crime to question crimes against humanity. The use by historical scholarship of the psychoanalytic concepts of "repression," "return of the repressed," "denial," "obliteration," and "amnesia" was a much-debated issue at the time. But even more crucial was the question of amnesty because of the civic issues at stake.

On various occasions, Loraux raises the possibility of an analogy with Vichy France or the "1940s." But it was a present-day combat she had in mind—the combat against the far right, first and foremost. She was a cofounder of the "Appel à la vigilance contre l'extrême droite et sa banalization" collective in 1993, signed by forty or so French and European intellectuals. This is evoked in *La cité divisée*: Athens forbade using trials to satisfy

238   *The Divided City*

a "memory opposed to forgetting," as she puts it, and did not envisage civic reconciliation through trials. Loraux forcefully argues that amnesty is not the same as forgetting because one cannot forget on being ordered to do so. Public peace, she writes, should not make do with monuments erected "to all the victims of the war."

These issues have since become vital matters at the heart of current debate, with the increasing number of "truth commissions" since the Truth and Reconciliation Commission was set up in South Africa in 1993. Loraux argues for the need for grieving, which, she writes, has never meant forgetting. Grieving means the "incorporation of a painful or conflictual past, not a rejection or distancing of it." Other major points made in this book also stand out today, such as the way civic debate in France refers to the Republic as an ideally indivisible and single entity, once again in the name of concord and consensus, or attempts in a country such as Tunisia to refound its democracy—an experience in which the question of stasis and the fears expressed by a political community, which thinks of itself primarily as a single and united body, that it might be divided, turns out to be primordial.

Jocelyne Dakhlia

Nicole Loraux, *La cité divisée: L'oubli dans la mémoire d'Athènes* (Paris: Payot ["Critique de la politique"], 1997). Republished by Payot et Rivages ("Petite Bibliothèque Payot"), 2005. Translated into English by Corinne Pache with Jeff Fort as *The Divided City: On Memory and Forgetting in Ancient Athens* (New York: Zone Books, 2001).

1998

ART AND AGENCY: GELL REDEFINES ART INDEPENDENTLY OF AESTHETICS

No book better embodies the ontological turn and the material turn, placing the object, its materiality, and associated forms of intentionality at the heart of anthropological thought, than *Art and Agency*, a fascinating and baroque work written by Alfred Gell (1945–1997) during the last year of his life and published posthumously. This provocative book is a rare combination of intellectual audacity and ethnological "classicism," rigorous logic and sweeping statements. Its radical critique of the ethnocentrism lurking within the history and sociology of art provoked adulation and exasperation in equal measures. Gell emphasizes the need to finally grant various non-Western art forms the importance they are due. But he further argues that this must not be a simple rebalancing and rehabilitating of these forms to fill in the "blanks" in the history of art as hitherto practiced. Nor is it a matter of simply using them to reexamine the meaning attributed to the notions of art, beauty, and aesthetics. To his mind, such an approach, even when steering clear of depreciating non-Western artistic products, even when historicizing its analyses by taking into account the cultural exchanges presiding over these creations, even when giving increasing room to "indigenous arts" in galleries, fairs, collections, and contemporary museums, ultimately has nothing to do with an anthropology of art worthy of the name. A genuinely anthropological approach cannot make do with applying the existing axioms and methods of the sociology and history of art to non-Western creations. Rather, it needs to describe and analyze how "objects" may be considered, in precise cultural contexts, as genuine "social agents," endowed with a specific status identifying them in practice to *persons*. Art is no more the vehicle for beauty than it is the expression of an aesthetic culture specific to a period or a society. Works of art are primarily specific forms of agency. This is Gell's working hypothesis. And it is not as far removed as he might suggest from Aristotle's idea of dramatic arts or from analyses by such renowned historians of art as Julius Schlosser, Aby Warburg, Ernst Gombrich, and David Freedberg (*The Power of Images*).

But Gell's true accomplishment resides less in the detail of the ethnographic analysis punctuating the work, such as his discussion of Trobriand canoes, nail fetishes, or the Mona Lisa, than in his establishing a combinatory logic capable of embracing, in formal terms, all possible situations in which an artifact may be identified with a person. Within his perspective, this amounts to fundamentally redefining the necessary and sufficient conditions for an object to effectively acquire the status of a work of art. What is fascinating about such an undertaking (and has inspired several philosophers and social scientists) is the extremely abstract formalization combined with the attempt to apprehend the infinitely fleeting reality stemming from the social, emotional, or cognitive impact of a singular object on those who encounter it, especially when the latter belong to cultural spheres deemed far removed from our aesthetic judgments.

The paradoxical nature of this work also resides in the way its developments partly overspill the conceptual framework and general line of argumentation laid down in the early chapters, a bit like a song whose lines increasingly wander from the initial refrain. Thus, when it came out, most commentators focused on the book's main thesis, sometimes questioning the relevance and exactness of the empirical examples deployed, the exclusive emphasis on the *agency* of works of art, and the risk of assimilating too many artifacts to such works, at the peril of making it impossible to apprehend the specificity of artworks. Lastly, certain critics emphasized the limits of anthropomorphism for thinking about the ontology of nonhumans. In so doing, they all too frequently overlooked many other arguments in the book that have nevertheless done much to stimulate fresh readings. Such is the case, for example, in Gell's remarkable analysis of the idea of style, based on forms of decorative art that long prevailed in the Marquesas Islands, and in

241   *Gell Redefines Art Independently of Aesthetics*

his profoundly original observations about the idea of a "distributed person," which he uses to shed light on Marcel Duchamp's entire body of work. Other equally inspired passages have fueled anthropological thought about the role artifacts play in religious and ritual practices, when it is a matter of communicating with invisible intentional entities or when the very idea of temporality is in play. The theoretical wealth of such analyses is nowadays better appreciated, especially as they have been discussed and expanded on in social sciences and the humanities alike. Thus, at a time when a great number of intellectual products rapidly become obsolete, it may be asserted, without fear of error, that this book is emblematic of this particular time in the 1990s when anthropologists switched their focus to the materiality of objects and their agency. Further, it continues to be a lively source of inspiration and dialogue for many of its readers and has every chance of remaining so.

Denis Vidal

Alfred Gell, *Art and Agency: An Anthropological Approach* (Oxford: Oxford University Press, 1998).

1999

THE NEW SPIRIT OF CAPITALISM: BOLTANSKI AND CHIAPELLO READDRESS THE ENIGMA OF CAPITALISM

Modern capitalism is an enigma and a challenge. Karl Marx was among the first to pierce the secret of the law of value informing this singular mode of production. In his wake, though in a slightly different light, Max Weber considered the historical oddity in comparison to other societies of the capitalist economy, emphasizing the existence of an elective affinity between the Protestant ethic issuing from the Reformation and early bourgeois entrepreneurs' ambition for boundless accumulation. Returning to the tradition of such large-scale thinkers, Luc Boltanski (born 1940) and Ève Chiapello (born 1965) tackle in turn the enigma of capitalism. In *Le nouvel esprit du capitalisme* (*The New Spirit of Capitalism*), they focus on the beliefs participating in the production and legitimization of the capitalist order, in the same fashion as Weber. But unlike him, their purpose is not to identify all the components of the capitalist mindset but rather to gauge its successive transformations, the better to ascertain where we now stand.

The plasticity of modern capitalism merits the closest attention and poses a fundamental challenge to sociological understanding. After a founding period that came to a close with the Great Depression of 1929, capitalism enjoyed a new lease of life after the Second World War. In France, the synergy between production and mass consumption drove a society in which big business had the upper hand. A new stage was ushered in after the events of May 1968. Against the backdrop of globalization and financialization, the end of the century saw the progressive revival of capitalist forces at the same time as a degradation in employment conditions and the drying up of critical imagination.

To make sense of this transformation, Boltanski and Chiapello adopt a pragmatic stance. It is a matter of considering how people engage in action, justify it, and give it meaning. The first stage in their argument is to compare two bodies of management work published thirty years apart. In the 1960s, management rhetoric promoted decentralization, meritocracy, and goal-driven management. Three decades later, bureaucracies and hierarchies were still in the firing line. But the watchwords were no longer the same. Flexibility, adaptation to change, and innovation were the new obsessions. What was needed to manage men and women effectively was to favor personal development, freedom, confidence—and, as a counterpart, to ensure employability and psychological security. While in the same discursive register the French no longer referred to *cadres* but to *managers*, "networks" were now the new model for development and excellence.

To model this new spirit of capitalism, the authors draw on the theoretical framework of "economies of worth" devised a few years earlier by Boltanski and Laurent Thévenot in *De la justification* (*On Justification*, 1991). They thus associate the system of values that predominated in the 1990s with an apparatus for justification, that of the "project-based city," codifying the principles of justice applicable in a networked world. The capacity to communicate, to increase connections, to move about, to accumulate social capital, and ultimately, to partake in multiple projects, are, to their eyes, determinants favoring access to high status and associated properties, such as indexing one's authority on skill, not hierarchical position.

With such underpinnings, the new spirit of capitalism could only acquire form and meaning in a specific historical context. In France, the post-1968 period provided a favorable context for circumventing many Fordian compromises taken up by the vanguard of social critique. Especially after the Great Depression of the 1930s, trade unions and political parties had been quick to denounce the anarchic system of production, weak collective protection, and exploitation of workers. They had negotiated and accepted a set of conventions and practices that, finally, allowed capitalism to go through a new phase of expansion. History repeated itself after 1968, but the main source of inspiration was no longer "social critique" but "artistic critique"—to use a term forged by Chiapello in *Artistes versus Managers*

244   *The New Spirit of Capitalism*

(1998). To break free of the moral precepts that had weighed down on the 1960s, those protesting the dominant order started calling on autonomy, creativity, and mobility. Capitalism, digesting this critique and turning it to its advantage, rapidly revealed once again its capacity to change spirit and rewrite its codes. Consequently, since the 1980s, the world of work has been overhauled. Since then, the invention of productive organizations caring little for workers' health, the expansion in precarious employment, the fragilization of salaried employment, the retreat of trade unions, and the deconstruction of social classes have provided fertile ground on which capitalism has flourished.

At the end of its analysis, which stands out for the salutary ambition to return to sociological understanding on the broadest scale, the book refuses all sense of inevitability. These artistic and social critiques, irrespective of their vicissitudes, and despite being deflected to serve other ends, have not yet had their final say. They are more useful than ever for diagnosing contemporary pathologies and helping us to collectively take our destiny in hand. In 1999, Boltanski and Chiapello argued that social critique seemed better armed than artistic critique to play this role. Such a statement is still open to discussion. The fact is that the book also shows that a further element needs to be factored into any consideration of this topic: capitalism's seemingly infinite capacity to turn to its own advantage moral aspirations opposing its expansion.

Michel Lallement

Luc Boltanski and Ève Chiapello, *Le nouvel esprit du capitalisme* (Paris: Gallimard ["NRF-Essais"], 1999). Republished by Gallimard ("Tel"), 2011. Translated into English by Gregory Elliott as *The New Spirit of Capitalism* (London: Verso, 2006). A new, updated edition was published by Verso in 2018.

2000

THE GREAT DIVERGENCE: POMERANZ EXPLAINS WHY CHINA "LAGGED" BEHIND THE WEST

The considerable success of *The Great Divergence* by Kenneth Pomeranz (born 1958) raises an interesting question: Why did earlier works by Bin Wong (*China Transformed*, 1997) and Li Bozhong (*Agricultural Development in Jiangnan*, 1998), on which it draws extensively, not reach a comparable readership? Perhaps the book's fortune is due not solely to its wonderfully seductive title but also to the very particular political and intellectual circumstances of the time: the rise of China and, after initial enthusiasm, attendant Western concerns that fostered keen interest in Chinese economic history among economists and political scientists.

Pomeranz's idea is simple. He starts from the main elements mentioned in conventional historical scholarship to explain why England—and Europe generally—succeeded while China "lagged" behind: private property, effective institutions, competitive markets, democracy, small families, demographic evolution, the shift from proto-industry to manufacturing industry, and the role of capital, the bourgeoisie, and towns. But he sets about gradually demonstrating that not only were all these elements to be found in China (more specifically, in part of China, Yangtze), but that they were even better established and developed than in England. Hence the divergence between Europe and Asia does not date from the fifteenth or the sixteenth century but rather from the nineteenth century, and it is not explained by different mentalities or by the corruption and despotism of the Chinese government but, quite simply, by a factor from which England, unlike China, benefited: colonialism. North America in particular provided

England with vast markets, raw materials (often by slavery), and above all, environmental resources. Pomeranz's approach reflects the fall of the Berlin Wall and the rise of a monolithic way of thinking about the world: It was no longer a matter of imagining multiple possible paths of development, as had been the case during the Cold War, but solely of assessing who best respected the parameters of the liberal economic and social model. Within this framework, China emerges as even more competitive and capitalist than England.

It is not by chance that debates have related primarily to the empirical proof for these statements. Many authors, including the historian Patrick O'Brien, strove to demonstrate that Pomeranz's data was wrong, especially about China. This has led to disputes over figures, which are still ongoing. Especially, as in Pomeranz's wake, others (including Joseph Inikori and Prisanan Parthasarathai) have sought to make the same argument for Africa and India. Debate has thus returned to a question that has in fact been discussed since the eighteenth century and especially since decolonization: Is poverty to be explained by local attitudes and insufficient resources or by external constraints?

While admitting the importance of these debates, one may nevertheless acknowledge their limits. First, these analyses rarely raise the question of how the data is constructed or of the cumulative nature of sources and data in quantitative approaches. Yet this is a crucial issue. Is it legitimate to collate data from heterogeneous sources—eighteenth-century chronicles, self-interested policy suggestions, scientific studies—taking different hypotheses as their starting points? A second problem relates to the fact that this quarrel is prisoner to a vision of history as competition, which endeavors to explain, retrospectively, the strengths of the winner and weaknesses of the losers. Such an approach associates progress with rises in certain indicators—gross domestic product, income per head—while setting distribution and inequality to one side.

The controversy also relates to scales of analysis. One of Pomeranz's innovations was to avoid comparing nation-states (China and England) and to first privilege regional comparisons (between Yangtze and Lancashire), followed by global analysis. This approach has the merit of bringing out profound regional disparities. But it has come in for criticism. Some, such

247   *Pomeranz Explains Why China "Lagged" behind the West*

as O'Brien, have pointed out that while behind Lancashire, the whole of the United Kingdom was experiencing significant growth, whereas behind Yangtze, China lay stagnant. Others have reproached Pomeranz for not having considered the role of Africa or Latin America or the rest of Asia. Let us note, however, that such criticisms conflate Pomeranz's style of global history with world history. For as Pomeranz has often repeated, these two approaches are clearly different. In his case, the pertinent scale of analysis is defined by the question asked, not by any globalizing premises.

Lastly, historians of area studies have pointed out Pomeranz's shortcomings in this respect. This debate goes over much familiar ground from the long-standing question of how to go about economic and social history for area studies. Is it a matter of chance that for decades, and from well before the rise of world history, there have been few studies of economic and social history in these fields? This may be seen as stemming from a pronounced tension between civilization-based approaches—emphasizing the role of language and situating history within the humanities—and studies of economic and social history that draw on categories used in the social sciences. Perhaps the time has come to transcend this divide. If it is preferable to justify and criticize models and transhistorical categories before using them, is this not also true of the supposedly "local" categories and "specificities" of area studies?

Alessandro Stanziani

Kenneth Pomeranz, *The Great Divergence: China, Europe, and the Making of the Modern World Economy* (Princeton, NJ: Princeton University Press, 2000).

2001

ACTING IN AN UNCERTAIN WORLD: CALLON, LASCOUMES, AND BARTHE RETHINK DEMOCRACY

Agir dans un monde incertain (*Acting in an Uncertain World*) is a major and surprising contribution to contemporary political theory. Surprising because it is by three authors seemingly unconnected to the venerable tradition of political thought. When the book came out, Michel Callon (born 1945) was a world-renowned sociologist of science and technology, promoting (with Bruno Latour) a radically new approach to scientific production. He had just completed a major study on the power of those suffering from myopathy. Yannick Barthe (born 1970) was working in a research unit run by the other two authors and had just completed his thesis on nuclear waste policies. Pierre Lascoumes (born 1948) was an experienced sociologist of law, the environment, and public action, as well as an activist working with an association for those suffering from AIDS. Their previous works were in the field of descriptive sociology, often written largely from the actors' point of view, far removed from any normative contribution to the transformation of contemporary democracies. And indeed, the book is constantly backed up by precise examples taken from their earlier inquiries.

But it sets itself a different objective, apparent as of the dedication: "This book is dedicated to all those who, by inventing technical democracy, reinvent democracy." It is a matter of participating in the invention of a new model of political decision making, in a context of profound transformation of the relations between science, techniques, and society. The book opens on the observation of an "increase in uncertainties" affecting contemporary societies. Mad cow disease, genetically modified organisms, nuclear risks, and AIDS are but some of the many areas in which scientists and politicians are overwhelmed and unable to produce the type of politically fair and scientifically based "clear-cut decisions" they always claim they can provide. On the one hand, the dissemination of technical innovations seems to produce ever less controllable consequences on nature and humans. On the other, grassroots movements are formed and dispute ever more directly the scientific assessments and political choices imposed from above.

The purpose of the book is thus to rethink from the bottom up the process for making political choices in such a context. According to the authors, acting in such a world entails using hybrid forums within which controversies may be set out, "lay expertise" heard, and the identity of actors redefined. The concept of a hybrid forum provides the conceptual pillar around which the argument is based: "forums, because they are open spaces where groups may mobilize to debate technical choices which engage the group; hybrid, because these engaged groups and the spokespeople claiming to represent them are heterogenous." Within these forums, the "great division" between experts and laypeople, on the one hand, and political representatives and the represented, on the other, may be brought into question. What, then, takes place is, indissociably, an exploration of "possible worlds" and of the type of political groups concerned and worthy of being represented. Within this framework, citizens must be able to get across their point of view through mobilization or association with the decision-making process: democracy must cease to be purely "delegative" and also become "dialogical."

The strength of the concept of a hybrid forum resides in its evocative power and its relative vagueness. At times, it refers to the many occasions when lay groups have managed to gain access to a decision-making process. At others it designates far more formal mechanisms able to organize or even institutionalize the pooling and contrasting of experience and knowledge, such as the much-discussed "citizens' conferences." On the basis of this empirical approach, the book goes on to reexamine such structural notions of modernity as representation, democracy, and expertise. This leads to thinking about political decision making as a continuous process for producing knowledge and exploring identities, rather than as a brute act of authority or sovereignty. It also announces that expertise is no longer the preserve of experts and that democracy needs to be judged by its capacity to represent minorities and conceived in ways far exceeding matters of voting. The reception of the book, published in English by the MIT Press in 2009, was on a par with its ambition. It influenced the field of science and technology studies, where questions about the possibility of "placing science in democracy" became a recurrent feature of international scholarship as of the early 2000s. The book's most serious opponents were researchers interested in the changing relation between science and society, such as Dominique Pestre, for whom authors interested in the "participative turn of science" (such as Christophe Bonneuil or Pierre-Benoît Joly) are too quick to occult the structural background of the market regulation of science and techniques and the power relations this tends to impose.

But the influence of *Agir dans un monde incertain* was also felt in another field of research that was emerging at the time of its publication: "participative democracy" and "deliberative democracy," two ideas the authors were careful to avoid. The book very quickly became a classic, used by authors and actors, and the concept of "lay expertise" gradually became established as a major concept alongside that of "hybrid forums."

Loïc Blondiaux

Michel Callon, Pierre Lascoumes, and Yannick Barthe, *Agir dans un monde incertain: Essai sur la démocratie technique* (Paris: Éditions du Seuil ["La Couleur des idées"], 2001). Republished by Points ("Essais"), 2014. Translated into English by Graham Burchell as *Acting in an Uncertain World: An Essay on Technical Democracy* (Cambridge, MA: MIT Press, 2009).

2002

THE SURVIVING IMAGE: DIDI-HUBERMAN MAKES TIME THE FUNDAMENTAL DIMENSION OF IMAGES

L'image survivante (*The Surviving Image*) completes an inquiry launched in *Devant l'image* (*Confronting Images*, 1990) and spawned by a worry about historical knowledge in its entirety. What is at stake? The deconstruction of (art) history models that unify when dispersion predominates, close when duration insists, and separate when everything holds together. Montage, survival (*Nachleben*), symptom, telescoping, *Pathosformel*—all are concepts that disarticulate the historicity of things by accounting for their appearance and presence. Walter Benjamin, Carl Einstein, Aby Warburg—the gods unearthed by Georges Didi-Huberman (born 1953) and in whose company he leads the assault—dashed the discipline's certainty in its science and in its art of reining in time itself. The forms of temporality bequeathed by historicist conceptions of history—periodization, chronology, continuity, linear or incidental causality, explanation in terms of a Zeitgeist, and so on—need replacing, not by some new body of doctrine but rather by a methodological "openness." That is, first, a matter of paying attention to the disorientation brought about by the object of knowledge. For images anachronize time, disassemble history.

Didi-Huberman's book takes one image as its starting point: a painting that survived and transcended its time and whose period—Florence, circa 1440—does not allow us to fix a meaning. At the very beginning is an experience when a young art historian, arriving in a corridor of San Marco convent, catches sight of Fra Angelico's *Madonna of the Shadows* and stops midstride, disconcerted by the "stars" in the lower part. Such spurts of paint, like the "faux marbles" painted beneath the *Holy Conversation*, were anachronistic to their time, the former no doubt stemming from the long-standing theological tradition of dissemblance as the ideal "figuring" of the divine, the latter from liturgical *memoria* of the "presence" of the sacred. Further, these stars were placed within a trompe l'oeil frame characteristic of Albertian perspective and may be seen as an act of modern mimesis. The work is an "extraordinary montage of heterogeneous times forming anachronisms"; anachronism thus becomes the best way of naming "the complexity, the overdetermination" of all images with regard to time.

Didi-Huberman sets about drawing out the full consequences of this "heterochronia." As artifacts may only be apprehended from within our present, itself impure and heavy with memory, we cannot deem ourselves to be external, to be not involved. Our method becomes permeated with unease. If Fra Angelico's flecks of paint remained invisible to experts, it is because a power of exclusion had long been at work—meaning we need to undertake a "critical archaeology" of the history of art. The first decades of the twentieth century had already seen a refounding of the discipline, but this was "broken by the Second World War" and its "memory buried after the war." Many scholars had put forward bold ideas. Aby Warburg, with the concept of "survival," posited the life of images as a principle of historicity and sought to understand their effectiveness or capacity to act by what he called "incorporation" (*Verkörperung*), operative whenever the life projected into the thing brought about an "energetic empathy." This really amounted to posing the anthropological problem of agency, of attributing artifacts (in particular those *resembling* life, such as effigies or masks) with an autonomous existence and pathetic agency. But Warburg's thought had been misunderstood and neglected, or at least adulterated by authorized scholarship: survival was understood as what survives from folklore or heritage (the influence or reception of antiquity in Renaissance works), whereas it was in fact the name for a temporal model specific to images, which thereby become of great heuristic value.

What caused this initial founding act to be neglected? To a large extent it was due to Panofsky confirming visual history to be a history of representation, with the prevalence of meaning over affect, and to the importance

253 *Didi-Huberman Makes Time the Fundamental Dimension of Images*

attached to *explanatory principles*, promoting the elucidation of a society's aesthetic forms by its vision of the world (and vice versa); that is, "euchronic explanation" as exemplified by the magisterial social art histories of Michael Baxandall and Svetlana Alpers—total, unified histories in which social facts engender visual dispositions, which are translated in turn into the "style" of works. But images are in fact wholly unlike this, for they are "open structures."

And if images are here paradigmatic, it is because Didi-Huberman, like Warburg and Benjamin before him, takes images to be the true dimension of history and time to be the true dimension of images. Of course, a poem or work of architecture also places us in front of a complex temporal phenomenon, a confusion of periods and motivations whose unity is merely an appearance, to such an extent that any trace questions the knowledge examining it and that the examiner is not obliged to respond, for otherwise this would bring historical undertaking to an end. But the success of Didi-Huberman's argument lies in disrupting how the problem and the project are rolled up together, by increasing in generality without losing in detail. His work forms part of a chorus with that of other bold critical minds— Marc Bloch recognizing the anachronistic nature of history (traveling back through time, asking questions of another period) and Fernand Braudel distinguishing between a time "almost outside time," the conjuncture, and the event (without, however, thinking that "within each historical object all times meet"). Yet Didi-Huberman places a demand on the *metis* of the historian: If the overdetermination of traces repeatedly exposes them to over-interpretation, historians must assume the poetic dimension to what they do. *L'image survivante* is the perfect illustration of this.

Gil Bartholeyns

Georges Didi-Huberman, *L'image survivante: Histoire de l'art et temps des fantômes selon Aby Warburg* (Paris: Minuit ["Paradoxe"], 2002). Translated into English by Harvey Mendelsohn as *The Surviving Image: Phantoms of Time and Time of Phantoms: Aby Warburg's History of Art* (University Park: Penn State University Press, 2016).

2003

THE PRICE OF MONOTHEISM: ASSMANN AND THE VIOLENCE OF MONOTHEISM

Jan Assmann (born 1938), known for his works on Ancient Egypt and his ideas on cultural memory and transmission, had already attracted the ire of critics with his 1997 book *Moses the Egyptian*. In it, he took up Freud's hypothesis that Moses was a disciple of Pharaoh Akhenaton and indexed monotheism to the destruction of images and the increasing emphasis placed on the truth of a single god. Everything held in a single word: *Unterscheidung*—an underlying, hence foundational distinction or separation. But specialists were unwilling to admit that monotheistic religions be deciphered on the basis of a distinction that introduced a new violence necessarily unknown to polytheistic cultures, or further, that this engendered a poor arrangement between the religious and the political domain, from whose deadly effects we still suffer. Further still, the controversy took a scandalous turn in accusing the founder of the Jewish people—a people who thus provided in advance the matrix of all the persecutions to which they were subsequently victim.

As is clear, Assmann's ideas had already traveled a long way. The power of *Die Mosaiche Unterscheidung*, published in 2003, stems from its taking on board all the criticisms of the earlier book and using them to strengthen the initial thesis. In a sort of deferred act that Freud would have recognized, and which echoed dramatically with the aftermath of the events of September 11, 2001, Assmann brought to light what he had previously only touched on. The scholarly controversy was magnified by its projection into current affairs, imposing further clarification.

One may recognize a single god without thereby debarring veneration of any other one. To reach the monotheist thesis of uniqueness, a negation was needed. God had to be separated from the world in all its dimensions—be it the cosmos, society, or the state—and had to enter into a privileged relation with humankind alone. Against polytheism and paganism, he was erected as the true God, with the qualifying term implying the exclusion of any other form of obedience as necessarily marked by falsity. This is the move by which the new regime of religious passion was invented that fuels radical politics: fidelity to God, the jealousy and anger of God, together with their obverses (not their opposites), the misericord and love that God grants exclusively to those who have chosen him and whom he has chosen. It is only at this stage that religion takes control over politics. The history of "political theology," being previously unthinkable, thus started with Jewish monotheism, a history whose late ramifications we periodically experience, be it under Christian or Islamic guise.

But this is where Assmann is more precise than previously. The adjective "true" applied to religion acquires a particular meaning. For it is a moral truth, not a cognitive one. True equates to that which is just and liberating, in accordance with the law. False equates to oppression, servitude, and injustice. Recognizing this leads us to a fruitful paradox, which helps us better diagnose our political violence. The monotheist counter-religion lay the foundation for this violence only after having asserted that it was a liberation. In and by exodus, it opposed a life conducted in the hold of a state that thought of itself as impregnated with divinized powers. It was established by breaking with politics as terrestrial power, in which the gods were involved in myriad ways, in the form of divinities that people evoked to capture and distribute or monopolize their vital forces, to manipulate and enlist them. For Assmann, despite certain misconceptions of his undertaking, it was never a matter of celebrating the forgotten virtues of this pagan backdrop and recommending its improbable return. Rather, it was a matter of better understanding the fate in which we became entangled on breaking with it. For this break took a surprising turn, consisting in removing itself from state policy, the focal point of power where terrestrial politics was conducted, to assert that only a single god, outside the world, was the source of justice. It

256   *The Price of Monotheism*

thus projected us onto a ridge: we are monotheists, for better or for worse, and we need to understand how to play the better off against the worst, within a tradition that is wholly ours.

There is a paradox we need to accept: The most violent forms our politics assume are a secondary derivative of asserting our freedom, our emancipation from a strictly terrestrial politics, with the injustice and oppression that come bound up with it. Monotheism was the reaction to this violence, which was purely sovereign violence, the emanation of a worldly power, pure domination. Yet this gave rise to the possibility of a different type of violence—our own. For the reaction had to take place by transferring sovereign despotism to the power of God—hence intrinsically just, absolutely founded, to be absolutely obeyed, and infinitely greater than any possible sovereign. We must resign ourselves to this and gauge the increasing number of religious conflicts by this yardstick: Our political grandeur, the longest-standing wellspring of our vocation for democracy, is also, and inseparably, the source of still present perils. It comes with an in-built theologico-political price, *der Preis des Monotheismus*, a reservoir of violence. It would be illusory to decree the end to this violence. Instead, we should identify its nature and control its outbreaks.

Bruno Karsenti

Jan Assmann, *Die Mosaische Unterscheidung: Oder der Preis des Monotheismus* (Munich: Carl Hanser Verlag, 2003). Translated into English by Robert Savage as *The Price of Monotheism* (Stanford, CA: Stanford University Press, 2009).

2003

LAW AND REVOLUTION: BERMAN AND THE REVOLUTIONS OF WESTERN LAW

It was not until twenty years after publishing the first volume of *Law and Revolution* that Harold Berman (1918–2007) published the second volume. He died in 2007, when he was eighty-nine, before having the time to complete the third volume, which ought to have been his crowning achievement. And yet even incomplete, the two volumes of this comprehensive survey, echoing its title, resounded like a revolutionary bomb in the backwaters of legal history.

The first volume, published in 1983, was all about the origins of law in the West, which Berman situates in the radical change imposed on European society by the great "papal revolution" of the Gregorian age. On this basis, the Protestant Reformation is considered as the second revolution in Western law, followed shortly after by the third, the English Civil War. The second volume, published in 2003, is about two transformations to European law that occurred between the sixteenth and the seventeenth centuries. The third volume was to focus on the three final stages in this arc stretching over a thousand years: the American and French Revolutions, finishing with the Russian Revolution in 1917.

He thus argues that it is wrong to place the beginning of the modern age in the sixteenth century. For law, European modernity got underway in the Gregorian age, when the Church imposed separation of the two "jurisdictions," designating law to regulate power relations and economic conflicts. We thus need to look to the papal revolution of the eleventh century for the true origin of the Western legal tradition. It is this revolution that likewise explains why the second millennium of our era presents such unity in its legal structures. Admittedly, this millennium was marked by major discontinuities—revolutions—but these either underpinned legal modernity (the first revolution) or else redirected it (the five following revolutions) while maintaining its fundamental identity. Thus, the founding innovation was not the creation of Roman law, or even its rediscovery in the eleventh century. Western law is a creation of the Roman Catholic Church, which between 1075 and 1122 became "the first modern state." If Roman law of course played a leading role, it is not because the rediscovered texts of the *Digest* had the capacity to revive an ancient legal mindset, but because they were redeployed within a completely new framework and subjected to an unparalleled project of renewal.

Berman builds up a long-term history based on the perceptions Western societies have had of themselves. Given that the starting point is the papal revolution, these perceptions mainly coincide with transformations in ecclesiology: first the advent of the *societas christiana* across all Europe, then the renewals imposed by new Protestant denominations. Over the course of his argument, he provides a sort of constitutional history of the West, in which revolutions do not overthrow the legal order but tend rather to renew it. Each time, the transformation in law coincided with a new ecclesiological awareness, leading to the formulation of a new social pact grounded in a religious basis. If this link between law and religion is clear for the three revolutions that Berman analyzes in his two volumes (the papal, Lutheran, and English revolutions), it was, to his mind, equally clear for those he planned to study in the final volume. After all, the Founding Fathers looked to God, and the French Revolution, despite its anticlericalism, was conceived under the auspices of a "supreme being." For Berman, even the Russian Revolution of 1917, despite its materialism, preserved the ideal Christian community, relaunched by Calvinism then realized by handing total control over the economy to the law. On this point, Berman was aware that his interpretation challenged the Marxist interpretation of history and especially Weber's famous theory on the origins of the capitalist spirit. But the challenge is laid down to European historical scholarship on the law, to his mind still too marked by its nationalist matrix and refusal to integrate the religious and legal spheres.

259 *Berman and the Revolutions of Western Law*

As was to be expected, *Law and Revolution* received contrasting views. It is true that the scale of its research had obliged Berman to rely on secondary literature, which was not always up to date, and limit himself to works in English. Several specialists in medieval legal history felt that some of the historical and philological data used in the first volume were out of date (particularly Peter Landau in the *Chicago Law Review* in 1984). But European researchers soon recognized the innovative strengths of their American colleague's work. The first volume was translated into German in 1991; ten years after the publication of the second, the land of the history of law and modern Roman law honored him with an extensive specialist discussion of his work (in the journal *Rechtsgeschichte*). In Italy, Il Mulino brought out the first volume in 1998 and the second in 2010, with an extensive introduction by Diego Quaglioni. The first volume was published in French in 2002 by the Librairie universitaire d'Aix-en-Provence and the second by Fayard in 2010.

Emanuele Conte

Harold J. Berman, *Law and Revolution*, vol. 1, *The Formation of the Western Legal Tradition* (Cambridge, MA: Harvard University Press, 1983); vol. 2, *The Impact of the Protestant Reformations on the Western Legal Tradition* (Cambridge, MA: Harvard University Press, 2003).

2003

REGIMES OF HISTORICITY: HARTOG AND EXPERIENCE OF THE PRESENT

If history is "the science of men in time," in Marc Bloch's words, the temporality of human existence also has its history. This is brought out by studying "regimes of historicity," relating to the singular ways in which societies link up the past, present, and future. The history of these regimes, for which François Hartog (born 1946) laid the groundwork, is necessarily reflexive, since its object is the collective representations of time, of which it is, for its own period, a privileged expression.

The publication of *Régimes d'historicité* (*Regimes of Historicity*) partook in a movement in historical scholarship dating back to 1980s. The emergence of the history of representations triggered new interest in the cultural foundations of historical knowledge, inspiring Hartog's early works on Herodotus and on Fustel de Coulanges. Yet the research program for the history of regimes of historicity had greater ambitions, since it left behind the study of solely historical science and, drawing on more diverse sources, particularly literature, put forward a description of the great mutations affecting the experience of historical time.

Yet Hartog's book does not put forward a new universal history, dividing up periods distinguished by the predominance of a particular way of linking up times. Rather, it presents regimes of historicity as ideal-types, in the Weberian meaning of the term. They are concepts built through comparison, starting from a research problem. His analysis is guided by examination of the specificity of present-day historical consciousness, which, to his mind, stands out by focusing on a present that alone sheds light on the past and future. This "presentism" may be seen in contrast to two earlier ways of relating to time. Whereas the old regime of *historia magistra vitae* compared the present to models from the past, the modern regime, appearing in the eighteenth century and consecrated by the French Revolution, discerned in the past and in the present the premises of a hoped-for future. Expanding on Reinhart Koselleck's description of this contrast, Hartog examines the "crisis of the future" affecting the twentieth century and the resulting break with the modern regime of historicity.

But studying regimes of historicity should not be limited to Western societies. Drawing on the work of Marshall Sahlins on Maori and Polynesian societies allows Hartog to identify a heroic regime of historicity that deciphers the present and future solely in the light of a mythical past. Sahlins's anthropological viewpoint also provides a way of envisioning regimes of historicity as structures of experience, conditioning individuals' reciprocal understanding. From this perspective, Hartog seeks to move beyond the ideal-type construction of different regimes to instead apprehend subjective experience through the tensions and variations affecting it, particularly during crises of temporality. This is the aspect he examines in his reading of Chateaubriand, caught between the old and modern regimes.

Historical and anthropological comparison thus helps sketch the portrait of contemporary presentism. The present is not the sole object of interest but the main source of intelligibility. Thus, Hartog interprets new forms of addressing the past as efforts to escape the present, but which in fact cause the present to cast longer shadows. The value placed on collective memory and remembrance are caught up in identity considerations and moral thought about the present. As for the ever more imperious injunction to safeguard heritage, it signals recognition of an irremediable break with the past, rather than our actively laying hold of it. The description of presentism does not therefore invite us to some nostalgic or moralizing denunciation of how we forget the past or neglect the future, for it shows that such criticisms end up reproducing what they seek to combat.

Yet should we consider presentism as a fully-fledged regime of historicity, or as a pathological form of the modern regime? In either case, it is not wholly comparable to other regimes. Whereas an external source of light, issuing from the past or the future, was used to elucidate the present, the presentist present seeks to cast light on itself, triggering the contradictions brought out in the book. Our present seems both eternal and governed by the ephemeral, repeatedly looking forward and backward without ever managing to leave itself behind. Claiming to apprehend our present solely on its own basis would amount to giving in to presentism, and that is why *Régimes d'historicité* avoids providing any definitive answer to this question.

This line of thought has stimulated many works on the specificity characterizing how our present relates to time, focusing on the idea of modernity—for instance, Christophe Charle's *Discordance des temps* (Discordance of times)—or on the contemporary period, as in the work of Henry Rousso, *La dernière catastrophe* (*The Latest Catastrophe*). Further thought is also needed to determine whether presentism is a crisis or a viable way of relating to time, if it is transitory or lasting. This would entail studying the social forms whence it emanates, for instance, and more generally examining how experience of time relates to social life. Expanding on this innovative study of the discursive manifestations of how we experience time would also involve building a social history of these regimes of historicity, an essential step for understanding our present.

Florence Hulak

François Hartog, *Régimes d'historicité: Présentisme et expérience du temps* (Paris: Éditions du Seuil ["La Librairie du XXIᵉ siècle"], 2003). Republished by Points ("Histoire"), 2012. Translated into English by Saskia Brown as *Regimes of Historicity: Presentism and Experiences of Time* (New York: Columbia University Press, 2015).

2004

LA SERVITUDE VOLONTAIRE: TESTART, THE GENESIS OF INEQUALITIES AND THE EMERGENCE OF THE STATE

In 2004, Alain Testart (1945–2013) took the bold move of reusing, for a work of anthropology, the title of an essay by La Boétie on subjection, dependence, and despotism, written over 400 years earlier. The purpose of the two volumes of this new *La servitude volontaire* (Voluntary servitude) is to set out a theory of the origins of power and of the state. His starting point is the presence at burial sites of what archaeologists call "accompanying dead"—that is, men and women who were intentionally killed when a person (normally of a certain social standing) died. This custom is attested in archaeology, in ethnology, and in history. It once existed across all continents, including in societies without any form of state organization. It was not specific to royalties, as was long believed, yet was not practiced in constituted states, which banished it. Until the late nineteenth century, the use of accompanying dead was still practiced in certain regions of sub-Saharan Africa uninfluenced by monotheism.

How are we to interpret such practices? According to Testart, describing them in terms of sacrifice (as historians, anthropologists, and subsequently archaeologists have done) is reductive: The person who ordered the death of his followers, slaves, or concubines sought, on the contrary, to retain them in his service after death. There is also no idea of an offering, no indication that accompanying retainers in the grave were intended for a supernatural power or a god.

This burial practice is primarily a political, not a religious phenomenon: It indicates rather the existence of ties of *personal loyalty* (voluntary or involuntary) within a society. It proves that a man had at hand other human beings ready to do anything for him, including die for him. This practice thus indicates specific social relations, already firmly in place in societies without a state: leaders, chiefs, and kings relied on a certain number of followers, whose number conferred political power and authority. In the ethnographic and historical sources, these followers were slaves, royal captives, clients, refugees, mercenaries, debtors, and concubines. In any case, in ancient societies, they were one of the most frequent bases for wielding political power. There are many examples of sovereigns in precolonial Africa or honorary chieftains on the northwest coast of America who were supported by such ties of personal loyalty. These ties could engender the personalized centralization of power and contribute to the emergence of a state, at least in its despotic form.

Accordingly, personal loyalties preceded the state. Yet the fact remains that while personal loyalties helped give rise to the state, this state, once constituted, helped suppress these same loyalties. Insofar as it becomes bureaucratized, the state tends to promote another form of loyalty—namely, *loyalty to principles*, consequently suppressing personal loyalties and, inevitably, canceling accompanying dead, its most spectacular illustration. This is what happened in China in the fifth and fourth centuries before our era, after nearly 1,000 years of mass accompanying dead.

This book expands on Testart's examination of the origin of inequalities, addressed in his other works: *Les chasseurs-cueilleurs ou l'origine des inégalités* (Hunter-gatherers or the origin of inequalities, 1982); *Des dons et des dieux* (On gifts and gods, 1993) on chremastic societies; *Aux origines de la monnaie* (At the origins of money, 2001); and *L'esclave, la dette et le pouvoir* (Slaves, debts, and power, 2001) on the institution of slavery. Testart notes that personal loyalties are not to be found among the aborigines of Australia or, apparently, during the Paleolithic period. The origin of these loyalties may be explained by the birth of wealth: In the ancient "wealth" societies—that is, those with a minimum level of techniques for storing food and with a "usufund" property, in which cultivating land ensures its ownership—a leader becomes rich not by controlling the means of production but by the allegiance of certain individuals who are economically dependent on him. Wealth was even more necessary for followers, given that standardized goods of value were indispensable during key moments in collective life (birth, marriage, funerals, illness, festivities, and conflict resolution) and that the associated payment in goods was stipulated by law or custom (blood money, bride prices, fines, etc.). In being indebted to an influential or powerful man, the economic dependent became, to an extent, an auxiliary of power.

Among the institutions providing debtors and dependents—such as slavery and clientelism, for instance—it is slavery for debts that is most likely to play a key role in the emergence of a despotic type of political power.

Testart's book is important for various reasons. It managed to set aside the excessive insistence on the religious and psychosocial interpretation of accompanying dead. It attributed full importance to the asymmetric nature of collective burial tombs and the hierarchy inherent to their being built. It shows, beyond the often-overestimated role played by kinship ties, the extent to which personal loyalties are decisive when studying ancient societies, and that they also lie at the origin of the development of inequalities and, probably, the emergence of the state.

Valérie Lécrivain

Alain Testart, *La servitude volontaire*, vol. 1, *Les morts d'accompagnement*, vol. 2, *L'origine de l'État* (Paris: Errance, 2004).

2005

EXPLORATIONS IN CONNECTED HISTORY: SUBRAHMANYAM CONNECTS THE EURO-ASIAN WORLDS

The two volumes of *Explorations in Connected History*, subtitled, respectively, *From the Tagus to the Ganges* and *Mughals and Franks*, clearly partake in a program set out in a paper published in 1997 in *Modern Asian Studies* by the Indian historian Sanjay Subrahmanyam (born 1961). In this paper, he criticized the program put forward by the historian of Burma, Victor Lieberman, advocating systematic comparison of state forms and cultural formations in six different areas in Eurasia. Subrahmanyam suggested an alternative, which he called "connected histories," based on looking for effective connections between different areas at certain privileged moments. Connected history has a complex relation to global history. Both are motivated by a desire to move beyond the boundaries of nation-states, a recent formation. Yet while most practitioners of global history look for often long-term syntheses, by comparing diverse secondary sources, the connected histories program focuses on comparing primary sources in original languages over a shorter period.

This stemmed from Subrahmanyam's personal trajectory. A specialist in the economic history of southern India and the Portuguese empire in Asia, he expanded his horizons to embrace a global history of the Indian Ocean, comparing Portuguese sources with those in other languages, primarily Persian, in the manner of the French Orientalist Jean Aubin (one of his sources of inspiration), and granting greater room to the cultural, religious, and political dimension in his works. Furthermore, as a professor at the École des hautes études en sciences sociales (EHESS) from 1995 to 2002, he had built up contacts with historians of other areas, particularly Serge Gruzinski studying Latin America, who were also influential in this broadening of perspective.

The two volumes contain fifteen or so articles. Taken as a whole, they provide an object lesson in method. Methodologically, the greatest challenge in the project for "connected histories" is the need for historians to venture outside their zone of competence, defined in terms of a "cultural area," which Subrahmanyam likens to a "box," to seek out "at times fragile threads that connected the globe." The first obstacle is of course linguistic, for each cultural area has its own language(s) for texts and archives (which are not always the same, as in southern Asia), and mastering the languages for several areas is not within everyone's grasp. He stands out for being able to read the sources in many Oriental and Western languages, as demonstrated in a certain number of articles in these two collections, in which he compares sources in Portuguese, Dutch, French, and Persian. The heuristic advantage of such comparison is clear when he contrasts several accounts of a given event, using two episodes in Indo-Portuguese history that he mentioned in the article called "On Indian Views of the Portuguese in Asia." It may be objected that comparing diverse sources is something all historians do. Still, in these two cases, it had never been done before, partly because historians of the "Portuguese expansion" often ignore the existence of sources in Persian while historians of the Mughal Empire consider the Portuguese point of view to be overly biased.

The most telling example of the advantages of the connected history approach is no doubt his analysis of the global millenarian conjuncture in the sixteenth century in which the several empires controlling most of Eurasia were brought into contact, an aspect only briefly sketched in his 1997 article and fully developed here ("Sixteenth-Century Millenarism from the Tagus to the Ganges"). Taking as his starting point a 1581 dialogue about the Final Judgment between the Mughal emperor, Akbar, and a Catalan Jesuit attending his court, Antonio Monserrate, Subrahmanyam unravels a thread that brings to light a Zeitgeist comprising eschatological expectations, largely shared by such varied political and religious worlds as the Iberian Catholic monarchy and its Habsburg cousin in Austria, the Sunni Sultanate of the

Ottomans, the Shiite virtual theocracy of the Safavids in Iran, and Akbar's regime marked by a largely unorthodox Sunnism not exempt of Shiite influences. It could be objected that Subrahmanyam's "global" conjuncture is heavily slanted toward the Catholic and Islamic worlds, neglecting the Protestant, Hindu, and Confucian worlds, even though Mughal millenarianism apparently incorporated certain Hindu traditions. Nevertheless, this analysis provides a valuable counterpoint to a certain strain of teleological Western discourse that views voyages by Europeans, described as "great discoveries" (neglecting the navigations by the Muslim Chinese admiral Zheng He in the years 1400–1430), as the initial steps toward capitalist globalization. In his own way, Subrahmanyam thus helped "provincialize" Europe.

The book made a great impact and, to an extent, established connected history in the scholarly landscape. Subrahmanyam has continued to explore this vein, as illustrated by several recent works. His growing interest in the figure of the nomad, the foreigner, those who cross political, intellectual, or spiritual boundaries, responds to one of the great questions raised by a period as tormented as ours.

Claude Markovits

Sanjay Subrahmanyam, *Explorations in Connected History: Mughals and Franks: From the Tagus to the Ganges* (New Delhi: Oxford University Press, 2005).

2005

BEYOND NATURE AND CULTURE: DESCOLA STEERS NATURE INTO THE SOCIAL SCIENCES

The legacy of structural anthropology in France seems to be shared between three main domains and distinct problems: the difference between the sexes, taken up by Françoise Héritier, the difference between classes, taking up by Maurice Godelier, and the difference between nature and culture, taken up by Philippe Descola (born 1949), especially in his most noteworthy book, *Par-delà nature et culture* (*Beyond Nature and Culture*). Each of these three research programs developed by mining a blind spot in Lévi-Strauss's structuralism, suggesting that what transpires in his work as a set of abstractly combined variables are, in fact, points around which the social dynamic crystallizes. From this point of view, Descola shares the same stated ambition as Héritier and Godelier, continuing the work of their common master but on political ground, since ecology is Descola's critical horizon, just as the inequality of the sexes and domination were likewise questioned by his fellow anthropologists.

The book took up a theoretical style that had fallen into disuse among social anthropologists by the early 2000s—namely, large-scale comparative synthesis. It thus completed the trilogy comprising the canon of an anthropological career, for in 1986 Descola published a monograph based on fieldwork among the Achuar in Amazonia, *La nature domestique* (*In the Society of Nature*), followed in 1993 by a first-person ethnographic account, *Les lances du crepuscule* (*The Spears of Twilight*). When viewed in the light of the history of scientific institutions, he thus cuts a classical figure, lost amid postmodern disputes over ethnological authority. Yet he also comes across as more in tune with the prevalent epistemology, for the book is firmly situated within the reworkings to the nature-couple pair initiated by the sociology of science as conducted by Bruno Latour and Donna Haraway. And it stood out within the intellectual landscape of the moment by introducing the anthropological usage of the concept of ontology, which went on to have an important yet disputed posterity.

The source of this book is the total indifference displayed by the Achuar—the Jivaroan group from the Andean foothills he studied as of the 1970s—for the intuitive division we make between, on the one hand, people capable of symbolic interaction and, on the other, natural things bound by blind physical determination. The symbolic ecology of the Achuar distributes the properties of personhood more liberally than in the modern context, since, for example, plants cultivated by women in gardens and prey hunted by men have a relation of kinship or of predatory and warlike reciprocity to their human alter egos. Descola chooses the concept of animism, taken from Edward Tylor, to characterize this system of relations. The heuristic power of Amazonian animism derives from the inversion it brings about to the modern (which Descola calls naturalist) way of organizing relations to the world: whereas we think of beings endowed with minds as marking a difference within a physical continuum, animist groups consider the materiality of bodies as operating a differentiation between different groups, all of which share the same status of personhood.

Par-delà nature et culture fleshes out and then systematizes the subversive potential of animism by describing two other ontological formulas—that is, two other ways of ordering the world and of managing differences and continuities—namely, analogism and totemism. Though many readers saw this move as a classificatory undertaking enclosing each human society in a cultural style defined from above by anthropologists, there are at least two ways of responding to this criticism. First, each mode of identification, or ontology, is only a variant, derived by comparison, within which diversity appears. What the author calls "modes of relation" designates institutional formations giving a specific orientation to a given ontology. Thus, animism is marked by predation or reciprocity, depending on the case, while naturalism occurs in versions in which production or protection may dominate. The

271   *Descola Steers Nature into the Social Sciences*

modes of relation are what bring about change, history, within ontologies that are, furthermore, described synchronically. Second, this four-term comparative framework radicalizes the provincialization of modern naturalism, transpiring not as a mere counterpart to a unique ontological alternative (as in Eduardo Viveiros de Castro's perspectivism) but as one social, political, and ecological arrangement among many others. It thus avoids the pitfall of idealizing the non-modern as a simple counter-model to instead start thinking about transformations to our cosmological structures inherited from the past.

From the point of view of the social sciences, the main contribution of *Par-delà nature et culture* has no doubt been its capacity to fundamentally redefine what we mean by "society." While its empirical and conceptual underpinnings seem to constitute a straightforward critique of this concept, insofar as the sphere of interactions instituted between humans no longer suffices to give rise to the very object of social science, the book should in fact be seen as returning to Durkheim's project of inquiring into the genesis of the social. Descola invites anthropologists, as well as sociologists, historians, and philosophers, to examine, as a priority, how relations to the natural environment are structured, because the process of group formation depends essentially on these relations. The legacy of this work (other than its profound impact on Amazonian ethnology) is to be found in work currently being conducted to conceive of ecology not as some immediately prescriptive or normative form but as a central anthropological and sociological problem.

Pierre Charbonnier

Philippe Descola, *Par-delà nature et culture* (Paris: Gallimard ["Bibliothèque des sciences humaines"], 2005). Republished by Gallimard ("Folio"), 2015. Translated into English by Janet Lloyd as *Beyond Nature and Culture* (Chicago: University of Chicago Press, 2013).

2006

CHARONNE, 8 FÉVRIER 1962: DEWERPE AUTOPSIES STATE VIOLENCE

Given that democratic regimes' police forces make ever less use of force in their daily activity, why do paroxysmic episodes of police violence break out at regular intervals and so clearly persist? How are we to explain that genuine state massacres occur within the bosom of *democratic states? And how are social science researchers to account for what the actors do,* assuming they wish to go beyond merely repeating what the latter have already said or wish to avoid the temptation of adopting an overarching top-down vision? Alain Dewerpe (1952–2015) provides illuminating and fundamental answers to these questions in *Charonne.*

The book is presented as the total analysis of an event: the February 8, 1962, demonstration in the Charonne district of Paris against the Organisation armée secrète (OAS). If this was part of an anti-OAS dynamic in full swing for several months, it had two particularities: It was reactive, since it was a response to a series of assassinations and bombings by the far-right organization; and it was banned, albeit equivocally, by the public authorities. The demonstration resulted in the massacre of nine people (without counting the very many injured) by the police units sent to maintain order.

Dewerpe's exploration starts, in the first part of the book, by meticulously reconstructing the twenty-five minutes of the police charge at the rue de Charonne/boulevard Voltaire crossroads. It then goes over the employment conditions of the police units dispatched to maintain order, the origins of their professional routines, the formation of their *habitus,* and the fabrication of their cognitive frameworks, particularly through their contact with the colonial experience. Dewerpe emphasizes the police and political decisions that allowed and even encouraged this outburst of brutality. His reconstruction is exemplary. Nothing is left to chance, nothing is overlooked, and he avoids reckoning any single reason as central and, hence, the many others as parasitical. He steers clear of all the pitfalls that would view the police solely as the armed wing of the state, that would imply the police force is a state within the state, that would hold Charonne to be an exceedingly rare but exceptionally serious accident, or that would detect an indication of some subjacent reality to the police institution. And if Dewerpe quite rightly views the preconditions for this explosion of paroxysmic violence as following on from routines of codified violence, he does not thereby take the former as the logical consequence of the latter but rather thinks of them interdependently. This approach allows him to sketch an anthropological history of this state massacre.

After all, state massacre is not just a matter of the number of dead. In order to exhaustively examine the event, Dewerpe seeks to make sense of the affair surrounding Charonne. This had three main dimensions. The first, which he calls the "civic scandal," relates to immediate reactions to the event, from the mobilization denouncing the murders through to the patient and solid fabrication of what would retrospectively be seen, without the slightest doubt, as a state lie: The demonstrators were said to be responsible for the massacre because of their audacious behavior in wishing to exert their right to demonstrate in a republic. The police hierarchy was also relieved of its responsibility, giving rise to a persistent false account of the immediate causes of death. Dewerpe's investigation of Charonne as a social fact includes the dead ends to which the judicial proceedings were deliberately led by the political authorities and the conditions presiding over the creation of a memory, from the somber ceremony of the funerals on February 13 through to the formation of a political and trade union memory of the act of repression.

Dewerpe's book provides the social sciences with a lesson in general methodology. It is currently fashionable to denounce the supposedly artificial distinction between event and structure. But such denunciation is rarely accompanied by any attempt to work through its consequences, and the ephemera of interactions are regularly dissolved in analysis of social structures. But *Charonne* successfully moves beyond the distinction. Social structures cannot fully account for the singularity of the event, nor should the event be understood as some autonomous floating occurrence. In many ways, this book shares in the sociological tradition initiated by Karl Mannheim: It provides one point of view among others on the case under study, while also providing a panoramic view that is thus particularly robust. If historical research fully validates the versions given by protesters at the scene, backed up by arguments and proof, Dewerpe does not merely provide academic legitimization. He goes a step further, providing a sociological vision of social and political processes that, by virtue of being examined, become describable. The work is both bound up with the object it seeks to analyze (in that it acts as a reminder and an analytical model of state violence, for example) and the result of an endeavor to reach an external point of view on that object. This is how one may make sense of the deeply moving sentence on which the introduction closes: "If being the son of a martyr of *Charonne* does not provide any lucidity, nor does it prevent one from doing one's *job* as a historian." One cannot but respect such a capacity to relinquish none of the scientific demands required by the social sciences while maintaining a normative perspective forged by an absolutely dramatic personal experience.

Cédric Moreau de Bellaing

Alain Dewerpe, *Charonne, 8 février 1962: Anthropologie historique d'un massacre d'État* (Paris: Gallimard ["Folio"], 2006).

2007

THE YEARS OF EXTERMINATION: FRIEDLÄNDER PUTS THE HOLOCAUST AT THE HEART OF SCHOLARSHIP ON NAZISM

Although it seems improbable today given the place the Holocaust has in our images of the past, the two volumes of *Nazi Germany and the Jews* were initially conceived as books to do battle against its oblivion. In the 1970s and 1980s, Saul Friedländer (born 1932) was worried by changes in German memory. He detected an attempt to erase Auschwitz from the historical record, as he explained in a 1976 article in which he sketched out a "global historical study" of the events (which he long put off), paying equal attention to the perpetrators, victims, and context. The famous controversy opposing him, ten or so years later, to Martin Broszat, the director of the Munich Institute of Contemporary History (Institut für Zeitgeschichte), gave his project renewed topicality.

Promoting a "historicization" of Nazism, Broszat voiced a wish to relegate Nazi criminality to the margins: Twelve years of German history could not be reduced solely to that. The debate was tense, violent, fascinating. It turned without a fight to Friedländer's advantage. His own life had been marked by the Holocaust. Both his parents had died in Auschwitz, and, in his early teens, he had only just escaped the same fate. Another issue was precisely the place to grant to records left by Jewish victims, which Broszat, adopting a diametrically opposed stance to Friedländer, ruled out as a source, claiming they were based on a "mythic memory"—to use an expression that now seems inconceivable, almost scandalous, revealing the full extent of the subsequent shift.

Over the course of 300 pages, the first volume, *The Years of Persecution* (1997), examines the prewar period, focusing therefore on the Reich. The account is less radical than might be expected, given Friedländer's previous ideas on how to make sense of an event pushing the question of representation to the limits. The novelty and fertility of the narrative stems from the alternation between the persecution decided on and implemented by the perpetrators and the persecution as experienced by victims or, in a more distanced way, observed by other social actors. All in all, Friedländer conducts a dual operation. In accordance with his original project, he confirms the centrality of the Holocaust in the history of Nazism but also invents—imposes even—a place for victims in this historical account. Of course, the Jews had not been totally absent from the historical narrative over the previous half-century. But the history of victims, often conducted on a local scale, had had limited impact, while the dominant history focused on the perpetrators, trying to understand how they had reached such a point. In such an account, the Jews were only present when necessary, as contingent figures. In Friedländer's book, on the contrary, the Jews, one may say, are not only dead: they are alive, and later only are killed.

They are killed. This happens in the second volume, *The Years of Examination*, running to 1,000 or so pages, published ten years later. The account becomes more complex, covering an entire continent, explaining what happened in Byalistok, Berlin, Brussels, and Bordeaux, for instance. The account is also more oppressive, for after 1941 it was solely a matter of killing or being killed. It is also oppressive because, in this second volume, Friedländer systematically uses sources less present in the first: that is, diaries left by persecuted Jews—so lively, so alive when they wrote, then dead the day after. We follow some of them from chapter to chapter, and then suddenly they stop, at an impromptu moment, on a final entry. Thus on August 4, 1942, in Warsaw, Chaïm Kaplan wrote: "If I die, what will happen to my diary?"

Nevertheless, Friedländer does not focus solely on the history of the victims. Concerning that of the perpetrators, he puts forward a set of insightful propositions. His concept of "redemptive anti-Semitism" is particularly useful, making it possible to distinguish the form of anti-Semitism advocated by Hitler in *Mein Kampf* from what had preceded and to explain the relentless ferocity with which everything was implemented: The "redemption" of the German people, said to be weakened and sullied by the Jewish presence in its midst, was supposed to occur only through the elimination of Jews, through their social exclusion, forced emigration, or murder. Equally, and through his authority, Friedländer did much to stabilize the chronological division that now dominates in scholarship concerning the evolution of the "final solution": The decision for total extermination was taken by Hitler in December 1941, against the backdrop of the globalization of the conflict and the United States joining the war; it was followed by a radical acceleration as of spring 1942.

The two volumes of *Nazi Germany and the Jews* were translated into many languages and won many prizes. They occupy a unique place, with their radical novelty in proposing an "integrated history." This was the case when they came out and is still the case today. But if this monumental work has left a lasting mark, it is not what one might have initially imagined. For it has not imposed a new canon, that of a multifocal account replacing the previously prevalent approaches. Rather, it has shown that using the appropriate form, combined with great dexterity of writing, it is possible to account more completely and more sensitively to this monstrous event that indelibly marked the tragic twentieth century.

Florent Brayard

Saul Friedländer, *The Years of Extermination: Nazi Germany and the Jews, 1939–1945* (New York: Harper Collins, 2007).

2008

VIOLENCE: COLLINS MAKES VIOLENCE AN EFFECT OF SITUATION

Drawing on rich and varied documentation about military battles, street fights, conjugal violence, mass massacres, and playground quarrels, *Violence* is an abnormal and exorbitant work that seeks to apprehend its subject with such distance that it at times displays a surprising hint of mischievousness. Its author, the sociologist (and novelist) Randall Collins (born 1941), currently a professor at the University of Pennsylvania, puts forth a hypothesis whose provocative nature he makes resoundingly clear: What if the cause of all violence was entirely rooted in the situation giving rise to it? The radicality of this approach is transparent in its codicil, for it amounts to holding the socialization of individuals and the group culture to which they belong to be secondary in the etiology of violence.

Collins's purpose was to supplement the study of "successful interaction rituals," addressed in an earlier work, *Interaction Ritual Chains* (2004), with that of "violent interactions," whose specificity is that they "go against the grain of normal interaction rituals." They start with situations of "confrontational tension," a sort of low-level hostility that takes hold between people, accompanied by negative emotions dominated by fear (hence his use of the phrase "tension/fear"). If this state is a precondition for resorting to violence, we further need to see that it also acts as a brake on it. Since fear gives rise to avoidance attitudes, most such situations cease, either because the protagonists disperse or because a normal interaction situation is reestablished. Violence, Collins insists, is a rare phenomenon.

For violence to occur, further conditions are needed, leading the participants to overcome the fear inspired. Collins thus emphasizes the importance of a set of incentivizing mechanisms: the presence of a public, for example, pushing protagonists to perpetrate acts of violence, or else belonging to a group or organization exerting an obligation to act violently. But the most important factor is asymmetrical forces: If one party feels it can crush the adversary, this considerably increases the probability of violence. These situations accentuate a trait characterizing all situations of violence: "forward panic," a state of rage giving violence its disordered and uncontrolled aspect, thereby making it difficult to have a strictly instrumental relation to it, a rule to which only high-powered professionals, such as snipers, are an exception.

Yet, to Collins's mind, sticking to this elementary scheme would entail overlooking that there is no opposition between positing situational (micro-sociological) determination and taking sociohistorical (macro-sociological) aspects into account, without which his ambition to put forward a general theory of violence would be doomed to failure. For him, situations belong to history and therefore take structured forms exerting constraints on the action of those caught up in them. He thus discusses at length the ways in which human groups seek to regulate and tame violence. Collins suggests the common principle to these efforts is that they seek to contain the risks of forward panic, and its potentially irreversible consequences, by favoring situations that prevent conflict by ensuring a certain balance of forces, thereby limiting the exorbitant step of resorting to violence (resulting, for example, in rules of fairness). Practices such as vendettas and duels, the norms of *jus in bello*, and the codes of honor of certain criminal groups are illustrations of this, just as recreational violence—particularly sport—is in contemporary societies.

Many of Collins's readers are not convinced by his arguments. They have sometimes considered that, in a given social situation, certain individuals and groups are more prone to use violence than others; they may feel that social organization is of such importance that, depending on its qualities, social relations take a more or a less peaceful turn, or else that the relation societies have with violence varies, depending on the general tendencies running through and transforming. Yet these are obvious statements that Collins feels absolutely no need to dispute. What he is aiming at lies on another plane. *Violence* is best read as the protocol for an experiment. He pushes the hypothesis of the situational determination of violence to its limits, not to

280　*Violence*

invalidate what he ironically calls "alternative theoretical approaches" (that is, dispositional approaches) but to put them in their true perspective. The move is daring, considering the hegemonic character of such approaches, not only in social sciences, which would be a lesser evil, but especially in the attitudes we commonly and spontaneously adopt toward violence. It is not just a theoretical counterproposition but a practical—hence political—alternative that Collins portrays: If, all things being equal, situations increase or decrease the probability of violence, this violence may be curbed by acting on the situations in which there is the strongest risk of it occurring. This paves the way to very different approaches to those targeting individuals and groups reputed to be most likely to resort to violence.

Dominique Linhardt

Randall Collins, *Violence: A Micro-Sociological Theory* (Princeton, NJ: Princeton University Press, 2008).

2009

THE ART OF NOT BEING GOVERNED: SCOTT AND THE ANTHROPOLOGICAL OUTCOME OF AN ANARCHIST HISTORY

From the moment it was published, *The Art of Not Being Governed* was enthusiastically received by a wide readership and debated by historians, anthropologists, and political scientists far outside the circle of Southeast Asia specialists. Its success owes much to its disputing the habitual evolutionary schema, according to which humanity progressively built up literate agricultural state-based civilizations from primitive forms of organization, the latter existing in residual form through tribes living on the margins. Drawing on documentary research into mountain populations in northern India, James Scott (born 1936) argues, on the contrary, that these populations' social morphology and livelihoods are better seen as forms of resistance to the regime of constraints that local states impose on the peasantry: slavery, statute labor, conscription, and taxation. Rather than being the archaic base on which state societies were built up, the sociopolitical organization of these marginal peoples is in fact an inverted derivative product—a counter-model of libertarian hue. Scott argues that these are "state-repelling" and "state-escaping" societies. As for the mountain dwellers, they do not hail from some stock of primitive settlement but descend mostly from peasants who fled the lowlands to be free of the overly heavy hand of the state.

Scott here draws on the legacy of Pierre Clastres's *La société contre l'État* (*Society against the State*, 1974). He also takes up the concept of "jellyfish tribes" set out in *Tribes and States in the Khyber, 1838–1842* by Malcom Yapp, for whom the high degree of segmentation and internal autonomy of tribal societies endow them with an amorphous, impalpable nature, making it hard to exert political control over them. However, in comparison to these two authors, Scott's perspective proceeds from a radical constructionism. He notes that slash-and-burn agriculture, practiced by Indochinese mountain dwellers in hard-to-reach zones, requires mobility and dispersal and generates low surpluses. He therefore argues that it is an *escape agriculture*, a deliberately dissuasive techno-economic system to ward off the predatory tendencies of plain states. For him, mountain dwellers have deliberately opted for principles combining a lack of political leadership with social segmentation and interchangeable identity. They reject writing, hence literacy: They are not preliterate but postliterate, where the lack of texts allows them to manipulate their genealogies, their past, and their identity so as to be less visible, hence lessen the control exerted by the administrative apparatus of modern states, empires, and kingdoms.

This theory, which, in comparison to civilizational and orientalist accounts, presents the advantage of making Asian mountain dwellers fully-fledged actors in their own history, is not a new facet to Scott's work, a pioneering political scientist whose earlier works in subaltern studies (*The Moral Economy of the Peasant* and *Weapons of the Weak*) were already built around the forms of resistance used by Southeast Asian peasantries to counter state-imposed forms of extortion. Nevertheless, whereas his earlier concern was to bring out sets of attitudes and strategies common to lowland peasantries under close state control, he now expands his focus to slash-and-burn farmers who escape this hold due to their place on the geographical margins. Further, he erects the philosophy of these clearance farmers into an alternative social model as part of a history that explicitly addresses anarchy. Far from accrediting the Hobbesian thesis that adherence to a Leviathan is the precondition for human progress, he depicts groups moving in the opposite direction, to find the means to be free and to thrive in a deliberately recomposed state of nature.

This is one of the reasons for the book's success. Just as *La société contre l'État* had lent academic backing to the libertarian theories in fashion in the 1970s, so Scott's book echoed with the legitimacy crisis affecting Western democratic governments as a result of the 2008 financial crisis, giving rise to the Indignados movement in 2011. In this context, the state looked less and less like the expression and guarantor of the Enlightenment social contract and more and more like the puppet of globalized financial capitalism. In reducing the state to a regime of constraints, Scott's book provided anthropological arguments for this disenchantment.

Yet his thesis came in for criticism, particularly from specialists of Southeast Asia. His constructionist interpretation seems somewhat speculative, given the lack of historical sources on the sociogenesis of mountain groups. Linking all these populations' characteristics solely to their rejecting the state model is highly reductive, especially as Scott only retains evidence supporting his argument. For the arc of mountains forming a border zone between southern China and the north of the Indochinese Peninsula has never been a zone of refuge beyond the reach of local potentates. The relief divides the area up into a multitude of valleys, occupied by rice-growing states, causing mountain dwellers there to be in close contact with other populations: groups of slash-and-burn farmers tended to respond to state pressure through alliances and compromise rather than opposition, resistance, and flight.

The book's most lasting contribution ultimately lies in its defining a new cultural area, Zomia (borrowed from the geographer Willem van Schendel), uniting many mountain peoples from Assam to Vietnam within the same field of study.

Bernard Formoso

James C. Scott, *The Art of Not Being Governed: An Anarchist History of Upland Southeast Asia* (New Haven, CT: Yale University Press, 2009).

2010

HOW CHIEFS BECAME KINGS: KIRCH ENDOWS POLYNESIA WITH ITS OWN ARCHAIC STATE

It was known that the earliest states appeared independently in the Egyptian, Mesopotamian, Indian, Chinese, Mesoamerican, and Andean civilizations before the Christian era. And it was previously considered that certain regions of the world had to await the arrival of Western trade in firearms for their aristocratic chieftains to mutate into territorial states. In publishing *How Chiefs Became Kings*, the archaeologist Patrick Kirch (born 1950) exploded this Eurocentric account. On the strength of fieldwork in Oceania and his reconstitution of Austronesian migrations in the Pacific from Taiwan, he identified the birth and development of an interstate system in the Hawaiian archipelago at a period (sixteenth to eighteenth century) when this set of eight islands existed in a state of complete autarky.

The argument that Kirch marshals is a magisterial synthesis of linguistic, archaeological, ethnological, and historical data about Hawaii and of comparative works by Gary Feinman, Joyce Marcus, Robert Carneiro, and Bruce Trigger on the origins of states. His methodology draws on glottochronology of vocabulary; excavations of fishponds, farmland, and monumental stone architecture; museum collections of bark clothing, double-hulled canoes, mats, and feathered adornments; diaries of European expeditions and texts by missionaries and traders in Honolulu; the oral traditions and historical accounts of indigenous elites; and the administrative archives of the nineteenth-century Hawaiian monarchy. As for his explanatory model, it elegantly combines *etic* and *emic* perspectives, causes operating at different scales, and many strategies and circumstances to account for the transformation of these chieftains into divine royal states.

The main point of his argument is precisely that the state originated in the type of divine king dear to James George Frazer, the descendant and incarnation of the gods on earth, ritually granting his subjects the energetic power (*mana*) founding the universe and life and put to death on his succession, in this instance by his victor who sacrificed him on the altar to *Kū*, the god of war, who was invoked whenever an enemy principality's territory was conquered. The whole question is to understand how the chief of one ancestral system among others came to represent this unique sovereign, the "tiger shark on earth," encircled by taboos and reigning over the population to the exclusion of others.

To do so, Kirch compares Hawaiian society, described once contact was reestablished in the late eighteenth century, with the Polynesian culture imported by the first colonists from the Marquesas Islands at the end of the first millennium. Initially, there were a few small kin groups practicing self-subsistence, differentiated by age, gender, and rank and headed by a chief who offered up the first harvest and memorized the genealogies justifying access to the coral reefs and cropland for recognized members. Eventually, there were several hundred thousand people divided into three administrative levels in a territory segmented by interlocking domains and temples. They were thus hierarchized into pariah servants with tattooed faces, commoner households that had to perform statute labor and render tributes to obtain the right to feed and dress themselves from the fruit of their work, and the endogenous group of hereditary chiefs (*ali'i*) and priests of the official form of worship, owners of the land and coastline, head craftsmen at court, and those holding the monopoly over warfare, ritual practice at temples, historical knowledge, and the redistribution and consumption of prestige goods stored at the palaces. What had happened between these two times?

The archipelago's population and demographic density increased until it was necessary to supplement lagoon aquaculture and irrigated cultivation of taro in the valleys of the western isles by colonizing the eastern isles to grow yams and sweet potatoes on the plains, an activity subject to fluctuating rainfall and the disadvantages of lower marginal labor productivity, thus needing large number of workers as farming became intensified. The growing number of kinship groups encouraged statutory rivalries between the growing number of chiefs, who were exposed to attempts by their younger relatives to usurp them or to acquire autonomy. This led to the extraction of ever larger surpluses, thereby reinforcing the intensification and expansion of food and craft production. These two intrinsically linked processes gave rise to a new situation in the late sixteenth century when the depletion of available land coincided with the exhaustion of the soil and decline in the marginal productivity of labor, particularly in the plains. Native Hawaiians launched wars of territorial conquest against the western isles to expand their tributary bases and be able to draw on the labor and ecological resources they lacked. They then innovated in the fields of religion and matrimony: first, by reserving for their warrior elites the divine privilege of reproducing by incest between brothers and sisters and marrying between aristocratic houses from one island to another; and second, by subverting the religious ideology to serve the warlord's interests, by building new temples to conduct an annual cycle of itinerant festivities (*mahaliki*) alternating between the gods of war and of agriculture, by ritualizing the payment of tributes and the opening of hostilities, and by replacing offerings of the first harvest and the domestic worship of ancestors with practices now centered on animals and plants.

If this Polynesian case confirms that there is no need for urbanization, metallurgy, and writing for states to arise, it forcefully illustrates that the monopolistic control of technologies of destruction, (re)production, and communication by a sovereign is accompanied by his divinization and the hypostasis of the political entity thereby created through incest and human sacrifice.

Laurent Berger

Patrick Vinton Kirch, *How Chiefs Became Kings: Divine Kingship and the Rise of Archaic States in Ancient Hawai'i* (Berkeley: University of California Press, 2010).

2011

DEBT: GRAEBER WISHES TO END THE VIOLENCE OF DEBT

It is hard to say to what discipline David Graeber's *Debt: The First 5,000 Years* belongs. Graeber (1961–2020) was an anthropologist specializing in Madagascar, a professor at the London School of Economics, and an activist. The book may be read as an essay in economic history and anthropology or, more precisely, as a critique of the anthropological underpinnings of classical economics. Yet, from the very first pages, the reader realizes that it has still greater ambitions: In going over the genealogy of the idea of "debt," Graeber is in fact following in the footsteps of Hobbes and Adam Smith, but also going against them in writing a new *Theory of Moral Sentiments*. He puts forward a complex and original theory centered on the struggle between two proposed forms of economy, the human economy and the market economy, linked over four great lengthy cycles: the age of credit (3500 BCE to 800 BCE), the axial age (800 BCE to 600 CE), the Middle Ages (600–1450), and the age of great capitalist empires (1450–1971).

The book is both a scholarly study and a political pamphlet, built on the latest major financial crisis, a systemic crisis initially relating to private debt in the United States (subprimes) yet disguised as a public debt crisis once it crossed the Atlantic to Portugal, Italy, Ireland, Greece, and Spain. It is often said that all debts ought to be reimbursed, whatever the cost. As an anthropologist, Graeber takes this commonplace as his starting point, but the entire volume sets out to disprove it. To this end, he deconstructs the notion of debt and strives to understand its origins, what economic relations it activates, what moral ties it establishes, and further, what forms of physical or impersonal violence it conceals.

The book is divided into three sections. The first is a critique of the theoretical presuppositions of classical political economy. Graeber holds that it is historically unjustified to think that the practice of exchange is a universal form of communal life. He further argues that it is anthropologically incorrect to take personal interest or egotism to be the driving force behind all sociality, a point on which works in comparative anthropology prove him right. Yet these are the presuppositions central to the economic institutions governing us and, still more seriously, central to our common sense. One need only think of Adam Smith: Graeber shows how arbitrary his decision is to place barter as the logical and historical antecedent to the market, whereas it is in fact a fairly recent form of exchange, and it is ritual, not economic, in nature. If one is looking for an antecedent to the modern configuration of the market economy, it is not to the ritual exchange of objects that one should turn but rather to the systematic usage of violence as an instrument of subjection. It is doubtless not by chance that the issuing of money, invented in the seventh century BCE in China, India, and Greece concomitantly, were initially to pay soldiers at war. Enslavement and the systematic use of physical violence are the two operations without which one cannot understand the structures shaping the changing relationship over the centuries between, on the one hand, forms of life, political power, and religious power and, on the other, the state and the market.

Classical economic science (with the exception of Marx) refuses to consider this uninterrupted chain of violence. It is so constructed to ignore it even and make the world, as thought by economists, transpire as the arithmetical result of rational choices and private interests. This is a vast defense mechanism (another of Marx's points), concealing the origins of a form of domination perpetuated through violence. Graeber also interprets it as the symptom of a deeper, anthropological transformation when, in the modern age, the monetary economy started to destroy the human economy, and when the impersonal logic regulating the accumulation of money turned into an authentically moral law.

The second section could function as a stand-alone book, being a brief treatise on the moral foundations of economic relations. Graeber identifies three: communism, exchange, and hierarchy, all three of which are always mixed and never exist in a pure state. Communism is an economic relation based on locality and concrete sharing (and, consequently, the foundation of all forms of human sociality); the exchange of goods designates an economic relation between peers at a distance, while hierarchy is an asymmetric power relationship based on the idea of precedence.

The third section is the most ambitious. Graeber sets out a comparative history of credit and debit relations in human societies, from the earliest Sumerian documents through to the present day. This is divided into four great periods, characterized either by the prevalence of virtual monies and systems of protection by credit or by the dissemination of metal monies and systems of oppression by debt. The "metallic" periods are generally more violent, with wars and ransacking of an intensity unknown during "crediting" periods, which are comparatively pacific. Yet over these alternating cycles one thing remains constant: the close relationship linking debt to physical violence and enslavement. This is at the heart of Graeber's book. The unceasing history of this relationship over the millennia may be detected everywhere, behind the terms "freedom" and "honor," and even in the form taken by our economic institutions. It is this genealogical approach, attentive to very long periods, grounded in anthropological analysis capable of cutting through economic theory as a whole, which allows Graeber to write what is fundamentally an essay on the ferocity of humankind and the enigma of a predatory destructiveness that still exists today in market mechanisms dressed up as game theory and algorithmic series.

Daniele Balicco

David Graeber, *Debt: The First 5,000 Years* (New York: Melville House, 2011).

2012

THROUGH THE EYE OF A NEEDLE: BROWN RETURNS TO THE ROOTS OF THE CHRISTIAN PROBLEM OF WEALTH

Peter Brown (born 1935) became established as one of the leading intellectuals in English-speaking academia in 1967 with his first book, a magisterial biography of Saint Augustine. His writings have inspired several generations of historians of the ancient world and, thanks to his idea of "late antiquity," helped reappraise the radical transformation affecting the Mediterranean world and its surrounding lands, from Brittany to Iran, encompassing within a single body of thought all the ideological and religious problems affecting this vast area from the fourth through to the sixth centuries.

Through the Eye of a Needle, published at the end of a career spent at Oxford, London, Berkeley, and Princeton (as of 1986), is a highly innovative study addressing the place of wealth—its acquisition, transmission, and social distribution—in the upheavals taking place during late antiquity. It is a complex book, of interest to medievalists and historians of antiquity alike, examining the elaboration of the ideological underpinnings on which much of Christendom was based in the Middle Ages, along with deeper changes affecting the West through to the twelfth century. In so doing, it tackles some of the most topical themes in present historical scholarship.

Brown takes as his starting point a fundamental cultural shift: Whereas fourth-century Roman society was preoccupied by matters of social hierarchy, reputation, and prestige, that of the sixth century placed salvation—that is, the fate of souls—above all other preoccupations. Problems that did not arise in the fourth century—the links between the church's wealth, caring for the poor, and the salvation of the soul—became crucial in the sixth century.

There was thus a Christian usage of wealth. This justified a change to the status of church wealth, which became holy and inalienable precisely because its purpose was to succor the poor. At the end of this shift, church wealth was considered as the way by which the poor could access property in this world, even though they were by definition excluded from it. The question of poverty is essential in this book about wealth, since it accompanies a radical change in how society represented itself.

Taking the poor into account and linking their fate to the salvation of the soul upended categories of social action. Gifts to the citizens, in the form of games, for example, were immediately recompensed by acclamation and admiration, consolidating the social prestige of the generous individual. Yet organizing games continued to be important in Roman life, particularly in Italy, at least through to the end of the fourth century, and euergetism continued to structure the political and social life of the Romans, even though rival models were emerging in a context of spiritual combat and intellectual competition. Ambrose of Milan, one of the first to consider poverty as a central element in Christianity and to talk about the matter, was a contemporary of Symmachus, one of the last great representatives of the old social elite, deeply pagan and certain that respecting rites practiced since the beginning of days was the only way to maintain the order of the world.

Contrarily, gifts to God and his church did not imply any immediate return. If the donor expected a recompense, it was deferred and could only occur after life on earth. Generosity was thus a way of building up an immaterial treasure to which the Christian could only have access in the afterlife, in infinite contemplation of God and eternal beatitude. The gift thus converted earthly riches into promises of salvation. The link between church property, salvation, and protecting the poor was slowly conceptualized through controversies conducted by figures from Ambrose to Salvian and the change in ethos of the aristocracy, for whom *otium* was given new content and poverty and withdrawal from the world were recognized social values. The fifth-century ascetic movement, particularly that which sprang up around Lérins, played a key role in transforming the aristocracy's social and mental attitudes toward ecclesial institutions and helped define what Foucault, duly cited by Brown, called *pastoral power*.

Present-day scholarship, particularly of the early Middle Ages, draws extensively on Brown's methods and lines of approach. Inquiry into gifts and the status of wealth, and in-depth analysis of how they were used by laypeople and ecclesiastics alike, are now in the foreground. Understanding the processes by which wealth was transformed into power is a central topic for medievalists, as it is for historians of antiquity, too. This involves consideration of such major ideas in the social sciences as preservation, reproduction, and transmission, all of which come in for close examination. At the heart of the debate lies the question of the existence of a Christian economy— that is, of whether production and exchange functioned in specific ways in ancient and medieval societies. Everything relating to transfers of wealth and modes of domination by elites in the early Middle Ages is encompassed by Brown's thought.

Laurent Feller

Peter Brown, *Through the Eye of a Needle: Wealth, the Fall of Rome, and the Making of Christianity in the West, 350–550 AD* (Princeton, NJ: Princeton University Press, 2012).

2013

CAPITAL IN THE TWENTY-FIRST CENTURY: PIKETTY DECRYPTS SHIFTS IN ECONOMIC INEQUALITIES OVER THE CENTURIES

Le capital au XXIe siècle (*Capital in the Twenty-First Century*) is the culmination of fifteen years of research by Thomas Piketty (born 1971), joined on the way by several colleagues, into historical shifts in income and asset inequalities. In the late 1990s, struck by the paucity of statistics and historical perspectives on the subject, Piketty set about reconstructing long data series, initially on France, to bring out changes in capital and income inequalities. The result contrasts with the optimistic vision claiming that inequalities diminish with economic development, instead showing the extent to which political decisions (relating to taxation in particular) and historical shocks (especially the two world wars) determined this distribution, thus contradicting any intangible economic law. Piketty's research then headed in two main directions: international comparison and the analysis of capital. With the world going through a disastrous economic crisis, the work echoed deeply with political debates and social movements (including Occupy Wall Street), especially in the United States where, as Piketty had already shown in various publications, the level of income inequality had nearly reached levels last seen in the pre-1914 days of "untamed capitalism" and "robber barons."

  Le capital expands on these analyses of income inequalities. It throws light on the recent reconstitution of wealth inequalities (though without these reaching pre-1914 levels) and diagnoses forces specific to changes in market economies that bring about increased wealth inequality when capital yields exceed growth rates. Piketty argues that there is nothing ineluctable about these forces and that they have been countered in the past. The book thus closes on suggestions, the most important of which is a progressive global tax on capital.

Yet while these arguments captured the most attention, they only represent one aspect of the book, whose greater ambition is to explain the processes of capital accumulation and how they depend on labor and social organization. Piketty devotes many pages to the history of slavery and to public debt. Dialoguing with classical economists such as Malthus, Ricardo, and Marx, he returns to the fundamental questions of political economy (the distribution of wealth, long-term economic growth, yield on factors of production, etc.) while devoting much of his analysis to national account statistics, which reflect the role society attributes to capital.

The book was published in late 2013 in France, translated in spring 2014 in the United States, and then nearly everywhere else in the world, soon becoming established as a major and singular work. It met with exceptional success for an academic work, selling several million copies, and resonated strongly in public debate and political commentary worldwide, though it was initially in the United States that it captured media attention. Although mainly covering inequalities in Western Europe and the United States, it sparked debate in many countries outside the usual academic networks, indicative of a new type of internationalization in the social sciences.

It should be noted that in addition to the print version, there is also a mass of data, bibliographical references, and appendixes available on Piketty's website. It is hard to tell whether this played a part in the book's success, but it certainly did much to shape debate about it: Many commentaries have been based on replicating and modifying its analyses by drawing on the statistical data thus made available. In the book, Piketty encourages such appropriations and reactions and has frequently replied in the press and in specialized journals.

In the early twenty-first century, *Le capital* stands out among academic economics publications because of its very format. Most economists—or mainstream ones, in any case—no longer view the book format as a valid scientific object, valuing only articles. Volumes by academic economists tend to be general-interest works, contributions to public debate, or collections of

295   *Piketty Decrypts Shifts in Economic Inequalities over the Centuries*

articles. *Le capital* is explicitly conceived against such stances. Piketty states this clearly in the introduction and conclusion, where he sharply criticizes economics as a discipline, accusing it of cleaving to sterile empirical and theoretical methods ignorant of the social sciences and political issues. In the same vein of his earlier 2001 book, *Les hauts revenus en France au xxe siècle* (*Top Incomes in France in the Twentieth Century*), but in a less linear and more ambitious manner, Piketty returns to the book format. Statistical analyses take on meaning within a historical and multidimensional study that alone brings out the social and political dimensions to changes in capital inequalities over time. In their criticisms of Piketty's book, economists tend to ignore this specificity, focusing primarily on the statistics and theory, without taking the institutional analysis into account. But it is this specificity that has brought the book into dialogue with the other social sciences, particularly sociology, history, political philosophy, and political science, as illustrated by the many reviews and borrowings by other disciplines.

Éric Monnet

Thomas Piketty, *Le capital au xxe siècle* (Paris: Éditions du Seuil ["Les livres du nouveau monde"], 2013). Translated into English by Arthur Goldhammer as *Capital in the Twenty-First Century* (Cambridge, MA: Harvard University Press, 2014).

2014

THE USE OF BODIES: AGAMBEN AND LIFE AS USE

When readers discovered *L'uso dei corpi* (*The Use of Bodies*), they felt as though a prophecy had come to pass. One of the greatest philosophical canvases of the second half of the twentieth century was now complete, the book being the ninth and crowning volume of *Homo Sacer*, bringing twenty years of research by Giorgio Agamben (born 1942) to a close. Yet despite being the "final" volume, the book is not so much a conclusion as a reprise of Agamben's main motifs, orchestrated like a chaconne—a baroque form of composition characterized by slowness, solemnity, and *ostinato*.

"How can use be translated into an *ethos* and a form-of-life? And what ontology and ethics would correspond to a life that, in use, is constituted as inseparable from its form?" The question on which *Altissima povertà* (*The Highest Poverty*, 2011) had closed is here answered, in the "definition of use in itself." It implies an ontology of non-operativity, together with an ethics and a politics liberated of the concepts of duty and will. To isolate "use" and form-of-life, Agamben proceeds in three stages, plus a prologue, an epilogue, and two interludes, the first about Heidegger and the second about Foucault.

The first part, on "the use of bodies," gives its title to the whole volume. It explores the full radicality of a dual thesis: Morality and politics need to be thought of starting from bodies; to do so, we need to replace the concept of action with that of use. The life of bodies, both secret and sacred, serves as a starting point for this undertaking, provided we do not apprehend this life abstractly but as bare life, captured, from the outset, as a means. This is the power of the concept of use. The expression "use of the body," borrowed from

Aristotle's analysis of slavery, indicates a nonproductive (idle) activity but also a gray zone between an artificial body and a living body, one's own body and the body of others, *zoé* and *bios*, *physis* and *nomos*. The verb *chresthai* (to use), in its strictest meaning, does not designate using something but rather the "relation one has to oneself." Whereas in Foucault, the concept of *chrésis* related to the self, for Agamben it may provide a way of moving beyond all hermeneutics of the subject, being linked to an "ontological adequation of self to the relationship." Hence subjectivity is no longer substantial and becomes more like a relation to relationship. What is at issue behind Foucault is also the long dispute with Heidegger. If "use" needs to be prized free of the Heideggerian conception, it is because Heidegger thought of it, once again, within the horizon of own-ness and authenticity. But using entails a relationship with the inappropriable, of which Agamben explores three figures: the body, language, and landscape. The difference stems from ontology, and a new ontology is necessary, implying a reinterpretation of the Stoic concept of *oikeiosis* to think of use not as activity but as "form-of-life"

What is needed is to take the "grandiose" path, which consists in resolving the aporia of hypostatic ontology by a modal ontology, for which instructions may be found in Spinoza and Leibniz. That is the purpose of the second part, which inquires whether "access to a first philosophy, that is, to an ontology, is today still—once again—possible." This was the approach taken by Leibniz in venturing the concept of "*vinculum substantiale*," a link uniting the multiplicity of monads within a single substance, which was picked up on by Alfred Boehm and Gilles Deleuze. For his part, Agamben insists on the concept of "requirement": If the link *requires* the monads, the requirement needs to replace substance as the central concept of ontology; being does not appropriate modes of being, it requires and is deployed in them—it is nothing other than its modifications. This new ontology is that of use. In the form-of-life, in the life that takes on and transpires as form, *zoé* and *bios* are no longer opposed but linked to each other—they require each other. They touch and are in contact.

This "ontology of non-relation and of use" calls for a new politics, for it makes it possible to move beyond the separations of "divided life" on which Western philosophy is built and frees the concept of form-of-life—that is, in its most rigorous definition, a "life where it is never possible to isolate and keep distinct something like bare life." Agamben describes as inseparable the link uniting life to its form, an "indivisible whole." What we call form-of-life corresponds to an ontology of style and designates the "mode in which a singularity bears witness to itself in being and being expresses itself in the singular body." In other words, it is also "disappropriated" in manner. The epilogue sets out a "theory of destituent potential."

If this work will come to be seen as a landmark, it is precisely because of its reorchestration of "use," of the ontology of "modality" and "requirement," and of the form-of-life in an ontological requirement that Agamben persistently addresses to the social sciences and to their conceptual toolkit for thinking about practices, modes of being, and ways of doing. It has already sparked debate in various fields, including ethics, metaphysics, aesthetics, and politics, and, above all, is driven by the ambition of joining them back together.

For the cover, Agamben selected Titian's *The Bacchanal of the Andrians*. This scene is at Andros. The libation is in full swing under blue skies of Cockayne. Bodies are enlivened by inebriety or giving into sleep. People dance. In the background a naked satyr is sleeping, his legs apart. In the foreground a young woman languishes, her bust graciously arched, her breasts raised slightly outward. Our eyes are drawn to her, "like a peaceful hamlet at the foot of the mountain." She blushes as she sleeps. A little boy raises his shirt to have a pee. The use of bodies? Sleeping, dancing, peeing, playing, and sexual enjoyment. And all these figures are lounging beneath the ragged tent of the sky, where Agamben wishes to lead us to take up the inquiry where he has left off.

Martin Rueff

Giorgio Agamben, *L'uso dei corpi. Homo Sacer, IV, 2* (Vicenza Neri Pozza ["La Quarta posa"], 2014). Translated into English by Adam Kotsko as *The Use of Bodies: Homo Sacer, IV, 2* (Stanford, CA: Stanford University Press, 2016).

2015

THE MUSHROOM AT THE END OF THE WORLD: TSING TRACKS LIFE IN THE RUINS OF CAPITALISM

Unlike Archimedes, it is not a fixed point to move the world that Anna Tsing (born 1952) needs but a single, strong-smelling, hard-to-find mushroom, the *matsutake*, which the Japanese prize highly. And it is surely not to move the world, a mighty dream that has always fired scientists and engineers, but rather to reveal the conduits by which capitalism inserts itself into the world and the behavior by which we may hope to survive it.

"We" is significant, because this book of anthropology works with a considerably expanded list of beings in a series of short chapters that overlap rather like the matsutake.

In this book, which is exemplary in its subject, investigation method, and style, Tsing profoundly modifies what is meant by "human." For her, being human means finding a provisional overlapping with many other species, and humans are not necessarily placed at the center. It would be a euphemism to say this book is not anthropocentric—it places humanity on another orbit.

Nor is it one of those books of natural science or popular works in which naturalists share their knowledge about the surprising existence of trees, microbes, whales, or intestinal flora. It is a work of social science through and through, and of the most demanding kind. Not for one instant does it lose from view its purpose of tracking the new nature of capitalism and exploring the possibility of living among its ruins.

Why should a mushroom make it possible to understand capitalism—better than the Internet, for example, or the arms trade, or the sale of grain?

The reason defines both the method and the object of this investigation: a problem of scale. It is not possible to cultivate this mushroom because it has a capricious life cycle and depends heavily on other factors; it is not a scalable object.

One of the major contributions of this book is that it redefines capitalism by its capacity to create local conditions that may be scaled up, and plantations are the precursor and the prototype. Gathering matsutake eludes all forms of scalability, as do those gathering it in Oregon or China, whose perilous economy Tsing tracks closely. Criticizing the disputed notion of the Anthropocene, Tsing could in fact put forward a serious candidate, as Donna Haraway suggests: the "Plantationocene."

But the truly ingenious thing about this book is that resistance to scalability also applies to its method of investigation. Tsing effectively rehabilitates what could be called "pure and simple" description—though there is nothing pure or simple about it. Describing is inventing a science of the concrete, which does not seek to generalize but to penetrate ever more deeply into the specificity of places and history. This specificity is so difficult to describe that "all terrain" sciences, which, like development projects, are obsessed by scalability, systematically fail to understand the ever so particular situation of overlapping species, thus multiplying the fields of ruins.

And becoming accustomed to living in the ruins, and knowing how to do so, is what this book is about. The reason is rooted in its object of investigation: this occluded mushroom that likes ruins, particularly pine forests laid waste by loggers. Its mode of life is devoid of the harmony and equilibrium of nature. Everything about it is artificial; everything in its development is counterintuitive. It resists all stable and lasting definition, all changes of scale. Additionally, like other members of its genus, it refuses to be defined as a species. The matsutake prospers amid disruption, a term to which Tsing imparts a positive meaning, against all hope of return to a "natural" situation.

In this book, which is far from espousing any catastrophist vision, the word *ruin* takes on a positive meaning, this time concerning the method. If the mushroom is "at the end of the world," it is not for some apocalyptic reason but because the time of development projects is now over. More exactly, it is the very notion of projection, bound up with the hope for indefinite scalability, which is no longer able to describe how the paths of all these actors and doers—pines, mushrooms, the Asian migrants gathering them, the Japanese loggers seeking to disrupt the forest to restore its fertility, the Canadian importers who manage to create an economy for luxury products in Japan despite destroying forests the world over—how these terrestrials (the word to describe them is lacking) end up crossing one another. Learning to live in the ruins of capitalism means learning to do without the notion of projects and, finally, moving on to an attentive description of situations that cannot easily change scale.

With her dog Cayenne, Donna Haraway had proved how far one could take analysis of relations between species. With her matsutake, Anna Tsing proves that we can go still further, modifying not only the landscape to be described but what we should expect of meticulous description.

Bruno Latour

Anna Lowenhaupt Tsing, *The Mushroom at the End of the World: On the Possibility of Life in Capitalist Ruins* (Princeton, NJ: Princeton University Press, 2015).

2016

MONEY: AGLIETTA UNVEILS THE CONTRADICTORY NATURE OF MONEY

La monnaie: Entre dettes et souveraineté (*Money: 5,000 Years of Debt and Power*), by Michel Aglietta (born 1938), is the culmination of work undertaken over a thirty-year period, including three previous books written with André Orléan: *La violence de la monnaie* (The violence of money), *La monnaie souveraine* (Sovereign money), and *La monnaie entre violence et confiance* (Money: Between violence and trust). Aglietta's 2016 book sets out an alternative theory of money to that of economic orthodoxy, yet its ambition is not limited to monetary theory. This innovative interdisciplinary work tackles the relation between currencies, debts, the economy, and society, effecting a radical break with the contractualist and market vision predominating among economists. By successively exploring "money as a relation of social belonging," "the historical trajectories of money," "crises and monetary regulation," and "the enigma of international currency," Aglietta shows that money is, in essence, a social link and a political relation. This analysis provides a way of leaving behind an exclusively individualist vision of social relations coordinated by the market. Economists advocating "efficient markets" were, for that matter, incapable of seeing the onset of the global financial crisis.

Against the thesis that money is a particular merchandise, Aglietta argues that money is a system of institutional practices born with the state. Money cannot be reduced to its traditional functions of payment, unit of account, and store of value, for the payment system it institutes is a way of belonging to a group, and it is strengthened by its dependency to the authorities, gods, ancestors, sovereigns, and political whole they embody.

This historical detour together with comparative analyses drawing on all the social sciences brings to light the fundamental role of debt in its various meanings: life debt, inherited debt, and social debt. The central importance accorded to debt leads to examination of what procures confidence in money and what legitimates its use in transactions through its difference of kind in comparison to other forms of wealth. Aglietta shows that the institutional architecture turns money into the *medium* of value, and that this generates three levels of confidence linked to three rules underpinning the payment system: ethical confidence in the continued existence of society (correlated to maintaining the unit of account), hierarchal confidence fused with state sovereignty (ensuring the principle of compensation and payment), and methodical confidence immersed in economic exchange (permitting the circulation of debts).

Aglietta additionally places the ambivalence of money at the center of his thought, bringing out the fatal weakness of the monetary order, which oscillates between violence and confidence. This oscillation stems from the contradictory nature of money, which may engender catastrophic crises. Indeed, money is at one and the same time the prototypical public good and principle of coordination (instituted in coinage and the payment system) and the most sought-after private good, since it may be appropriated and hoarded as a means for constituting wealth and power (liquidity).

The history of institutional changes thus raises the recurrent problem of knowing how to ward off financial and deflationist crises, on the one hand, and monetary and inflationist crises, on the other, and avoiding that either imperil the very existence of society by exacerbating rivalries between creditors and debtors. Periods of monetary and financial disorder have always been phases of acute political trouble and social conflict, and it is in the wake of debates and events correlated to these crises in the West that banks acquired their importance and the central bank's role as lender of last resort gradually came to be accepted.

Aglietta's approach to monetary phenomenon is singular, especially because it is underpinned by joint research: Many researchers from different disciplines contribute directly or indirectly, and they have also drawn inspiration from it, as evidenced by Bruno Théret's work on crises, for instance.

The approach shows the influence of Louis Dumont—a critic of economism who introduced Karl Polanyi's thought to France—for whom money cannot be considered a merchandise. It also draws on theses of the philosopher René Girard on mimetic violence, of Charles Malamoud on existential debt as conceptualized in Vedic texts, of Daniel de Coppet on the religious origin of primitive currencies, and of Carlo Benetti and Jean Cartelier on money as payment system.

This work, a benchmark study of the regulation school, applies its theory to thought about the euro and the sovereignty of states currently in the European Union, setting out the possible foundations for a new international monetary order. The role of key international currencies, and the need for a hierarchy between monies and for regulating globalized capitalism, are carefully examined in a bid to understand the 2008 financial crisis, the future of the eurozone, and the possibilities for relaunching long-term European growth. Firmly setting aside the German solution, which would perpetuate the asymmetry between the North and South in the name of conserving its ordoliberal model, Aglietta completes his great portrayal of money by exploring different ways to relaunch European construction, including altering the mandate of the European Central Bank, creating a budgetary authority capable of drawing up multiannual policies, and initiating an industrial plan grounded in developing technological solutions to environmental damage. In short, *La monnaie* is a dense and at times difficult work, but one of startling unity of purpose.

André Tiran

Michel Aglietta (with Pepita Ould Ahmed and Jean-François Ponsot), *La monnaie: Entre dettes et souveraineté* (Paris: Odile Jacob, 2016). Translated into English by David Broder as *Money: 5,000 Years of Debt and Power* (London: Verso, 2018).

List of Books Covered

Adorno, Theodor W., and Max Horkheimer. *Dialectic of Enlightenment*. 1947.

Agamben, Giorgio. *The Use of Bodies: Homo Sacer, IV, 2*. 2014.

Aglietta, Michel. *Money: 5,000 Years of Debt and Power*. 2016.

Althusser, Louis, Étienne Balibar, Roger Establet, Pierre Macherey, and Jacques Rancière. *Reading Capital*. 1965.

Anderson, Benedict. *Imagined Communities: Reflections on the Origin and Spread of Nationalism*. 1983.

Arendt, Hannah. *The Origins of Totalitarianism*. 1951.

Ariès, Philippe. *Centuries of Childhood: A Social History of Family Life*. 1960.

Assmann, Jan. *The Price of Monotheism*. 2003.

Austin, John L. *How to Do Things with Words: The William James Lectures Delivered at Harvard University in 1955*. 1962.

Balandier, Georges. *The Sociology of Black Africa: Social Dynamics in Central Africa*. 1955.

Barth, Fredrik, ed. *Ethnic Groups and Boundaries: The Social Organization of Culture Difference*. 1969.

Barthes, Roland. *Mythologies*. 1957.

Beck, Ulrich. *Risk Society: Towards a New Modernity*. 1986.

Becker, Howard S. *Art Worlds*. 1982.

Benveniste, Émile. *Problems in General Linguistics*. 1966.

Berger, Peter L., and Thomas Luckmann. *The Social Construction of Reality: A Treatise in the Sociology of Knowledge*. 1966.

Berman, Harold J. *Law and Revolution*. 1983, 2003.

Boltanski, Luc, and Ève Chiapello. *The New Spirit of Capitalism*. 1999.

Bourdieu, Pierre. *Distinction: A Social Critique of the Judgement of Taste*. 1979.

Braudel, Fernand. *The Mediterranean and the Mediterranean World in the Age of Philip II*. 1949.

Brown, Peter. *Through the Eye of a Needle: Wealth, the Fall of Rome, and the Making of Christianity in the West, 350–550 AD*. 2012.

Butler, Judith. *Gender Trouble: Feminism and the Subversion of Identity*. 1990.

Callon, Michel, Pierre Lascoumes, and Yannick Barthe. *Acting in an Uncertain World: An Essay on Technical Democracy*. 2001.

Canguilhem, Georges. *Knowledge of Life*. 1952.

Castel, Robert. *From Manual Workers to Wage Laborers: Transformation of the Social Question*. 1995.

Certeau, Michel de. *The Practice of Everyday Life*. 1980.

Chartier, Roger. *The Cultural Uses of Print in Early Modern France*. 1987.

Collins, Randall. *Violence: A Micro-Sociological Theory*. 2008.

Corbin, Alain. *The Foul and the Fragrant: Odor and the French Social Imagination*. 1982.

Davidoff, Leonore, and Catherine Hall. *Family Fortunes: Men and Women of the English Middle Class, 1780–1850*. 1987.

Derrida, Jacques. *Of Grammatology*. 1967.

Descola, Philippe. *Beyond Nature and Culture*. 2005.

Desrosières, Alain. *The Politics of Large Numbers: A History of Statistical Reasoning*. 1993.

Dewerpe, Alain. *Charonne, 8 février 1962: Anthropologie historique d'un massacre d'État*. 2006.

Didi-Huberman, Georges. *The Surviving Image: Phantoms of Time and Time of Phantoms: Aby Warburg's History of Art*. 2002.

Douglas, Mary. *Purity and Danger: An Analysis of the Concepts of Pollution and Taboo*. 1966.

Duby, Georges. *The Legend of Bouvines: War, Religion, and Culture in the Middle Ages*. 1973.

Dumézil, Georges. *Mythe et épopée: L'idéologie des trois fonctions dans les épopées des peuples indo-européens*. 1968.

Dumont, Louis. *Essays on Individualism: Modern Ideology in Anthropological Perspective*. 1983.

Elias, Norbert. *The Court Society*. 1969.

Favret-Saada, Jeanne. *Deadly Words: Witchcraft in the Bocage*. 1977.

Febvre, Lucien. *Combats pour l'histoire*. 1953.

Foucault, Michel. *History of Madness*. 1961.

Friedländer, Saul. *The Years of Extermination: Nazi Germany and the Jews, 1939–1945*. 2007.

Furet, François. *Interpreting the French Revolution*. 1978.

Galbraith, John Kenneth. *The Affluent Society*. 1958.

Garfinkel, Harold. *Studies in Ethnomethodology*. 1967.

Geertz, Clifford. *The Interpretation of Cultures: Selected Essays.* 1973.

Gell, Alfred. *Art and Agency: An Anthropological Approach.* 1998.

Ginzburg, Carlo. *The Cheese and the Worms: The Cosmos of a Sixteenth-Century Miller.* 1976.

Godelier, Maurice. *The Making of Great Men: Male Domination and Power among the New Guinea Baruya.* 1982.

Goffman, Erving. *The Presentation of Self in Everyday Life.* 1959.

Goody, Jack. *The Domestication of the Savage Mind.* 1977.

Graeber, David. *Debt: The First 5,000 Years.* 2011.

Guha, Ranajit. *Elementary Aspects of Peasant Insurgency in Colonial India.* 1983.

Habermas, Jürgen. *The Structural Transformation of the Public Sphere: An Inquiry into a Category of Bourgeois Society.* 1962.

Haraway, Donna J. *Primate Visions: Gender, Race, and Nature in the World of Modern Science.* 1989.

Hartog, François. *Regimes of Historicity: Presentism and Experiences of Time.* 2003.

Héritier, Françoise. *L'exercice de la parenté.* 1981.

Hirschman, Albert O. *Exit, Voice, and Loyalty: Responses to Decline in Firms, Organizations, and States.* 1970.

Hobsbawm, Eric J. *Age of Extremes: The Short Twentieth Century, 1914–1991.* 1994.

Hoggart, Richard. *The Uses of Literacy: Aspects of Working-Class Life with Special Reference to Publications and Entertainments.* 1957.

Kantorowicz, Ernst. *The King's Two Bodies: A Study in Medieval Political Theology.* 1957.

Kirch, Patrick Vinton. *How Chiefs Became Kings: Divine Kingship and the Rise of Archaic States in Ancient Hawai'i.* 2010.

Koselleck, Reinhart. *Futures Past: On the Semantics of Historical Time.* 1979.

Kuhn, Thomas S. *The Structure of Scientific Revolutions.* 1962.

Labov, William. *Language in the Inner City: Studies in the Black English Vernacular.* 1972.

Latour, Bruno. *The Pasteurization of France.* 1984.

Leach, Edmund. *Political Systems of Highland Burma: A Study of Kachin Social Structure.* 1954.

Le Goff, Jacques. *Saint Louis.* 1996.

Leroi-Gourhan, André. *Gesture and Speech.* 1964.

Lévi-Strauss, Claude. *The Elementary Structures of Kinship.* 1949.

Lombard, Denys. *Le carrefour javanais: Essai d'histoire globale.* 1990.

Loraux, Nicole. *The Divided City: On Memory and Forgetting in Ancient Athens.* 1997.

Marin, Louis. *Portrait of the King.* 1981.

Mauss, Marcel. *Sociologie et anthropologie*. 1950.

Mead, Margaret. *Male and Female: A Study of Sexes in a Changing World*. 1949.

Meillassoux, Claude. *Maidens, Meals, and Money: Capitalism and the Domestic Community*. 1975.

Merton, Robert K. *Social Theory and Social Structure*. 1949.

Mills, Charles Wright. *The Power Elite*. 1956.

Panofsky, Erwin. *Meaning in the Visual Arts*. 1955.

Patterson, Orlando. *Slavery and Social Death: A Comparative Study*. 1982.

Piketty, Thomas. *Capital in the Twenty-First Century*. 2013.

Pomeranz, Kenneth. *The Great Divergence: China, Europe, and the Making of the Modern World Economy*. 2000.

Ricœur, Paul. *Time and Narrative*. 1985.

Sahlins, Marshall. *Stone Age Economics*. 1972.

Said, Edward W. *Orientalism*. 1978.

Sartre, Jean-Paul. *Situations II*. 1948.

Scott, James C. *The Art of Not Being Governed: An Anarchist History of Upland Southeast Asia*. 2009.

Strathern, Marilyn. *The Gender of the Gift: Problems with Women and Problems with Society in Melanesia*. 1988.

Subrahmanyam, Sanjay. *Explorations in Connected History: Mughals and Franks: From the Tagus to the Ganges*. 2005.

Testart, Alain. *La servitude volontaire*. 2004.

Thompson, Edward P. *The Making of the English Working Class*. 1963.

Touraine, Alain. *The Post-Industrial Society: Tomorrow's Social History: Classes, Conflicts and Culture in the Programmed Society*. 1969.

Tsing, Anna Lowenhaupt. *The Mushroom at the End of the World: On the Possibility of Life in Capitalist Ruins*. 2015.

Vernant, Jean-Pierre. *Myth and Thought among the Greeks*. 1965.

Veyne, Paul. *Bread and Circuses: Historial Sociology and Political Pluralism*. 1976.

Wachtel, Nathan. *The Vision of the Vanquished: The Spanish Conquest of Peru through Indian Eyes, 1530–1570*. 1971.

Wallerstein, Immanuel. *The Modern World-System: Capitalist Agriculture and the Origins of the European World-Economy in the Sixteenth Century*. 1974.

White, Harrison C. *Identity and Control: A Structural Theory of Social Action*. 1992.

White, Richard. *The Middle Ground: Indians, Empires, and Republics in the Great Lakes Region, 1650–1815*. 1991.

List of Contributors

Frédérique Aït-Touati
Historian of literature and modern science, chargée de recherche, Centre national de la recherche scientifique (CNRS)
f.aittouati@gmail.com

Étienne Anheim
Historian, directeur d'études, École des hautes études en sciences sociales (EHESS)
etienne.anheim@ehess.fr

Daniele Balicco
Theory and critical studies, visiting fellow, Roma Tre University
balicco@gmail.com

Yannick Barthe
Sociologist, directeur de recherche, CNRS
yannick.barthe@ehess.fr

Gil Bartholeyns
Historian, maître de conferences, Université de Lille
gil.bartholeyns@univ-lille.fr

Jacques-Olivier Bégot
Philosopher, maître de conferences, Université Paris Diderot
jacques-olivier.begot@univ-rennes1.fr

Laurent Berger
Anthropologist, maître de conferences, EHESS
laurent.berger@ehess.fr

Romain Bertrand
Historian, directeur de recherche, Fondation Nationale des Sciences Politiques (FNSP)
romain.bertrand@sciencespo.fr

Loïc Blondiaux
Political scientist, professeur, Université Paris 1 Panthéon-Sorbonne
loic.blondiaux@free.fr

Guillaume Boccara
Anthropologist, chargé de recherche, CNRS
boccara.guillaume@gmail.com

Pascale Bonnemère
Anthropologist, directrice de recherche, CNRS
pascale.bonnemere@univ-amu.fr

Pascal Bouchery
Anthropologist, maître de conferences, Université de Poitiers
pascal.bouchery@univ-poitiers.fr

Pierre Bouretz
Philosopher, directeur d'études, EHESS
pierre.bouretz@ehess.fr

Jean Boutier
Historian, directeur d'études, EHESS
jean.boutier@ehess.fr

Florent Brayard
Historian, directeur de recherche, CNRS
Florent.Brayard@ehess.fr

Guillaume Calafat
Historian, maître de conferences, Université Paris 1 Panthéon-Sorbonne
gcalafat@gmail.com

Cléo Carastro
Historian, maîtresse de conferences, EHESS
cleo.carastro@ehess.fr

Marion Carel
Linguist, directrice d'études, EHESS
marion.carel@ehess.fr

Giovanni Careri
Art historian, directeur d'études, EHESS
giovanni.careri@ehess.fr

Pierre Charbonnier
Philosopher, chargé de recherche, CNRS
pierre.charbonnier@ehess.fr

Roger Chartier
Historian, professeur, Collège de France, and directeur d'études, EHESS
roger.chartier@ehess.fr

Julia Christ
Philosopher, chargée de recherche, CNRS
julia.christ@ehess.fr

Emanuele Conte
Legal historian, professor, Roma Tre University, and directeur d'études, EHESS
emanuele.conte@ehess.fr

Jean Copans
Anthropologist, professeur émérite, Université Paris Descartes

Jocelyne Dakhlia
Historian, directrice d'études, EHESS
Jocelyne.Dakhlia@ehess.fr

Vincent Debaene
Literary scholar, professeur assistant, University of Geneva
vincent.debaene@unige.ch

François Denord
Sociologist, chargé de recherche, CNRS
francois.denord@cnrs.fr

Vincent Descombes
Philosopher, directeur d'études, EHESS
Vincent.Descombes@ehess.fr

Emmanuel Désveaux
Anthropologist, directeur d'études, EHESS
emmanuel.desveaux@ehess.fr

Christine Détrez
Sociologist, professeure, École Normale Supérieure (ENS) Lyon
christine.detrez@ens-lyon.fr

Laurent Dousset
Anthropologist, directeur d'études, EHESS
laurent.dousset@pacific-credo.fr

Laura Lee Downs
Historian, professor, European University Institute, and directrice d'études,
    EHESS
laura.downs@eui.eu

Francis Dupuy
Anthropologist, professeur, Université Toulouse 2 Jean Jaurès
francis.dupuy@univ-tlse2.fr

Pierre Encrevé †
Linguist, directeur d'études, EHESS

Jean-Louis Fabiani
Sociologist, directeur d'études, EHESS
jean-louis.fabiani@ehess.fr

Laurent Feller
Historian, professeur, Université Paris 1 Panthéon-Sorbonne
Laurent.Feller@univ-paris1.fr

Serena Ferente
Historian, senior lecturer, King's College London
serena.ferente@kcl.ac.uk

Bernard Formoso
Anthropologist, professeur, Université Paris-Nanterre
bernard.formoso@orange.fr

Michel de Fornel
Linguist, directeur d'études, EHESS
michel.de-fornel@ehess.fr

Béatrice Fraenkel
Anthropologist, directrice d'études, EHESS
beafraenkel@gmail.com

Laurent Gabail
Anthropologist, maître de conferences, Université Toulouse 2 Jean Jaurès
laurentgabail@gmail.com

Édouard Gardella
Sociologist, chargé de recherche, CNRS
edouardgardella@yahoo.fr

Delphine Gardey
Historian, professor, University of Geneva
delphine.gardey@unige.ch

Jean-François Gossiaux
Anthropologist, directeur d'études, EHESS
gossiaux@msh-paris.fr

315 *List of Contributors*

Frédéric Gros
Philosopher, professeur, Sciences Po
frederic.gros@sciencespo.fr

Michel Grossetti
Sociologist, directeur de recherche, CNRS, and directeur d'études, EHESS
michel.grossetti@univ-tlse2.fr

Patrice Gueniffey
Historian, directeur d'études, EHESS
patrice.gueniffey@gmail.com

Andréa-Luz Gutierrez Choquevilca
Anthropologist, maîtresse de conferences, École pratique des hautes études
    (EPHE)
andrea-luz.gutierrez-choquevilca@college-de-france.fr

François Hartog
Historian, directeur d'études, EHESS
Francois.Hartog@ehess.fr

Gilles Havard
Historian, directeur de recherche, CNRS
gilles.havard@ehess.fr

Yves Hersant
Historian, directeur d'études, EHESS
Yves.Hersant@ehess.fr

Thierry Hoquet
Philosopher, professeur, Université Paris-Nanterre
t.hoquet@parisnanterre.fr

Florence Hulak
Philosopher, maîtresse de conferences, Université Paris 8 Vincennes-
    Saint-Denis
florence.hulak@gmail.com

Romain Huret
Historian, directeur d'études, EHESS
Romain.Huret@ehess.fr

Bruno Karsenti
Philosopher, directeur d'études, EHESS
bruno.karsenti@ehess.fr

Christiane Klapisch-Zuber
Historian, directrice d'études, EHESS
Christiane.Klapisch-Zuber@ehess.fr

Michel Lallement
Sociologist, professeur, Conservatoire national des arts et métiers (CNAM)
michel.lallement@lecnam.net

Bruno Latour
Sociologist, philosopher, professeur, Sciences Po
bruno.paul.latour@gmail.com

Valérie Lécrivain
Anthropologist, chercheuse associée, Université de Bourgogne
lecrivain.valerie@wanadoo.fr

Cyril Lemieux
Sociologist, directeur d'études, EHESS
cyril.lemieux@ehess.fr

Antoine Lilti
Historian, directeur d'études, EHESS
antoine.lilti@ehess.fr

Dominique Linhardt
Sociologist, chargé de recherche, CNRS
dominique.linhardt@ehess.fr

Sabina Loriga
Historian, directrice d'études, EHESS
Sabina.Loriga@ehess.fr

317   *List of Contributors*

Judith Lyon-Caen
Historian, maîtresse de conferences, EHESS
judith.lyon-caen@ehess.fr

Arnaud Macé
Philosopher, professeur, Université de Franche-Comté
amace@univ-fcomte.fr

Marielle Macé
Literary scholar, directrice de recherche, CNRS, and directrice d'études,
    EHESS
marielle.mace@gmail.com

Patrice Maniglier
Philosopher, maître de conferences, Université Paris-Nanterre
patrice.maniglier@gmail.com

Claude Markovits
Historian, directeur de recherche, CNRS
claumark@club-internet.fr

Alain Messaoudi
Historian, maître de conferences, Université de Nantes
alain.messaoudi@univ-nantes.fr

Eric Mielants
Sociologist, associate professor, Fairfield University
emielants@fairfield.edu

Philippe Minard
Historian, professeur, Université Paris 8 Vincennes-Saint-Denis, and direc-
    teur d'études, EHESS
philippe.minard@ens.fr

Éric Monnet
Economist, chercheur, Banque de France and École d'économie de Paris
eric.monnet@ehess.fr

318   *List of Contributors*

Cédric Moreau de Bellaing
Sociologist, maître de conferences, ENS
cedric.moreau.de.bellaing@ens.psl.eu

Serge Paugam
Sociologist, directeur de recherche, CNRS, and directeur d'études, EHESS
serge.paugam@ehess.fr

Jean-Luc Paul
Anthropologist, maître de conferences, Uuniversité des Antilles-Guyane
jean-luc.paul@univ-antilles.fr

Patrick Peretti-Watel
Sociologist, directeur de recherche, Institut national de la santé et de la
recherche médicale (INSERM)
patrick.peretti-watel@inserm.fr

Dominique Pestre
Science historian, directeur d'études, EHESS
pestre.dominique@gmail.com

Perig Pitrou
Anthropologist, chargé de recherche, CNRS
perig.pitrou@college-de-france.fr

Jacques Pouchepadass
Historian, directeur de recherche, CNRS
jacques.pouchepadass@gmail.com

Louis Quéré
Sociologist, directeur de recherche, CNRS
louis.quere@ehess.fr

Jacques Revel
Historian, directeur d'études, EHESS
jacques.revel@ehess.fr

Yann Rivière
Historian, directeur d'études, EHESS
yann.riviere@ehess.fr

Philippe Roger
Historian, literary scholar, directeur de recherche, CNRS, and directeur
   d'études, EHESS
philippe.roger@ehess.fr

Paul-André Rosental
Historian, professeur, Sciences Po
rosental@sciencespo.fr

Martin Rueff
Literary scholar, professeur, Université de Genève
martin.rueff@unige.ch

Arnaud Saint-Martin
Sociologist, chargé de recherche, CNRS
arnaud.saint-martin@cnrs.fr

Gildas Salmon
Philosopher, chargé de recherche, CNRS
gildas.salmon@ehess.fr

Gisèle Sapiro
Sociologist, directrice de recherche, CNRS, and directrice d'études, EHESS
gisele.sapiro@ehess.fr

Jean-Frédéric Schaub
Historian, directeur d'études, EHESS
Jean-Frederic.Schaub@ehess.fr

Nathan Schlanger
Archaeologist, professeur, École nationale des Chartes
schlanger1@gmail.com

Jean-Claude Schmitt
Historian, directeur d'études, EHESS
jcsvialas@gmail.com

Alessandro Stanziani
Historian, directeur d'études, EHESS
alessandro.stanziani@ehess.fr

Anne-Christine Taylor
Anthropologist, directrice de recherche émérite, CNRS
anchumir@gmail.com

Clément Thibaud
Historian, directeur d'études, EHESS
clement.thibaud@ehess.fr

André Tiran
Economist, professeur émérite, Université Lumière Lyon 2
andre.tiran@univ-lyon2.fr

Francesca Trivellato
Historian, professor, Yale University
ft@ias.edu

Sylvain Venayre
Historian, professeur, Université Grenoble-Alpes
sylvain.venayre@univ-grenoble-alpes.fr

Cécile Vidal
Historian, directrice d'études, EHESS
Cecile.Vidal@ehess.fr

Denis Vidal
Anthropologist, directeur de recherche, Institut de Recherche pour le Développement (IRD)
Denis.Vidal@ehess.fr

Arundhati Virmani
Historian, enseignante-chercheuse, EHESS
arundhati.virmani@ehess.fr

Michel Wieviorka
Sociologist, administrateur, Fondation Maison des sciences de l'homme
(FMSH), and directeur d'études, EHESS
michel.wieviorka@ehess.fr